Security selection
and
active portfolio
management

Security selection and active portfolio management

Edited by
Peter L. Bernstein

Institutional Investor Books
New York

"It is not sensible to pay 25 for an investment, of
which you believe the prospective yield to justify a
value of 30, if you also believe that the market will
value it at 20 three months hence."

John Maynard Keynes

Contents

SECURITY SELECTION AND
MODERN PORTFOLIO THEORY

Security selection: A new look to an old tradition

Peter L. Bernstein

Once upon a time, an investor who was known as a "stock picker" carried his head high, walked with pride, and was the envy of his peers. In the tumbling crash that followed the go-go days of the late 1960's, however, terrifying concepts like the random walk, efficient markets, alphas and betas came in successive blows and crushed him to bits. He seemed all too easy a target for the dart-throwers. After that, anyone who still had pretenses to being a stock picker had to hide in the closet while practising his craft.

But something funny happened on the way to the complete obliteration of stock picking as an honored profession. Major purveyors of index funds started to offer something called "active management" or "noncore portfolios," which were nothing more than fancy names for the old game of picking stocks that would outperform the averages. William Sharpe, one of the pioneers in the development of modern portfolio theory, explained in a textbook published in 1978 that stock picking was a legitimate objective, so long as you knew what you were doing when you tried it. Computer screens, valuation models, Value Line techniques, and old shoe methods inherited from Graham and Dodd began to find a new vogue.

As Editor of The Journal of Portfolio Management, I have been astonished to see how dramatically the winds of change have been blowing. In our first issue, published in October 1974, only one author dared to stand up and proclaim his doubts about the total efficiency of the market; all the other writers warned our readers that stock selection was a waste of time. Exactly three years later, we published an entire issue devoted to arguments against the efficient market hypothesis. And, as I looked back through the material that we had been carrying, and have carried more recently, the increasing frequency of articles on stock selection was readily apparent.

As Part I of this book makes clear, the controversy has by no means been resolved. These first articles reflect the nature of the debate; all of them stress the extraordinary difficulty inherent in the game of stock selection. Part II shows, however, that traditional techniques of security valuation still offer profitable opportunities, even for the investor who has had little exposure to modern investment technologies and theories. But perhaps most significant of all, the final sections are vivid examples of how the investor can employ these new techniques, once used to justify the random walk, to beat the dart-throwers at their own game.

All of this, I suppose, is just another example of how the investment process is a continuous blending of old concepts with new concepts. After nearly thirty years of earning my living by investing other people's money, I find that I can never dare forget anything that I learned from the past — but that I had also better be sure to learn everything that the present has to teach me. Anytime I forget one or the other, I tend to make a mess of the future.

For that reason, the selections in this book are designed to provide the proper blend between the lessons of the past and the new discoveries of the present. Taken together, they should help to provide profits in the years ahead.

CONTROVERSY:
IS SECURITY SELECTION
POSSIBLE?

Timing versus selection: Which holds the key?

"The game of timing . . . is worth more than the game of trying to forecast future earnings and dividends. The real question is what are the probabilities of success for either game."

Russell J. Fuller

This paper deals with the questions of market timing and security analysis by presenting a range of possible rates of return that can hypothetically be achieved based on market timing versus stock selection. I make no attempt to assess the probabilities of achieving the various rates of return — the reader may assess his own chances of success using either strategy. By knowing what the range of possible outcomes is for each approach to investing, however, the investor will be better able to determine how to allocate his efforts and resources in the investment process.

Timing strategies basically consist of two decisions — when to buy and when to sell. Stock selection, for the purposes of this paper, was considered to be based on the determination of the growth rate of common stock dividends. While for individual stocks there is obviously more to security analysis than just the security's dividend growth rate, capital market theory suggests that investors should hold well-diversified portfolios; the dividend growth rate for such portfolios is clearly a distinguishing characteristic for security analysis purposes. Thus, for analyzing timing strategies, the purchase price and sale price are considered; for stock selection purposes, the dividend growth rate is considered. Using this simplified approach, we can use the dividend discount model to determine the range of possible rates of return that can hypothetically be achieved from market timing versus stock selection.

THE DIVIDEND DISCOUNT MODEL

The dividend discount model proposed by Williams[1] in his classic book and elaborated on by Gordon[2] and others suggests the following formula for determining the price of common stocks:

$$P_0 = \frac{D_1}{1 + R} + \frac{D_2}{(1 + R)^2}$$

$$+ \ldots \ldots + \frac{D_n}{(1 + R)^n} \quad (1)$$

Where:

P_0 = current stock price
D_i = dividend received in the ith year
R = return required by investors

Thus, R is the rate of return investors require to justify the purchase price (P_0) of a common stock given its expected dividend stream over the life of the company. (D_n includes any liquidating dividend in the last year of the company's existence.)

If the dividend is expected to grow at a constant rate (G) for a reasonably long period of time, the following equation[3] is a reasonable approximation of Equation 1:

$$P_0 = \frac{D_1}{R_0 - G_0} \quad \text{or more generally} \quad P_n = \frac{D_{n + 1}}{R_n - G_n} \quad (2)$$

Equation 2 is a particularly useful formula, because it allows one to estimate the price of a stock at some

1. Footnotes appear at the end of the article.

point in the future (P_n). Since most investors do not intend to hold a stock for the life of the company, they must estimate a future sale price in order to determine the return on the purchase price (P_o), given the holding period (n years), the dividends received during the holding period

$$\left(\sum_{i=1}^{n} D_i \right),$$

and the sale price at the end of the holding period (P_n). In equation form:

$$P_o = \sum_{i=1}^{n} \frac{D_i}{(1 + r)^i} + \frac{P_n}{(1 + r)^n} \tag{3}$$

By solving for r in Equation 3, one can determine the compound annual rate of return on a common stock investment.

THE DISCOUNT FACTOR (R-G)

Equation 2 is a powerful tool for analyzing the factors which influence stock prices. In a more simplified form, Equation 2 becomes:

$$P = \frac{D}{R - G} \tag{4}$$

According to this equation, stock prices are determined by two factors: (1) The current dividend, and (2) The difference or "spread" between the rate of return required by investors and the expected growth rate of dividends. This spread (R-G) will be referred to as the discount factor. By transposing Equation 4, the discount factor can be shown to be equal to the dividend yield:

$$R - G = \frac{D}{P} \tag{5}$$

Thus the dividend yield provides a handy yardstick for measuring the discount factor. According to Holmes,[4] dividend yields have averaged 4.8% over the past 100 years. In a more recent time period (1946-74), the S&P 425 dividend yield averaged around 4.0%.

With respect to market timing, it is the discount

SECURITY
SELECTION
AND ACTIVE
PORTFOLIO
MANAGEMENT

factor or dividend yield at market tops and market bottoms that is of most interest. In a recent article, Jahnke[5] indicates that the discount factor has ranged from 2.6% at market tops to 6.0% at market bottoms, based on the peaks and troughs in the S&P 425 from the 1946 top to the 1974 bottom, as shown in Table 1.

For the purposes of this paper, three possible discount factors were used to determine purchase and

TABLE 1

DISCOUNT FACTORS (R-G) AT MARKET TOPS AND BOTTOMS

Date	Discount Factor (R-G)
1946 Top	3.5%
1947 Bottom	6.0%
1952 Top	5.1%
1953 Bottom	5.9%
1956 Top	3.4%
1957 Bottom	4.6%
1961 Top	2.7%
1962 Bottom	4.0%
1966 Top	2.9%
1966 Bottom	3.8%
1968 Top	2.7%
1970 Bottom	4.2%
1973 Top	2.6%
1974 Bottom	5.1%

Source: Jahnke and standard sources.

sale prices: a high price discount factor of 2.6%; an average discount factor of 4.0%; and a low price discount factor of 6.0%. The high price and low price discount factors cover the extremes reached at market tops and bottoms since 1946, and 4% is about the average dividend yield or discount factor for the same period.

THE DIVIDEND GROWTH RATE (G)

Three possible dividend growth rates are considered for this paper: a high dividend growth rate of 9%; an average dividend growth rate of 6%; and a low growth rate of 3%. Cohen, Zinbarg and Zeikel[6] have

TABLE 2

DIVIDEND STREAMS ASSUMING VARIOUS
LEVELS OF CONSTANT GROWTH RATES

Year (n)	$G_0 = 3\%$	$G_0 = 6\%$	$G_0 = 9\%$
0	$3.79	$3.68	$3.58
1	3.90	3.90	3.90
2	4.02	4.13	4.25
3	4.14	4.38	4.63
4	4.26	4.64	5.05
5	4.39	4.92	5.51
6	4.52	5.22	6.00
7	4.66	5.53	6.54
8	4.80	5.86	7.13
9	4.94	6.22	7.77
10	5.09	6.59	8.47
11	5.24	6.98	9.23
12	5.40	7.40	10.06
13	5.56	7.85	10.97
14	5.73	8.32	11.96
15	5.90	8.82	13.03
16	6.08	9.35	14.21
17	6.26	9.91	15.48
18	6.45	10.50	16.88
19	6.64	11.13	18.40
20	6.84	11.80	20.05
21	7.04	12.51	21.86
22	7.26	13.26	23.82
23	7.47	14.05	25.97
24	7.70	14.90	28.31
25	7.93	15.79	30.85
26	8.17	16.74	33.63
27	8.42	17.74	36.66
28	8.67	18.81	39.96
29	8.93	19.94	43.55
30	9.20	21.13	47.47
31	9.47	22.40	51.74
32	9.76	23.74	56.40
33	10.05	25.17	61.48
34	10.35	26.68	67.01
35	10.66	28.28	73.04
36	10.98	29.98	79.61
37	11.31	31.77	86.78
38	11.65	33.68	94.59
39	12.00	35.70	103.10
40	12.36	37.84	112.38
41	12.73	40.11	122.50

suggested that 6% is a reasonable approximation of
the average dividend growth rate. With respect to the
S&P 425, Jahnke[7] found that for overlapping ten-year
periods from 1947-73, the dividend growth rate averaged 5.6% with a range of 3.9% to 9.3%. Thus a range
of 3-9% dividend growth fairly well encompasses the
actual experience of the S&P 425, and 6% is reasonably
close to the average growth rate. Obviously for indi-

vidual stocks the dividend growth rates will cover a considerably wider range, but for well-diversified portfolios, a 3-9% range appears reasonable.

Table 2 illustrates the stream of future dividends, assuming growth rates (G_0) of 3%, 6%, and 9%. As a starting point for D_1, $3.90 was used because this is reasonably close to the mid-1976 annual rate of dividends for the S&P 425 industrial average. (Note: Any positive, non-zero figure can be used for D_1 without affecting the rates of return calculations since the purchase and sale price would then be scaled up or down in the same proportion as D_1.)

THE RANGE OF POSSIBLE RETURNS

Given the assumptions of three possible discount factors for both the purchase and the sale price (2.6% = Hi; 4.0% = Avg; 6.0% = Lo) and three possible dividend growth rates (3%, 6%, 9%), a range of possible compound annual rates of return can be calculated using Equation 3. The starting point is the dividend to be received in the first year (D_1) which was assumed to be $3.90. Assuming G_0 to be constant over the entire holding period of n years, the stream of dividends

$$\left(\sum_{i=1}^{n} D_i \right)$$

can be calculated, as was done in Table 2.

Using Equation 2, the purchase price (P_0) is determined by dividing D_1 by the discount factor (R_0-G_0). Given a dividend of $3.90, P_0 could vary from $65 to $150 using a range of 2.6% to 6% for the discount factor; an average discount factor of 4% gives a purchase price of $97.50. Table 3 lists the possible purchase prices given excellent timing (Bi-Lo), average timing (Bi-Avg), and poor timing (Bi-Hi).

Compound annual rates of return were calculated for holding periods of 1, 5, 10, 25, and 40 years. A one-year holding period would normally be considered too short a time horizon for serious investors. Forty years is probably too long, since it would stretch past the life expectancy of an investor in his 30's. However, the one-year and forty-year periods were included in order to demonstrate the effect time has on investment returns. Whether 5, 10, or 25 years is the

TABLE 3

POSSIBLE PURCHASE PRICES

Timing	Discount Factor (R_0-G_0)	Purchase Price $(P_0)^*$
Bi-Lo	6.0%	$65
Bi-Avg	4.0%	$97.50
Bi-Hi	2.6%	$150

*Solving Equation 2 where $P_0 = \dfrac{D_1}{R_0-G_0}$ and $D_1 = \$3.90$

more appropriate holding period depends on each investor's personal situation.

The sale price for poor timing (Sell-Lo), average timing (Sell-Avg), and excellent timing (Sell-Hi) at the end of each holding period (year n) is calculated by dividing D_{n+1} by the three discount factors (R_n-G_n), once again using 6%, 4%, and 2.6% as the possible discount factors. Table 4 lists the possible sale prices for 1, 5, 10, 25, and 40-year holding periods and dividend growth rates of 3%, 6%, and 9%.

If the S&P 425 being over $1,000 in the next 25-40 years, as shown in Table 4, seems implausible, pause to consider that this is the same approximate increase experienced during the past thirty-some years. The S&P indexes were constructed to equal $10, with 1941-43 as the base period and the industrials subsequently peaked at $135 in 1973.

Having determined the dividend stream under assumptions of 3%, 6%, and 9% dividend growth rates, as well as purchase prices and sale prices under assumptions of 6%, 4%, and 2.6% discount factors, the compound annual rates of return for various holding periods can be calculated by solving for r in Equation 3. Table 5 lists the compound annual rates of re-

SECURITY
SELECTION
AND ACTIVE
PORTFOLIO
MANAGEMENT

TABLE 4

POSSIBLE SALE PRICES

Sale Price (Pn)* in $'s

Timing	Discount Factor (Rn-Gn)	Year 1 Dividend Growth			Year 5 Dividend Growth			Year 10 Dividend Growth			Year 25 Dividend Growth			Year 40 Dividend Growth		
		3%	6%	9%	3%	6%	9%	3%	6%	9%	3%	6%	9%	3%	6%	9%
Sell-Lo	6.0%	67	69	71	75	87	100	87	116	154	136	279	560	212	669	2042
Sell-Avg	4.0%	101	103	106	113	131	150	131	175	231	204	419	840	318	1003	3063
Sell-Hi	2.6%	155	159	163	174	201	231	202	268	305	314	644	1293	490	1543	4712

*Solving Equation 2 where $P_n = \dfrac{D_{n+1}}{R_n - G_n}$ with D_{n+1} taken from the appropriate column in Table 2.

TABLE 5

THE HYPOTHETICAL RANGE OF
COMPOUND ANNUAL RATES OF RETURN

Timing	Discount Factor For Purchase Price (R₀-G₀)	Discount Factor For Sale Price (Rn-Gn)	1 Year Dividend Growth 3%	6%	9%	5 Years Dividend Growth 3%	6%	9%	10 Years Dividend Growth 3%	6%	9%	25 Years Dividend Growth 3%	6%	9%	40 Years Dividend Growth 3%	6%	9%
Bi-Lo, Sell-Hi	6.0%	2.6%	143.9	150.4	157.4	26.2	29.8	33.3	16.3	19.6	22.8	10.9	14.0	17.1	9.8	12.8	15.9
Bi-LO, Sell-Avg	6.0%	4.0%	60.6	64.9	69.5	16.9	20.1	23.4	12.4	15.5	18.6	9.9	12.9	15.9	9.4	12.3	15.4
Bi-Lo, Sell-Lo	6.0%	6.0%	9.0	12.0	15.0	9.0	12.0	15.0	9.0	12.0	15.0	9.0	12.0	15.0	9.0	12.0	15.0
Bi-Avg, Sell-Hi	4.0%	2.6%	62.6	66.9	71.7	15.7	18.9	22.2	10.9	14.0	17.1	8.2	11.2	14.3	7.5	10.6	13.6
Bi-Avg, Sell-Avg	4.0%	4.0%	7.0	10.0	13.0	7.0	10.0	13.0	7.0	10.0	13.0	7.0	10.0	13.0	7.0	10.0	13.0
Bi-Avg, Sell-Lo	4.0%	6.0%	-27.3	-25.4	-23.4	-0.3	2.4	5.2	3.7	6.5	9.4	6.1	9.0	12.0	6.6	9.6	12.5
Bi-Hi, Sell-Hi	2.6%	2.6%	5.6	8.6	11.6	5.6	8.6	11.6	5.6	8.6	11.6	5.6	8.6	11.6	5.6	8.6	11.6
Bi-Hi, Sell-Avg	2.6%	4.0%	-30.4	-28.6	-26.6	-2.4	0.3	3.1	1.8	4.7	7.5	4.3	7.3	10.3	5.0	8.0	10.9
Bi-Hi, Sell-Lo	2.6%	6.0%	-52.7	-51.5	-50.1	-9.2	-6.6	-4.1	-2.0	0.9	4.0	3.4	6.3	9.2	4.5	7.5	10.4

Solving for r in Equation 3 where $P_o = \sum_{i=1}^{n} \frac{D_i}{(1+r)^i} + \frac{P_n}{(1+r)^n}$

turn for all possible combinations of assumed purchase prices, sale prices, and dividend growth rates for 1, 5, 10, 25, and 40-year holding periods.

Using Table 5, one can examine the impact above average or below average success with respect to timing of the purchase and sale decisions and stock selection can have on investment returns for various holding periods. Note that the specific assumptions underlying the construction of Table 5 are not particularly crucial to the general conclusions drawn from the analysis which follows: the reader is welcome to reconstruct Table 5 with his own assumptions. (He might, however, find computing internal rates of return, based on up to 40 uneven cashflows, for the 135 different combinations a little tedious.) As long as his particular assumptions are a reasonable approximation of realized investor experience, he will probably reach conclusions similar to those that follow.

TIMING OF THE PURCHASE DECISION

Figure 1 illustrates the impact that the timing of the purchase decision can have on investor returns if the dividend growth rate is held constant at an average 6% rate and the sale price is held constant by assuming an average discount factor of 4%. It is obvious that the timing of the purchase decision has a tremendous impact on the rate of return if the holding period is relatively short. But even assuming a 25-year holding period, there is still a 5.6% difference in the compound annual rate of return for exceptional purchase timing versus very poor purchase timing (Bi-Lo return @ 25 years = 12.9%; Bi-Hi = 7.3%). To illustrate the magnitude of the impact of the purchase decision timing, $1,000 invested at 12.9% compounds to $20,776 over a 25-year holding period versus only $5,821 if the rate of return is 7.3%. (For the Buy-Avg return of 10%, $1,000 compounds to $10,835 in 25 years.)

At forty years, the Bi-Lo and Bi-Hi curves appear to "flatten out" and, in fact, if the holding period is extended further the Bi-Lo curve would approach a constant 12% and the Bi-Hi curve a constant 8%.

Thus, *no matter how long the holding period, time will not "bail out" poor timing of the purchase decision, relative to good timing.*

The Bi-Avg return in Figure 1 is a constant 10%. Referring back to Equation 4 where

$$P = \frac{D}{R - G}$$

a simple algebraic transformation will reveal that the investor's rate of return is equal to the dividend yield

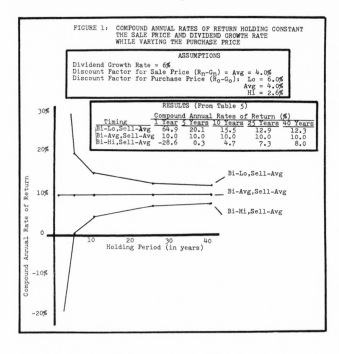

FIGURE 1: COMPOUND ANNUAL RATES OF RETURN HOLDING CONSTANT THE SALE PRICE AND DIVIDEND GROWTH RATE WHILE VARYING THE PURCHASE PRICE

ASSUMPTIONS

Dividend Growth Rate = 6%
Discount Factor for Sale Price (R_n-G_n) = Avg = 4.0%
Discount Factor for Purchase Price (R_o-G_o): Lo = 6.0%
Avg = 4.0%
Hi = 2.6%

RESULTS (From Table 5)

Timing	Compound Annual Rates of Return (%)				
	1 Year	5 Years	10 Years	25 Years	40 Years
Bi-Lo,Sell-Avg	64.9	20.1	15.5	12.9	12.3
Bi-Avg,Sell-Avg	10.0	10.0	10.0	10.0	10.0
Bi-Hi,Sell-Avg	-28.6	0.3	4.7	7.3	8.0

at the time of purchase plus the growth rate of dividends.

$$R = \frac{D}{P} + G \qquad (6)$$

This relationship assumes that the discount factor (R-G) is the same on the date of purchase and the date of sale, which was the case in Figure 1 for Buy-Avg,

Sell-Avg. Equation 6 may help put historical rates of return into perspective. In the post-war era, the average growth rate of dividends for stocks as a group has been 5-6% and dividend yields have averaged 3-4%, resulting in an average return to common stock investors of 8-10%, which is verified by the studies of Fisher and Lorie[8], Holmes,[9] and others.

TIMING OF THE SALE DECISION

Figure 2 illustrates the impact that the sale decision can have on investment returns if the dividend growth rate is held constant at 6% and the purchase price is held constant by assuming an average discount factor of 4%. In a fashion somewhat similar to

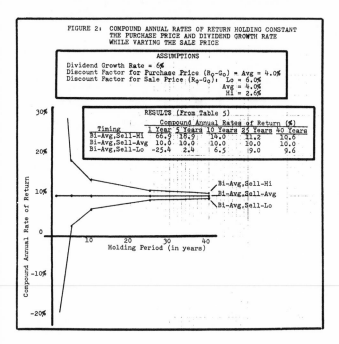

FIGURE 2: COMPOUND ANNUAL RATES OF RETURN HOLDING CONSTANT THE PURCHASE PRICE AND DIVIDEND GROWTH RATE WHILE VARYING THE SALE PRICE

ASSUMPTIONS

Dividend Growth Rate = 6%
Discount Factor for Purchase Price (R_0-G_0) = Avg = 4.0%
Discount Factor for Sale Price (R_0-G_0): Lo = 6.0%
Avg = 4.0%
Hi = 2.6%

RESULTS (From Table 5)

Timing	Compound Annual Rates of Return (%)				
	1 Year	5 Years	10 Years	25 Years	40 Years
Bi-Avg,Sell-Hi	66.9	18.9	14.0	11.2	10.6
Bi-Avg,Sell-Avg	10.0	10.0	10.0	10.0	10.0
Bi-Avg,Sell-Lo	-25.4	2.4	6.5	9.0	9.6

the purchase decision, the impact of the timing of the sale decision on investment returns is quite large if the holding period is relatively short and the impact tends to diminish as the holding period lengthens. However, a poor sale decision will not have near the impact of a poor purchase decision if the holding period is relatively long. For a 25-year holding period there is only a 2.2% difference in the annual rate of return for exceptional sale timing (Sell-Hi = 11.2%) versus very poor sale timing (Sell-Lo = 9.0%). If $1,000 were invested at 11.2% for 25 years it would compound to $14,211; invested at 9.0% for 25 years, $1,000 would compound to $8,623.

COMBINATIONS OF TIMING FOR THE PURCHASE AND SALE DECISIONS

In Figure 3 the rates of return for the combinations of Bi-Lo with Sell-Hi, Sell-Avg, and Sell-Lo are compared with the combinations of Bi-Hi with Sell-Hi, Sell-Avg, and Sell-Lo, holding the dividend growth rate constant at 6%. (The other possible timing combinations of Buy-Avg with Sell-Hi, Sell-Avg, and Sell-Lo are not illustrated in order to simplify the graph. The Bi-Avg Group would lie between the Bi-Lo

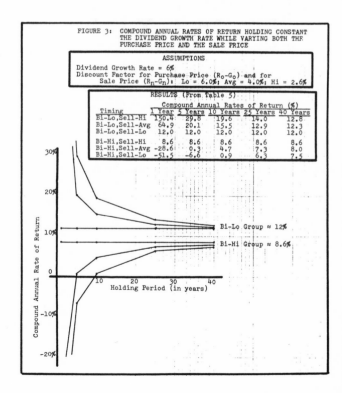

FIGURE 3: COMPOUND ANNUAL RATES OF RETURN HOLDING CONSTANT THE DIVIDEND GROWTH RATE WHILE VARYING BOTH THE PURCHASE PRICE AND THE SALE PRICE

ASSUMPTIONS

Dividend Growth Rate = 6%
Discount Factor for Purchase Price (R_0-G_0) and for
    Sale Price (R_n-G_n): Lo = 6.0%; Avg = 4.0%; Hi = 2.6%

RESULTS (From Table 5)

Timing	Compound Annual Rates of Return (%)				
	1 Year	5 Years	10 Years	25 Years	40 Years
Bi-Lo,Sell-Hi	150.4	29.8	19.6	14.0	12.8
Bi-Lo,Sell-Avg	64.9	20.1	15.5	12.9	12.3
Bi-Lo,Sell-Lo	12.0	12.0	12.0	12.0	12.0
Bi-Hi,Sell-Hi	8.6	8.6	8.6	8.6	8.6
Bi-Hi,Sell-Avg	-28.6	0.3	4.7	7.3	8.0
Bi-Hi,Sell-Lo	-51.5	-6.6	0.9	6.3	7.5

SECURITY
SELECTION
AND ACTIVE
PORTFOLIO
MANAGEMENT

and Bi-Hi Groups and trend toward 10%.)

From Figure 3 it is apparent that, given enough time, the Bi-Lo Group trends toward 12% while the Bi-Hi Group trends toward 8%. Using Equation 6, where

$$R = \frac{D}{P} + G \, ,$$

as a rough guide to analyze the results of the two groups, the initial dividend yield of the Bi-Lo Group is 6.0% versus 2.6% for the Bi-Hi Group. Assuming the same growth in dividends (G) for both groups, Bi-Lo will always have *at least* a 3.4% greater compound annual rate of return than Bi-Hi, *regardless of the sale price and the length of the holding period.* Thus the timing of the purchase decision is far more important than the timing of the sale decision.

THE DIVIDEND GROWTH RATE

Figure 4 illustrates the effect changes in the dividend growth rate have on rates of return, while holding constant the discount factor at 4.0% (Buy-Avg, sell-Avg).

As Figure 4 illustrates, when it is assumed that the discount factor is constant, then the difference in rates of return is simply the difference in dividend

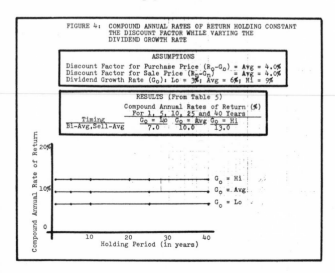

FIGURE 4: COMPOUND ANNUAL RATES OF RETURN HOLDING CONSTANT THE DISCOUNT FACTOR WHILE VARYING THE DIVIDEND GROWTH RATE

growth rates, regardless of the holding period. Because Figure 4 is not as dramatic as the previous illustrations with their curves and so forth, one might tend to underestimate the importance of the dividend growth rate. If so, consider that $1,000 invested at the 13% rate indicated for $G_0 = $ Hi compounds to $21,231 in 25 years; at the 7% rate indicated for $G_0 = $ Lo, $1,000 only compounds to $5,427 in the same time period. And, as the following section will demonstrate, superior stock selection can offset poor market timing — but only if the holding period is extremely long.

MARKET TIMING VERSUS STOCK SELECTION

In order to illustrate the impact market timing can have on rates of return versus the impact of stock selection, Figure 5 graphs the combination of the best possible timing with the worst dividend growth (Bi-

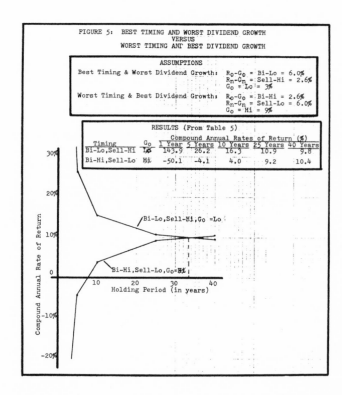

FIGURE 5: BEST TIMING AND WORST DIVIDEND GROWTH
VERSUS
WORST TIMING AND BEST DIVIDEND GROWTH

ASSUMPTIONS	
Best Timing & Worst Dividend Growth:	$R_0-G_0 = $ Bi-Lo = 6.0%
	$R_n-G_n = $ Sell-Hi = 2.6%
	$G_0 = $ Lo = 3%
Worst Timing & Best Dividend Growth:	$R_0-G_0 = $ Bi-Hi = 2.6%
	$R_n-G_n = $ Sell-Lo = 6.0%
	$G_0 = $ Hi = 9%

RESULTS (From Table 5)

Timing	G_0	Compound Annual Rates of Return (%)				
		1 Year	5 Years	10 Years	25 Years	40 Years
Bi-Lo,Sell-Hi	Lo	143.9	26.2	16.3	10.9	9.8
Bi-Hi,Sell-Lo	Hi	-50.1	-4.1	4.0	9.2	10.4

SECURITY
SELECTION
AND ACTIVE
PORTFOLIO
MANAGEMENT

Lo, Sell-Hi, G_0 = Lo) versus the combination of the worst possible timing with the best possible dividend growth (Bi-Hi, Sell-Lo, G_0=Hi).

It is obvious to most stock market participants that timing dominates dividends in determining the investor's return when the holding period is relatively short. Notice, however, that in Figure 5, it is 33 years before the combination of an excellent growth rate in dividends and poor timing results in a higher return than the combination of excellent timing and poor dividend growth. Therefore, given the assumptions underlying Figure 5, it is clear that the value of perfect information with respect to timing is far greater than the value of perfect information with respect to future dividend growth rates, given any reasonable holding period. The question is not whether the game of timing is worth playing — it is, and it is worth more than the game of trying to forecast future earnings and dividends. The real question is what are the probabilities of success for either game.

THE RANDOM WALK VERSUS HIGGLEDY-PIGGLEDY GROWTH

The weak form of the efficient market hypothesis[10] suggests that stock prices follow a random walk with no significant correlation between past prices and future prices. Academicians have tested a great number of trading techniques to see if they can produce above normal profits. Given a long enough time horizon, most trading strategies have been shown to do no better and generally worse than a simple buy-and-hold strategy.[11]

Unfortunately, the evidence presented by Linter and Glauber[12] and others[13] suggests that the chances of forecasting superior earnings and dividend growth are not much better than the chances of achieving superior timing. Thus, the literature suggests that the market is reasonably efficient. Given enough chances, most investors will get average results, which in the case of Bi-Avg, Sell-Avg, G_0 = Avg, would be a compound annual return of 8-10%.

TO TRY OR NOT TO TRY?

One conclusion that is frequently drawn from the efficient market hypothesis is that the best investment strategy is a passive strategy — that is, buy and hold a well-diversified portfolio and keep costs at a minimum by not expending resources in trying to outperform the market by either security selection or market timing. Obviously there are many market participants who do not accept this conclusion, and this paper should aid them in determining where the potential rewards lie in trying to outperform the market. Figure 5 suggests that the greatest benefits lie in improving the timing aspect of the total return equation. And of the two timing decisions, the purchase decision is by far the most important. (If one can Bi-Lo, he has it made.) However, each market participant will have to evaluate his personal skills in deciding whether to allocate his time and resources on market timing, security analysis, or some combination of both.

[1] John Burr Williams, *The Theory of Investment Value* (Cambridge, Mass: Harvard University Press, 1938.)

[2] M. J. Gordon, "Dividends, Earnings and Stock Prices," *Review of Economics and Statistics* (May, 1959), pp. 96-105.

[3] For a proof of this equation see most college level texts on finance or investments. For example, see J. Fred Weston and Eugene F. Brigham, *Managerial Finance* (4th ed.; Hinsdale, Ill.: The Dryden Press, 1972), p. 285.

[4] John Russell Holmes, "100 Years of Investment Experience With Common Stocks," *Financial Analysts Journal* (November-December, 1974), p. 42.

[5] William W. Jahnke, "What's Behind Stock Prices?" *Financial Analysts Journal* (September-October, 1975), p. 71.

[6] Jerome B. Cohen, Edward N. Zinbarg and Arthur Zeikel, *Investment Analysis and Portfolio Management* (Homewood, Ill.: Richard D. Irwin, 1973), pp. 225-227.

[7] Jahnke, *op. cit.*, p. 70. Note: For the 10-year period of 1947-56, the dividend growth rate was 11.1%; however, this growth

SECURITY
SELECTION
AND ACTIVE
PORTFOLIO
MANAGEMENT

rate was significantly affected by the unusually depressed level of dividends in 1947.

[8] Lawrence Fisher and James H. Lorie, "Rates of Return on Investments in Common Stocks: The Year-By-Year Record, 1926-1965," *Journal of Business* (July, 1968), pp. 291-316.

[9] Holmes, *op. cit.*

[10] For a discussion of the efficient market hypothesis see James H. Lorie and Mary T. Hamilton, *The Stock Market: Theories and Evidence* (Homewood, Ill.: Richard D. Irwin, 1973), pp. 70-112.

[11] For a discussion of studies testing the value of timing formulas and other trading techniques, see Lorie and Hamilton, *op. cit.*; also see Richard A. Brealey, *An Introduction to Risk and Return from Common Stocks* (Cambridge, Mass.: The M.I.T. Press, 1973), pp. 55-77.

[12] John Lintner and Robert Glauber, "Higgledy Piggledy Growth," an unpublished paper prepared for the Seminar on the Analysis of Security Prices, University of Chicago, May, 1967.

[13] For a discussion of earnings as a random walk, see Brealey, *op. cit.*, pp. 77-104.

Can selectivity pay in an efficient market?

It does pay to be selective, but you must diversify among your best selections.

Keith P. Ambachtsheer

Selectivity is an important dimension of an "active" approach to the management of stock portfolios. It implies being overweighted in undervalued stocks and industry groups and underweighted in ones which are overvalued. The *profitability* of a selectivity strategy depends on:

1. The accuracy with which the predictions of over- and undervaluedness are being made.
2. The reward associated with a prediction of a given level of accuracy.
3. The degree to which "slippage" in getting these judgments correctly reflected in portfolios can be eliminated. This typically implies balancing less than perfect predictions against transaction costs and desired levels of market sensitivity and diversification.

In a study published in an earlier issue of this Journal,[1] we reported the finding that a group of in-

1. Footnotes appear at end of the article.

stitutional investors achieved a low but significantly positive level of predictive ability in making judgments on stock and industry group over- and undervaluedness over a two-year period.

The measurement technique used was to correlate their expectations (expressed as ratings) against subsequent actual experience. The average correlation coefficient (called "information coefficient" or "IC" in this context) found was 0.15.

The "slippage" question in this study was addressed by using the PRECAST selection model[2] to relate the low quality predictions to the existing portfolio in the context of transaction costs and market sensitivity and diversification requirements. The model was able to rebuild the existing portfolios into new portfolios which, on average, outperformed both the old portfolios and the market by 2% per annum.

This level of realized incremental reward was consistent with prior expectations, given:

1. An assumed accuracy of the predictions equal to achieved accuracy (i.e., an "IC" of 0.15).
2. An assumed switch cost of 4% and the specification that the rebuilt portfolios have market sensitivities and diversification characteristics equal to that of the original portfolios.
3. An assumed *equal* level of reward potential associated with all stocks and industry groups having a given rating (with that rating expressing the *degree* of over- or undervaluedness).[3]

THE KEY QUESTIONS

This third assumption, while consistent with "ex post" experience in the study in aggregate, is obviously an oversimplification. It begs important questions, such as:

1. Is the reward potential from aggregate *stock selectivity* equal to the reward potential from aggregate *industry selectivity*, given equal predictive ability?
2. Is the reward potential from *stock selectivity* equal *within each industry group*, given equal predictive ability?

3. Is the reward potential from *industry selectivity* equal for *each industry group,* given equal predictive ability?
4. What implications do answers to questions 1, 2, and 3 have for (a) the allocation of research resources, and (b) portfolio construction?

ANSWERING THE QUESTIONS

A study was designed to answer some of these questions. The data[4] used in the study are annual stock returns (capital gains/losses) with the market effects removed. These return measures will be called "residual returns," and will be taken as proxies of the *relative* degrees of over- and undervaluedness of stocks at various points of time. The objective of security analysis is presumably to predict these "residual returns."

The specifics of the study design were:

1. Create two 100-stock samples by selecting the top four (by weight) stocks in 25 major S&P 500 groups and the top five (by weight) stocks in the twenty TSE groups.

WITHIN- VS. ACROSS-INDU

	1971		1972	
	Can.	U.S.	Can.	U
Total Variability	23	28	35	
Within-Group Variability	16	19	29	
Across-Group Variability	16	23	17	

* as measured by standard deviations of annual "residual ret

2. Calculate the "residual returns" for each of the 200 stocks for the calendar years 1971, 1972, 1973, and 1974.
3. Divide the total "residual return" for each stock into a company and industry component by: (a) calculating the average "residual return" for each group and defining that as the industry component; and (b) calculating the difference between the

SECURITY
SELECTION
AND ACTIVE
PORTFOLIO
MANAGEMENT

total "residual return" for each stock and the "industry component" and defining that as the company component for each stock.

4. Calculate, for each of the two samples for each year, the standard deviations of the company and industry "residual returns." These standard deviations will serve as the "reward potential" measures in the study. Clearly, there is more potential reward associated with forecasts, assuming equal predictive ability, made on groups of stocks which exhibit great variability of return than on groups which exhibit little variability.

5. Calculate, for each of the two samples, the standard deviation of the four one-year industry residual returns around their four-year average. This set of standard deviations will provide insight into the relative variability (and hence reward potential) of industry groups over time.

THE VARIABILITY OF TOTAL, INDUSTRY, AND COMPANY RESIDUAL RETURNS

By splitting total "residual returns" into com-

ARD POTENTIAL*

	1973		1974		Average	
n.	U.S.	Can.	U.S.	Can.	U.S.
9	29	16	19	26	26
0	17	12	15	19	18
0	24	11	13	16	20

pany and industry components for the 100-stock Canadian and U.S. samples, the standard deviation of both return components were calculated. Should within-group (company) variability greatly exceed across-group (industry) variability, potential rewards from selectivity would largely lie with individual stock selectivity. A reverse finding would of course indicate the opposite. The table below summarizes the actual findings in each of the four one-year periods.

Observations:
1. The potential gains from stock and industry selectivity were, on average, about the same during the last four years in both the Canadian and U.S. stock markets.
2. The *total* potential gains from selectivity appear to vary significantly. They were much greater during the 1972 bull market than during the 1974 bear market. This is consistent with a previous finding that betas are much better predictors of stock price movements during falling markets than during rising markets.[5]
3. Although there may be better methods of classifying groups, the traditional methods used by Standard and Poor's and the Toronto Stock Exchange are quite effective in grouping stocks having similar price movement characteristics. Analysis of variance tests strongly rejected the hypothesis that all industry group residual returns come from the same underlying return distribution.[6]

THE ALLOCATION OF RESEARCH RESOURCES

While the potential gains from stock and industry selectivity, *in aggregate,* appear to be of the same order of magnitude, given equal predictive ability, this is not necessarily the case on a disaggregated group by group basis. Which groups offer large potential gains from stock selectivity *within* the group? Which groups offer little? Which groups offer large potential gains from selectivity *among* groups? Which groups offer little?

Again, the standard deviations of the company and industry residual returns were used as the basis for categorizing the 20 Canadian and 25 U.S. groups into "high," "medium," and "low" reward potential categories. The following matrixes categorize individual industry groups simultaneously on the basis of within-industry group (company) variability and in-

SECURITY
SELECTION
AND ACTIVE
PORTFOLIO
MANAGEMENT

dustry group variability over time. The data on which the construction of the two matrixes is based are shown in brackets following the industry group name. The first number in the brackets is the average of the four one-year within-industry (company) standard deviations; the second number is the standard deviation of the four one-year (industry) group "residual returns" around their four-year mean:

Observations:

1. On a left to right basis, the categorization gives some indication of the importance of having an industry view for each of the groups. Not surprisingly, evidence of greater to lesser industry cyclicality (from left to right) is present in the "categorization" in both markets.

2. On a top to bottom basis, the categorization gives some indication of the importance of having a view on individual companies *within* each of the groups. Not surprisingly, evidence of lesser to greater homogeneity and size (from top to bottom) among companies within the groups is present in the categorization scheme.

3. The matrix gives some indication of where, assuming equal predictive ability, security analysis (i.e., the top of the matrix) and industry analysis (i.e., the left hand side of the matrix) will produce the greatest potential rewards.

IMPLICATIONS FOR PORTFOLIO CONSTRUCTION

To this point we have treated "residual return" variability very positively, calling it a measure of *reward* potential. Clearly, it is also a measure of *loss* potential. The foregoing analysis assumes that investors face each year cross-sectional distributions of within- and across-industry "residual returns." These distributions can be characterized as having a mean of 0% and an average standard deviation (using 1971-1974 results) of about 18%. In making their "residual return" predictions, assume investors define

UNITED STATES

Reward Potential From Group Selectivity

	HIGH	MEDIUM	LOW
HIGH		Machinery (23, 14) Tobacco (25, 15) Entertainment (25, 21)	Chemicals (23, 11)
MEDIUM	Airlines (21, 40) Forest Products (20, 43) Steels (15, 23) Containers (19, 23) Aerospace (21, 26)	Integrated Oils (15, 14) Textiles (19, 19) Beverages (16, 20) Building Materials (20, 19) Paper (18, 18)	Foods (21, 14) Soaps (17, 9) Drugs (16, 9) Merchandising (17, 13) Business Equip. (18, 16) Electronics (17, 12) Miscellaneous (21, 10)
LOW	Industrial Mines (10, 35)	Autos (13, 15) Rubber (6, 20) Railroads (12, 19)	Utilities (11, 5)

Reward Potential From Stock Selectivity Within Groups

SECURITY
SELECTION
AND ACTIVE
PORTFOLIO
MANAGEMENT

CANADA

Reward Potential From Group Selectivity

		HIGH	MEDIUM	LOW
Reward Potential From Stock Selectivity Within Groups	HIGH	Golds (35, 73)	Western Oils (25, 17) Real Estate (29, 18)	Base Metals (24, 5) Chemicals (23, 13) Miscellaneous (26, 6)
	MEDIUM	Communications (19, 22) Merchandising (19, 27) Industrial Mines (20, 28) Forest Products (19, 27) General Manuf. (19, 23)	Integrated Oils (17, 18) Steels (21, 15)	Foods (21, 8) Trust & Loan (22, 7) Pipelines (16, 13) Beverages (16, 10)
	LOW		Utilities (7, 15)	Construction (9, 4) Banks (9, 12)

"good" companies and industries as those that they judge likely to perform one standard deviation better than the mean (i.e., have a residual return of 18%). However, if their "information coefficient" in making these judgments is, as in the previously quoted study, 0.15, the *expected* residual returns of the "good" companies or groups is not 18% but 18% × 0.15 = 2.7%[7]. The variability associated with each prediction remains at a standard deviation level close to 18%.[7]

We are now set up to make a crucial point. The only way investors can "lock in" the 2.7%[8] increment is to diversify away the variability associated with the low quality predictions. This will, given the standard deviation of 18% associated with each prediction, require a lot of "good" stocks, or "good" industries. Using the square root rule,[9] a relationship between the number of "good" stocks or industries and the remaining variability around the expected incremental return of 2.7% is easily developed:

NUMBER OF PREDICTIONS VS. REMAINING VARIABILITY
AROUND EXPECTED INCREMENTAL RETURN

No. of "good" stocks or industries	1	10	25	50	100
Remaining variability	18%	5.9%	3.6%	2.6%	1.8%

The table suggests that the long-term attainment of 2.7% of incremental return per year through stock or industry selection *without subjecting the portfolio to a significant possibility of realizing a negative return in any one year* requires over 100 "good" stocks (for stock selectivity) or over 100 "good" industries (for industry selectivity). But, given the way we have defined a "good" stock or "good" industry, they must represent significantly less than 50% of the *total* number of stocks or industries. This *total* number then must be well over 200.

The crucial point should now be obvious. While investors use selection universes which often approach or exceed 200 stocks, these stocks are typically categorized into the 20 to 25 groups used in this study. This implies that the achievement of significant gains from selectivity requires far greater risk exposure through the industry selectivity route than through the stock selectivity route. This is so despite the documented assumptions of (a) equal predictive ability, and (b) equal reward potential per prediction. It is simply a question of the *number* of predictions: there are, at any time, far more undervalued companies than undervalued industries, simply because there are many more companies than industries *in total*.[10]

[1] See Keith Ambachtsheer, *Profit Potential In an Almost Efficient Capital Market*, Journal of Portfolio Management, Fall, 1974.

[2] The PRECAST selection model is a Canavest House adaptation of the single index stock portfolio selection models originated by W. Sharpe and J. Mao.

[3] The PRECAST system converts stock and industry group ratings into final ratings and converts the resulting rating distribution into a distribution of residual returns. This latter distribution was assigned a standard deviation of 18%. This estimate was based on analysis of residual return variability during the late 1960s and early 1970s. Our data for 1971, 1972, 1973, and 1974 suggest the 18% to have been an underestimate of annual residual return variability during the last four years. Accordingly, the standard deviation now being used in the system is 26%.

[4] The data on which this study is based are available from Canavest on request.

[5] See Robert Levy, *Beta As A Predictor of Return*, Financial Analysts Journal, Jan./Feb., 1974.

[6] The F values for the eight ratios of across-industry to within-industry variance ranged from 11.0 to 1.6. Any value over 1.7 indicates significant differences between group means at the 0.05 level.

[7] See Hodges, Brealey, *Dynamic Portfolio Selection*, Financial Analysts Journal, March/April, 1973, for a detailed explanation of the relationship between prior return distributions

and the adjustments that should be made to them on the basis of forecasting ability assumptions.

[8] Transaction costs would reduce the 2.7% expectation. Annual switch costs of 3% on 30% of the portfolio would reduce the 2.7% to 1.8%, for example.

[9] Specifically, the standard deviation of sample means is related to the standard deviation of the original distribution by the formula $\sigma/\sqrt{n}$ where n is the sample size. This estimate would understate the true standard deviation if the "residual returns" are not independent. To the degree stock "residual returns" are more likely to be independent than industry "residual returns," the conclusions of this section would be reinforced.

[10] Jack Treynor has pointed out that our conclusions in this section are dependent on an assumption that the *costs* of making the predictions are negligible relative to total assets under management. There is no doubt that the stock selectivity route would lose a great deal of its "comparative advantage" if significant costs per prediction are assumed.

Two tiers — but how many decisions?

Big stocks and the general market have frequently followed separate paths. What does this mean for portfolio management?

Marshall E. Blume

T he popular financial press has coined the phrase "the two-tier market" to describe the often substantial differences in returns that have been realized by different kinds of stocks in recent years. As one illustration, the equal-weighted Value Line Composite Index declined 64.8% from March 11, 1968 to September 30, 1974, while the value-weighted New York Stock Exchange (NYSE) Composite Index declined only 33.2% over the same period. It might be expected that those investors, like banks, that have concentrated their holdings in the larger issues, as measured by the market value of the shares outstanding, would have realized greater returns on their stock investments during these years than many other investors, at least before management and commission costs.

According to some observers, the predilection of institutions, particularly banks, to invest their huge inflows of new pension fund money in a limited number of "favored" stocks, the so-called "upper tier," has supported the prices of these issues. Since many institutional investors invest primarily in the larger issues for reasons of liquidity, most of these "favored" stocks would be larger companies. Thus, the great differences between the returns on large and small companies are said to be explained.

Without judging the validity of this explanation, it does seem to suggest that the recent behavior of returns is unique in an historical perspective. The results in this paper, however, show that this recent behavior of returns is not unique to recent years and, moreover, that the differences in returns between large and small issues was even greater prior to the rapid growth of institutional investors. Nonetheless, the evidence gives no reason to believe that the past will repeat itself and that large issues will necessarily outreturn small issues in the future.

These findings mean that a portfolio to be well-diversified must contain investments in both large and small issues. In other words, portfolios invested primarily in larger issues, which are common to many institutions, are probably not well-diversified even though they contain many issues. While such portfolios will and have performed in some markets very well, there is substantial risk that they will perform poorly in other markets, a risk which can be avoided through proper diversification.

The often substantial differences in realized returns have profound implications for traditional portfolio management. A traditional portfolio manager must not only find securities of above average investment value but must also evaluate the contribution of each security to the overall risk of a portfolio. The results of this paper suggest that this second task is much more difficult than often perceived. Merely holding a large number of securities with not too much invested in each, for instance, does not guarantee a fully diversified portfolio.

Finally, the results of this paper have a direct

bearing on how a fund designed to replicate the return on some index, a so-called index fund, should be constructed. Any index fund should contain both large and small issues. An important remaining issue, which is often debated, is how many issues should be included. Simulations of various strategies to replicate the returns on the Standard and Poor's Composite Index of 500 stocks over the fourteen years ending June 30, 1974 suggest that as many stocks as possible should be included. Over these fourteen years, an index fund restricted to 200 stocks would have experienced much larger deviations in returns from the index and at the same time greater trading costs than a fund unrestricted as to the number of holdings. Since the charges of many custodians are based primarily on the market value of the portfolio, there appears to be no valid reason to restrict the number of securities in an index fund.

THE RELATIONSHIPS OF RETURNS TO SIZE

One of the most straightforward ways to analyze the relationship of returns on common stocks to the market value of the shares outstanding is to compare the returns from various indexes constructed under different weighting schemes. To this end, monthly returns for four differently weighted indexes of NYSE common stock were calculated over the 45 years from July, 1928 through June, 1973. One of these indexes was the familiar equal-weighted index in which the weight assigned to each stock is the same. Another was the familiar value-weighted index in which the weight assigned to each stock is proportional to the market value of the shares outstanding less treasury stock. This index is particularly important since it measures the returns realized by all investors in the aggregate on their NYSE investments.

The final two indexes were a more than value-weighted index and a less than equal-weighted index. The weights assigned to stocks in the more than value-weighted index were taken to be proportional to the square of the market values of the stocks, while the weights in the less than equal-weighted index were taken to be proportional to the reciprocal of the market values of the stocks.[1]

The percentage of each index attributable to the largest ten stocks by market value at any point in time

TABLE 1

SUMMARY STATI

Description

A. Percentage of Index on June 30, 1972
    Attributable to
      IBM
      Top 10 Stocks by Market Value
      Top 50 Stocks by Market Value
      Top 100 Stocks by Market Value

B. Returns on Indexes
    Terminal Value of an Initial Investment of $1.00
      July, 1928 — June, 1973
      July, 1928 — December, 1950
      January, 1951 — June, 1973

    Annual Geometric Rate of Return
      July, 1928 — June, 1973
      July, 1928 — December, 1950
      January, 1951 — June, 1973

provides a feel for the actual weights assigned to specific stocks. Using June 30, 1972 as an example, the weight given to these largest ten stocks in the less than equal-weighted index was 0.01% of the weight given to all stocks in the index; the weight for these same ten stocks in the equal-weighted index was 1.05%; 31.53% in the value-weighted; and 83.92% in the more than value-weighted. Table 1 presents these percentages and similar percentages for the same date for IBM, the largest fifty stocks, and the largest 100 stocks by market value. Of course for years prior to 1972, the weights

1. Footnotes appear at the end of the article.

would have been different, and IBM would not always have been the largest company.

One dollar invested in the less than equal-weighted index at the end of June, 1928 would have increased to $22.21 by June, 1973 (Table 1). In comparison, a dollar invested in an equal-weighted index or a

ARIOUS INDEXES

	Kinds of Index		
ss than al-Weight	Equal-Weight	Value-Weight	More than Value-Weight
0.00%	0.11%	7.67%	37.98%
0.01%	1.05%	31.53%	83.92%
0.09%	5.25%	57.17%	96.65%
0.36%	10.52%	68.61%	98.39%
$22.21	$52.34	$53.94	$110.80
$ 2.54	$ 4.61	$ 3.92	$ 6.84
$ 8.74	$11.35	$13.74	$ 16.20
7.1%	9.2%	9.3%	11.0%
4.2%	7.0%	6.3%	8.9%
0.1%	11.4%	12.4%	13.2%

value-weighted index would have increased to $52.34 or $53.94, respectively, while a dollar in a more than value-weighted index would have increased to $110.80. Thus, a dollar in a more than value-weighted index would have resulted in a terminal value over the 45-year period of more than double that from a value-weighted or equal-weighted index and approximately five times that from a less than equal-weighted index.

Furthermore, the terminal value of an initial investment of $1.00 in the more than value-weighted index would have been larger than that from any other index in each half of this 45-year period. What is perhaps even more interesting is that the relative difference for the first 22½ years ending in 1950 between the returns from the more than value-weighted index and those from the other indexes was greater than in the second 22½ years ending in 1973. One dollar invested in the more than value-weighted index from June, 1928 through December, 1950 would have yielded a terminal value 74% larger than if invested in the value-weighted index, while the difference would have been only 18% in the period from the end of 1950 through June, 1973. The superiority of the more than value-weighted index over the entire 45 years 1928-1973 was thus primarily due to the returns realized *prior* to 1950.

The comparative returns on these four differently weighted indexes suggest the following: First, if the market can be characterized as consisting of two tiers, this characterization is stronger prior to 1950 than after. Second, if there is a single reason for the larger returns on the more than value-weighted index, that reason cannot be the growth of institutions since institutions did not become an important force in the marketplace until sometime after 1950. It is, of course, possible that institutions caused a two-tier market after 1950 and something else was responsible for the two tiers, if there were indeed two tiers, prior to 1950. While possible, an alternative explanation is that the observed returns are consistent with random chance. The next section examines this possibility.

A MORE DETAILED STATISTICAL ANALYSIS OF THE INDEXES

What makes stocks risky is that their rates of return are subject to a great amount of variability in the short-run, say a month or a year, and contrary to the views of some, this variability does not average or "wash out" in the long-run.[2] To illustrate, consider two investors who realize the same returns month by month on their investments from now to eternity ex-

SECURITY
SELECTION
AND ACTIVE
PORTFOLIO
MANAGEMENT

cept for the initial month in which one makes 0% and the other 10%. No matter how long it is to eternity, the latter investor will always have 10% more wealth than the other even though it is true that the differences between their geometric average or compounded rates of return will become infinitesimally small.

It is thus possible that the substantially larger terminal values of the more than value-weighted index may be purely due to the chance occurrence of a few months of very favorable returns. One appropriate test of this proposition is to ascertain whether the mean monthly returns of the four indexes are significantly different (Table 2). No statistically significant differences could be found over the entire 45 years or in either half.[3]

Intuitively the differences in the mean returns are generally small relative to the standard errors of the means. Thus, if the mean monthly return for the more than value-weighted index, 1.02%, were reduced by 0.12 percentage points, just over one-half its standard error, the mean return on this index would have been the smallest of the four indexes. Since confidence intervals are usually given in terms of plus or minus two standard errors, a half a standard error is well within the usual margins of error.

In addition to the mean monthly returns, two standard risk measures were calculated (Table 2). The first was the beta coefficient using the value-weighted index as the measure of the market. The second was the standard deviation of monthly returns. As measured by standard deviation, the level of risk inherent in the indexes decreases as more weight is given to the larger issues at the expense of the smaller. This relationship implies, of course, that smaller issues are on average more risky than larger issues — a not too surprising result. If known risk is measured by the beta coefficient, only for the overall period and the first half of that period is the same relationship observed.

What is perhaps a more interesting result for portfolio management is that these risk measures

TABLE 2

AVERAGE MONTHLY RETURNS AND [

Description
_____

_____

A. July, 1928 — June, 1974

    Beta Coefficient[1]
    Standard Deviation of Monthly Returns[1]
    Diversified Portfolio Standard Deviation
    Correlation of Returns with Value-Weighted Index

    Average Monthly Return[2]
    Standard Deviation of the Average

B. July, 1928 — December, 1950

    Beta Coefficient[1]
    Standard Deviation of Monthly Returns[1]
    Diversified Portfolio Standard Deviation
    Correlation of Returns with Value-Weighted Index

    Average Monthly Return[2]
    Standard Deviation of the Average

C. January, 1951 — June, 1973

    Beta Coefficient[1]
    Standard Deviation of Monthly Returns[1]
    Diversified Portfolio Standard Deviation
    Correlation of Returns with Value-Weighted Index

    Average Monthly Return[2]
    Standard Deviation of the Average

[1] The beta coefficients and the standard deviations of monthly returns were estimated from the monthly returns over the same period used in calculating the average monthly returns. The index used in calculating the beta

show that the less than equal-weighted and the more than value-weighted indexes were not as well-diversified as the other two indexes. In an efficient market, in which securities are correctly priced, expected rates of return vary only with nondiversifiable risk, so that any portfolio containing some diversifiable risk bears some risk for which there is no compensation.

    Specifically, the standard deviation of returns

SECURITY
SELECTION
AND ACTIVE
PORTFOLIO
MANAGEMENT

	Kinds of Index		
Less than Equal-Weight	Equal-Weight	Value-Weight	More than Value-Weight
1.38	1.17	1.00	0.90
11.52%	7.05%	5.62%	5.45%
7.76%	6.57%	5.62%	5.04%
0.67	0.93	1.00	0.93
1.14%	0.98%	0.90%	1.02%
0.50%	0.30%	0.24%	0.24%
1.49	1.21	1.00	0.90
15.62%	9.10%	7.06%	6.84%
10.49%	8.52%	7.06%	6.37%
0.67	0.94	1.00	0.93
1.39%	0.98%	0.76%	0.95%
0.95%	0.55%	0.43%	0.42%
0.99	1.03	1.00	0.87
4.64%	4.08%	3.66%	3.56%
3.64%	3.78%	3.66%	3.20%
0.78	0.92	1.00	0.90
0.91%	0.99%	1.04%	1.10%
0.28%	0.25%	0.22%	0.22%

coefficients was taken to be the value-weighted index as constructed in this paper.

[2] The average monthly returns are arithmetic averages.

for a fully diversified portfolio can be shown to be the product of its beta coefficient and the standard deviation of returns on the market portfolio. Any standard deviation in excess of this theoretical amount represents undiversified risk. A comparison of the actual standard deviations with their theoretical values for a comparable fully diversified portfolio shows the substantial lack of diversification in the less than equal-weighted portfolio.

THE IMPLICATIONS OF A MULTI-FACTOR MODEL

The often substantial differences in returns as between large and small companies, as well as much other evidence,[4] lead to the strong conclusion that there are at least two and perhaps many market-wide forces shaping the returns of individual securities. In contrast, most commercial applications of beta-related theory make the implicit assumption that the variability in returns of an individual security stems from only two sources: a single market-wide force or factor common to all securities and an effect unique to each individual security. Assuming such a one-factor model is, for instance, tantamount to assuming that there are no industry factors, or more subtly, a size-related factor.

While the one-factor model may not provide an adequate description of how returns on securities are generated, it does provide some theoretical insights which are of value in understanding the implications of a two- or multi-factor model. Through diversification, an investor can eliminate virtually all of the risk unique to individual securities and thus be exposed only to the risk of fluctuation in the one common market factor, a risk which cannot be diversified away. This non-diversifiable risk can be summarized by the beta coefficient, which measures the exposure, or more precisely, the extent to which the returns of a portfolio will diminish or amplify general market-wide movements. If the beta coefficient is greater than 1.0, the variability of the returns on a diversified portfolio will be greater than on the market; if the beta coefficient is less than 1.0, the variability will be less.

In a one-factor model, the beta coefficient thus summarizes everything about the level of risk associated with a diversified portfolio. It makes no difference how the value of the portfolio beta coefficient is obtained — whether from a portfolio of a large number of securities with the same risk or from a portfolio of a large number of securities with the same risk or from a portfolio of a large number of securities

SECURITY
SELECTION
AND ACTIVE
PORTFOLIO
MANAGEMENT

with widely differing risks. Indeed, there is a direct and certain relationship between the return realized by the market and the return realized on a diversified portfolio. If, for instance, the portfolio beta is greater than 1.0, a fully diversified portfolio will necessarily increase at a faster rate than the market when the market is increasing and fall at a faster rate in a downturn.

This certain relationship between the return on a diversified portfolio and the return on the market as a function of beta in the case of a one-factor model underlies many commercial applications of beta-related theory. For example, several financial institutions provide one-parameter measures of investment performance. The rationale underlying these measures is that any randomly selected portfolio in which unique effects have been diversified away will return a known amount, once the return on the market is known. If an actual portfolio returns more than this amount, it is said to have experienced favorable performance; if less, unfavorable performance. For similar reasons, in a one-factor model, the beta coefficient can be used as a sophisticated timing device. In a rising market, diversified portfolios with betas greater than 1.0 are certain to do better than the market.

If, however, returns on individual securities are described by two- or multi-factor models, the concept of diversification, as well as the relationship of realized returns to market returns, becomes more complicated. A portfolio can be completely diversified as to the unique risks specific to individual companies without being fully diversified. Moreover, there is no longer a predictable relationship between the return on a portfolio diversified as to unique risk and the return on the market as a function of beta. Two portfolios diversified as to unique risk and having the same beta coefficient may experience widely different returns over the same period of time. It is even possible, and indeed it has happened, that in a rapidly rising market, the returns on most high beta portfolios diversified as to unique risk may be much smaller than the return on the market portfolio.

Without delving into the mathematical details, given in the appendix, a multi-factor model assumes that there are two or more factors common to at least two or more securities. In the case of a two-factor model, there might be two factors common to all securities which generate deviations from their expected returns or possibly one factor common to all securities and another common to a subset. To be concrete, one factor might be associated with the general level of economic activity and the other with monetary policy. The return on each security will tend to respond differentially to each of these risks. Some securities might be highly sensitive to monetary policy; others to economic activity. Still others might be relatively insensitive to each factor. The degree to which the return of a security is exposed to each of these risks can be measured by a response coefficient. The greater the response coefficient to a specific factor, the more sensitive the return of that security is to that factor. In order to establish a reference point, each factor or risk might be defined so that the response coefficient to that factor in the market portfolio is 1.0.

The beta coefficient of a security can be shown to be a weighted average of the response coefficients to each of the common risks. The weights are proportional to the importance of the risk in the market portfolio. Thus, a security with a large response coefficient to a risk which has a small chance of occurring could have the same value for its beta coefficient as a security which has a small response coefficient to a risk which has a large probability of occurring. In this case, the expected rates of returns of both securities would be the same.

More generally, in a multi-factor model, expected returns are an increasing function of beta as in a one-factor model. The beta coefficient serves as a summary of the overall level of risk exposure to market-wide risks. The relationship of realized returns on the market and those on a portfolio diversified as to unique risk is no longer a certain function of the beta

SECURITY
SELECTION
AND ACTIVE
PORTFOLIO
MANAGEMENT

coefficient. Such realized returns depend upon the specific market-wide risks or factors to which a portfolio is exposed. One can no longer be certain that in a rising market high beta portfolios will necessarily do better than the market. Beta loses its interpretation as a timing tool, and performance measures, which assume a one-factor model, become difficult to interpret.

Under a two- or multi-factor model, the concept of diversification itself becomes more complicated. An investor must not only consider the elimination of risks due to unique effects but must consider the level of exposure or the values of the response coefficients to each common market-wide effect. It is no longer simply possible to obtain a fully diversified portfolio merely by investing in a large number of issues, although such a policy will still minimize the impact of unique risks.

To minimize the risks of market-wide effects for any particular level of beta, the response coefficients on each market-wide factor should be the same, as shown in the mathematical appendix. To understand the reasoning underlying this statement, consider a portfolio exposed to one market-wide risk which has very little chance of occurring. To achieve a specific level of beta, the response coefficient of the portfolio to that factor would have to be much larger than it would if the risk had a high probability of occurring. Most of the time, such a portfolio would experience very small fluctuations in returns, but occasionally the fluctuations would be very great. It would seem less risky to increase the risk of moderate fluctuations while decreasing the risk of an occasional large fluctuation by reducing the response coefficient on the low-probability risk and increasing the response coefficient on the high-probability risk. Indeed, such changes will continue to reduce risk until the response coefficients to each factor are equal.

In less technical terms, securities in a fully diversified portfolio should be selected to minimize the risks unique to individual securities as well as to minimize the maximum exposure to any common market-wide risk. In other words, a portfolio should be exposed equally to every and all risks. In this way, the return on a portfolio will be less subject to the extreme fluctuations associated with specific sectors of the economy. If, for instance, one of the common market-wide factors is associated with size of a company, a fully diversified portfolio must include both large and small issues.

THE IMPLICATIONS FOR PORTFOLIO MANAGEMENT

The existence of two or more market-wide forces shaping the returns of individual securities complicates the traditional investment process of trying to obtain better than average performance. Not only must a portfolio manager find undervalued securities, but he must also attempt to structure a portfolio which is not disproportionally exposed to any one market-wide risk. It has been thought that holding a large number of securities with not too much invested in each will by itself take care of diversification. Diversification, however, will not take care of itself if the securities held are not representative of all market-wide risks. Such would be the case for a portfolio confined to the larger, readily marketable stocks, so typical of some institutional portfolios.

In view of the apparent difficulty of finding undervalued securities in the first place, as evidenced by the performance of many institutional investors, this added complication in obtaining full diversification would make the goal of beating the market seem even more difficult. It is thus not surprising that some institutional investors, particularly pension funds, are giving up the goal of trying to beat the market by investing in index funds.[5] The sole purpose of an index fund is to approximate the returns on the market portfolio, never doing much better nor much worse than the market. For reasons of historical tradition, the index usually picked to represent the market is the Standard and Poor's Composite Index of 500 stocks, although a good case could be made for a more broadly based index.

If there were no cash dividends, if the companies in the index never changed, and if stock dividends or splits were the only reason for changes in the number of shares outstanding of each company, it would be a simple matter to replicate the returns on the index. One would merely have to buy each stock in the index in proportion to the market value of its stock outstanding and hold these shares with no further transactions. The reason no further transactions would be required is that changes in the weights in the index, due only to movements in the prices of individual securities, would exactly parallel changes in the market values of the stocks held.[6]

Cash dividends, however, are paid and need to be reinvested. Companies are added or dropped from the index. Stock dividends or splits are not the only reason for changes in the number of shares outstanding. Furthermore, an actual fund would be subject to occasional additions or withdrawals of capital. All of these circumstances would require frequent trading in virtually every issue to keep the proportions in the index fund identical to those implicit in the index. Consider, for instance, the trading which would have been required when Johnson and Johnson was added to the Standard and Poor's Index on May 30, 1973.

The way to reduce transaction costs is to drop the requirement that the proportions in the fund be identical at every instant in time to those implicit in the index. Once this requirement is dropped, the returns on an index fund will only approximate the returns on the index. The critical choice is the degree of approximation one is willing to accept relative to the potential reduction in trading and custodial costs.

One approach which has been used in managing an index fund is to restrict the number of securities held to a fixed number, say for illustrative purposes, 200 stocks. In selecting these 200 stocks, a manager of an index fund can be viewed as picking a stratified sample of 200 stocks from a universe of 500 stocks to mirror the performance of the omitted 300 stocks. In the terminology of a multi-factor model, these 200 stocks should be selected so as to make the response coefficients on each of the market-wide risks identical. On the assumption that 200 stocks can be so selected, the changing characteristics of the individual securities will eventually make these 200 stocks non-representative, so that some trading might be required for rebalancing.

Unfortunately, the current state of financial knowledge yields little insight into the nature of these market-wide factors. Without empirically tested multi-factor models, about the best that can be done in selecting 200 stocks is the following: If returns are never related to the size of an issue, the optimal strategy would be to invest in the largest 200 stocks in proportion to their market values. In this way, each dollar is invested in those stocks which have the greatest effect in determining the return on the index. If, however, returns are sometimes related to the size of an issue, the 200 stocks should consist not only of large stocks but also of stocks with medium and small market values. Without a tested theory, it is impossible to determine beforehand the optimal distribution of securities as between issues of different sizes.

With the state of the art as it is, the most reliable method to evaluate different investment strategies is to simulate their returns on historical data. To this end, the returns from an initial investment of $25,000 under various 200 stock strategies were calculated over the 14.5 years ending June 30, 1974. These returns are adjusted for commission charges[7] and assume that the portfolio weights are revised quarterly and that dividends are reinvested at the revision time. To prevent trading in each of the 200 stocks, lower limits were placed upon the value of any purchase or sale.[8]

After much experimentation with the concentration of stocks as between large and small issues and with the size of the limits on purchases and sales, it appeared that the best strategy involved a heavy concentration in the top 100 stocks, with the remaining stocks distributed over the smaller stocks in the S & P Index. Excluding the first six months of 1960 in which the funds were initially invested, the average annual absolute deviation from the result on the index for these kinds of strategies was around 75 basis points per year, and the maximum annual absolute deviation was around 200 basis points, regardless of the specific limits placed on the minimum sizes of purchases and sales. The amount of trading activity, however, was highly sensitive to the specific limits.

The set of limits producing the closest correspondence to the index resulted in an annual average turnover rate[9] of 10% each year and an average of 25 issues traded per quarter.

An alternative to trying to replicate the returns on the index with a sample of stocks is just to buy all the stocks in the index. Over the period of simulation, the 500 stock strategy appears to be superior to a 200 stock strategy. Regardless of the limits tried for the minimum sizes of purchases and sales, the average annual absolute deviation was about 25 basis points, and the maximum annual absolute deviation was slightly more than 50 basis points. The set of limits producing the closest correspondence to the index resulted in an annual average turnover rate of slightly less than 2% and an average of 18 issues traded per quarter. Since many custodians base their fee primarily on the market value of the portfolio, the 500 stock strategy clearly dominates the 200 stock strategy.

CONCLUSION: THE MORE THE MERRIER

The recent differences in returns between large and small issues is not a new phenomenon. It is quite likely that in the future there will again be substantial differences, but the past gives no indication of which group will do better. The implication for the traditional portfolio management process is that a manager must concern himself not only with finding securities of above average investment value but also with structuring a portfolio to expose it to all market-wide risks equally. There is no guarantee that a portfolio spread fairly evenly over a large number will be fully diversified.

In view of the apparent inability of many portfolio managers to outperform the market averages, some institutional investors are beginning to place some of their assets in funds designed to approximate the returns on the Standard and Poor's Composite Index of 500 stocks. The question arises in forming such an index fund of how many securities should be held. Simulation results over the fourteen years ending the middle of 1974 suggest that there is no reason to restrict the number of securities held. Indeed, restricting the number of securities from the maximum of 500 tends to result in greater deviations from the index and at the same time greater costs.

---

[1] To develop the monthly returns for each of the indexes, the market values of the shares outstanding less treasury stock of all stocks listed on the NYSE at the end of June, 1928 were calculated as of that date. For each kind of index, a portfolio was formed based upon the weights implicit in the index. It was then assumed that this portfolio was held for the next twelve months. Any cash dividends were assumed to be reinvested in the stocks which paid them. Any stock delisted was assumed sold at the last available price and the proceeds reinvested in the remaining stocks in proportion to the value of each remaining stock in the portfolio at the time. From the monthly values of the portfolio, twelve monthly returns were calculated for each index.

At the end of June, 1929, this procedure was repeated. However, only stocks in existence on June, 1928 were used, and the market values of the stocks were estimated by multiplying the month-end prices in June, 1929 by the shares outstanding less treasury on June, 1928 adjusted for any splits or stock dividends. In a similar fashion, using 1928 information on shares but current information on prices, returns were calculated for each of the next three years. This process yielded sixty monthly returns for the period July, 1928 through June, 1933 for each index. The number of shares for each stock listed on the NYSE as of the end of June, 1933 was collected as of that date. Using these stocks and their shares outstanding less treasury, sixty more monthly returns were calculated for each index in the same manner as the preceding five years. Every five years thereafter, the process was repeated to yield in total 540 monthly returns for each index.

[2] The perhaps intuitive, but incorrect, notion that the short-run variability in returns somehow "washes out" in the long-run is probably at the heart of the recommendation that investors for the long-run should invest in those stocks with the larger expected rates of return, even though such a policy would clearly entail more short-run variability. M. E. Blume and I. Friend, "Risk, Investment Strategy, and the Long-Run Rates of Return," *The Review of Economics and Statistics,* (August, 1974) have examined the fallacy of this recommendation in more detail.

[3] A joint test of the equality of the mean monthly returns was performed by running the regression

$$r_{it} = \alpha_0 + \sum_{i=1}^{3} \alpha_i \delta_i + \epsilon_{it}$$

where r_{it} is the return on index i in month t, δ_i is a dummy variable defined as 1.0 for index i and 0.0 otherwise, and ϵ_{it} is a mean-zero normal disturbance independent of δ_i. This regression was estimated using generalized least squares and assuming that Cov $(\epsilon_{it}, \epsilon_{it'})$, $t \neq t'$, was zero, that Cov $(\epsilon_{it}, \epsilon_{jt})$, $i \neq j$ was proportional to the Cov (r_{it}, r_{jt}), and that Var (ϵ_{it}) was proportional to Var (r_{it}). The F-statistics, which test the hypotheses that the coefficients on the dummy variables are jointly zero, were all insignificant at the 5% level in the overall period and each half.

[4] Cf. B. F. King, "Market and Industry Factors in Stock Price Behavior," *Journal of Business,* XXXIX (January, 1966), Part II, pp. 139-190; S. L. Meyers, "A Re-Examination of Market and Industry Factors in Stock Price Behavior," *The Journal of Finance,* XXVIII, No. 3 (June, 1973), pp. 695-705; D. Rie, "Security Valuation Formulae: Their Relationship to Estimates of the Risk-Return Tradeoff," Working Paper No. 29-73, Rodney L. White Center for Financial Research, University of Pennsylvania, The Wharton School.

[5] "More Pension Funds Try to Tie the Market Instead of Beating It," *Wall Street Journal,* November 12, 1975.

[6] Any stock split or dividend will be associated with a commensurate change in the price of the stock, so that no trading is necessary.

[7] No adjustments were made for custodial or management costs. A detailed analysis of the simulation results suggests

that the returns would be insensitive to the initial amount, provided it were in excess of, say, $10,000,000.

[8] In addition to commission expenses, a trade in a security involves accounting and custodial costs, but perhaps even more important, the potential costs in terms of administrative time of an error in the execution of the trade.

[9] Annual turnover rate is defined as the ratio of the minimum of purchases or sales to the average value of the fund.

MATHEMATICAL APPENDIX

Since the essential results for a multi-factor model can easily be derived from an analysis of a two-factor model, the following will be couched in terms of a two-factor model. A two-factor model assumes that returns on individual securities are generated by:

$$(1)\ R_i = E(R_i) + b_{1i} \pi_1 + b_{2i} \pi_2 + \epsilon_i$$

where R_i is the realized return on security i;

π_1, π_2 are random factors common to all securities and thus not subscripted by i;

b_{1i}, b_{2i} are the response coefficients of security i to the two common factors which are subscripted by i since they can vary from security to security; and

ϵ_i is a random disturbance specific to security i.

Let it further be assumed that the random variables have means of zero and are independent of each other and finally that π_1 and π_2 are scaled such that $\Sigma x_{im} b_{1i}$ and $\Sigma x_{im} b_{2i}$ equal 1.0, where x_{im} is the ratio of the market value of security i to all securities. This last assumption is not trivial. For instance, if $b_{1i} = 1 - b_{2i}$, it would not be possible to rescale π_1 and π_2 so that both the summations of b_{1i} and b_{2i} would equal 1.0.

If there are n securities, the returns on the market portfolio, R_m, will be given by:

$$(2)\ R_m = \sum_{i=1}^{n} x_{im} R_i = \pi_1 + \pi_2 + \sum_{i=1}^{n} x_{im} \epsilon_i$$

The beta coefficient of security i, β_i, is given by:

$$(3)\ \beta_i = \frac{\text{Cor}(R_i, R_m)}{\text{Var}(R_m)}$$

$$= \frac{b_{1i}\text{Var}(\pi_1) + b_{2i}\text{Var}(\pi_2) + x_{im}\text{Var}(\epsilon_i)}{\text{Var}(\pi_1) + \text{Var}(\pi_2) + \sum_{i=1}^{n} (x_{im})^2 \text{Var}(\epsilon_i)}$$

If there are a large number of securities in the market with each one representing only a small proportion of the total market value, the terms involving x_{im} will be negligible in value relative to the remaining terms. In this case, β_i can be interpreted as a weighted average of the two response coefficients, b_{1i} and b_{2i}, the weights being proportional to the variances of π_1 and π_2.

If x_i represents the proportion of a specific portfolio invested in security i, the portfolio beta, β_p, will be $\Sigma x_i \beta_i$. According to the capital asset pricing model, the expected return on such a portfolio should be only a function of β_p. If an investor holds an efficiently diversified portfolio with a beta of β_p, the proportions invested in each security will be the same as the proportions in these same securities which minimize the variance of the return on this portfolio subject to the constraint that the average portfolio beta be β_p. Incorporating a Lagrange multiplier, the proportions x_i will be such as to minimize the function h:

(4) $h = (\Sigma x_i b_{1i})^2 \text{ Var } (\pi_1) + (\Sigma x_i b_{2i})^2 \text{ Var } (\pi_2)$
$\qquad + \Sigma x_i \text{ Var } (\epsilon_i) - 2\lambda \text{Var } (R_m) [\beta_p - \Sigma x_i \beta_i]$

Substituting (3) into (4) and setting $\dfrac{\partial h}{\partial x_i}$ to zero, we have:

(5) $b_1 b_{1i} \text{ Var } (\pi_1) + b_2 b_{2i} \text{Var } (\pi_2) + x_i \text{Var } (\epsilon_i)$
$\qquad + \lambda [b_{1i} \text{ Var } (\pi_1) + b_{2i} \text{Var } (\pi_2) + x_{im} \text{Var } (\epsilon_i)] = 0$

where b_1 is $\Sigma x_i b_{1i}$ and b_2 is $\Sigma x_i b_{2i}$. Equating the values of λ from the equations associated with $\dfrac{\partial h}{\partial x_i}$ and $\dfrac{\partial h}{\partial x_k}$, we finally obtain:

(6) $\dfrac{b_1 b_{1i} \text{Var } (\pi_1) + b_2 b_{2i} \text{Var } (\pi_2) + x_i \text{Var } (\epsilon_{i1})}{b_{1i} \text{Var } (\pi_1) + b_{2i} \text{ Var } (\pi_2) + x_{im} \text{Var } (\epsilon_i)}$

$\qquad = \dfrac{b_1 b_{1k} \text{Var } (\pi_1) + b_2 b_{2k} \text{Var } (\pi_2) + x_k \text{Var } (\epsilon_k)}{b_{1k} \text{Var } (\pi_1) + b_{2k} \text{Var } (\pi_2) + x_{km} \text{Var } (\epsilon_k)}$

Equation (6) shows how x_i and x_k are related in a fully diversified portfolio with a beta of β_p. Let us for the moment assume that the terms involving $\text{Var}(\epsilon_i)$ and $\text{Var } (\epsilon_k)$ are sufficiently small relative to the other terms that they can be dropped. In this case, equation (6) reduces to:

(7) $b_1 (1-\gamma_i) + b_2 (\gamma_i) = b_1 (1-\gamma_k) + b_2 \gamma_k$

where γ_j is the ratio of $b_{2j} \text{ Var } (\pi_2)$ to the sum of $b_{1j} \text{ Var } (\pi_1)$ and $b_{2j} \text{ Var } (\pi_2)$. Since γ_i would typically not equal γ_k, the only way equation (7) can hold in general is if b_1 equals b_2, so that in a diversified portfolio the response coefficients should all be equal.

Security analysts:
Some are more equal*

"It would appear that the researcher one chooses to listen to could well have some real impact on one's investment results."

John C. Groth, Wilbur G. Lewellen, Gary G. Schlarbaum, and Ronald C. Lease

A reputation for providing high quality securities research and investment advice is arguably the most sought-after objective of every Wall Street institution. Although the message is often subtly phrased, brokerage houses, bank trust departments, investment advisory services, and mutual funds all heavily orient their promotional activities toward creating such an image of expertise. In the aggregate, however, the hard data on actual portfolio performance histories,[1] and analyses of the apparent payoffs from trading on issued stock recommendations,[2] are less than encouraging about the value of professional counsel. Passive investments in the popular market indexes would seem to be about as worthwhile.

SELECTION
AND ACTIVE
PORTFOLIO
MANAGEMENT

* Research support from the National Bureau of Economic Research, the Investment Company Institute, and the Purdue Research Foundation is gratefully acknowledged.

1. Footnotes appear at the end of the article.

Within the mass of these findings, there nonetheless have been occasional instances of detectable differences in acumen across organizations — as judged by the observed *ex post* returns associated with the investment suggestions of those organizations.[3] We provided, in an earlier paper, such evidence on the securities recommendations of one of the nation's largest retail brokerage houses, for a seven-year period ending with 1970; intimations of superior overall returns therefrom were found.[4] Our purpose here is to carry the investigation the logical one step further: to examine the performances of the *individual* securities analysts within the firm, and address the matter of differential expertise at that level as well.

THE DATA

The underlying information base consists of the some 6000 common stock investment advisories released to its customers by the cooperating brokerage house between January, 1964 and December, 1970. They were compiled directly from the source documents in the firm's files, and the set is exhaustive for the period. Of these reports, 4,638 could be identified clearly as "buy" recommendations;[5] they will be the focus of our analysis. The remainder were "sell" suggestions, were offered "for information only," advocated the establishment of particular tax-loss positions, highlighted securities as potential candidates for "trading" accounts, or were simply unclassifiable.[6]

When we arrayed the "buy" recommendations according to the analysts listed as their authors, 25 different individuals emerged as having prepared at least thirty such recommendations for the firm during the time period in question. These individuals comprise the study group, and their histories encompass a total of 3,953 research reports. A minimum eligibility requirement of thirty observations was imposed for inclusion in the group merely to ensure that sufficient data would be available as to allow a meaningful assessment for each analyst of the quality of his or her aggregate research output. While alternative thresholds could be debated, thirty recommendations seem to us a respectable basis for judgment.

PERFORMANCE EVALUATION

The appraisal of "quality" will deal with the investment returns associated with the securities that were the subject of the recommendations, in the vicinity of the dates of their release. We will compare these returns with those that could have been realized concurrrently from the broader population or equivalent risk equity securities. Individual analysts then are rated by the extent to which their stock suggestions provided returns superior to that broader population.

For this purpose, we shall use the linear equilibrium risk-return prescriptions of the capital-asset-pricing model as the basis of our performance standards.[7] Pursuant to the now well-accepted "two factor" version of that model,[8] the return which *should* be expected to be observed on security j during period t is

$$R^*_{jt} = a_{1t} + a_{2t}\beta_j$$

where a_{1t} and a_{2t} represent, respectively, the intercept and slope of the overall (ex-post) risk-return profile in the market during t, and β_j is a measure of the systematic risk of the security — the latter being defined as the specific structural linkage, $Cov(R_j,R_m)/\sigma^2(R_m)$, between the returns on j and those on the fully diversified "market" portfolio (m) of all risky assets.

In that framework, our interest centers on the discrepancies, if any, between the *actual* periodic returns on the recommended stocks and the indicated concurrent *expected* returns that emerge from the capital-asset-pricing model for securities of equivalent risk (matching β). A positive, and statistically significant, mean difference in returns for the stock selections of a given analyst thereupon denotes superior market performance by his or her recommendations and will be interpreted here as evidence of research skill on the part of the analyst.

Values of the cross-sectional risk-return

parameters a_{1t} and a_{2t} were generated for each of the 84 months in our 1964-70 study interval by procedures that are described in detail in our other paper[9] and that follow the standard dictates of the literature. The core "market" portfolio involved was a value-weighted composite of all NYSE and ASE common stocks. These were arrayed into twenty sub-portfolios of descending relative risk, whose observed monthly returns and computed betas were utilized in 84 cross-sectional regressions to obtain estimates of the a_{1t} and a_t for each month under study.[10] Both the portfolio betas and those for the individual recommended securities were derived from regressions of their returns on the indicated market index over the seven-year period of concern.[11] All such returns encompassed dividend receipts as well as price changes. A monthly unit of account was adopted simply because the available securities-price-and-dividend master file, developed for the larger study of which the present investigation comprises just one segment, was so constructed; month-end closing prices are the ones recorded therein.[12]

Our examination of the performance of the investment suggestions of the analyst sample is organized around the specific months in which those recommendations appeared. In every case, return discrepancies — or, in the vernacular, return "residuals" — were computed for the security involved, for the month of its recommendation, and for the preceding and following six months. Thus, the test interval applies to a variety of different *calendar* dates but is centered throughout on the report release month. The thirteen-month period covered was found, in the cited predecessor analysis of the cooperating brokerage firm's total research output, to be sufficient to treat the pertinent securities return phenomena.[13] We shall expand upon this point further.

WHEAT VS. CHAFF

Table 1 provides evidence of noticeable variations in talent across the analyst-group sample — at

Table 1

PERFORMANCES OF STOCK RECOMMENDATIONS,
BY SECURITIES ANALYSTS

Analyst	Rank[a]	Mean Annualized Excess Return on Recommended Securities:			No. of Stocks	Mean Beta
		Months -6 to -1	Month t=0[b]	Months +1 to +6		
A	# 1	--	53.08%	--	34	1.49
B	# 2	32.24%	46.52	--	120	1.51
C	# 3	7.87	46.14	--	198	1.47
D	# 4	13.13	42.16	9.17%	242	1.29
E	# 5	17.22	41.09	18.92	188	1.55
F	# 6	13.20	40.64	10.16	191	1.09
G	# 7	17.44	31.55*	--	112	1.37
H	# 8	13.72	25.78	--	275	1.10
I	# 9	13.65	21.45	--	406	1.26
J	#10	5.83*	19.54	--	165	0.96
K	#11	12.83	18.31*	--	239	1.62
L	#12	13.59	17.64	--	391	1.33
M	#13	--	15.52*	--	228	1.02
N	-	27.30	--	--	30	1.42
O	-	26.89	--	--	67	1.19
P	-	19.32*	--	--	56	1.46
Q	-	14.62*	--	--	32	1.75
R	-	--	--	--	188	1.21
S	-	--	--	--	34	1.40
T	-	--	--	--	143	1.66
U	-	--	--	--	73	1.47
V	-	--	--	--	175	1.38
W	-	--	--	--	31	1.06
X	-	--	--	--	36	1.02
Y	-	--	--	--	299	1.57

[a] By recommendation-month mean excess return.

[b] The month of recommendation.

* Significant at the .05 level; all other listed values significant at the .01 level.

least by our definition of the term. The figures listed record, in the form of annualized percentage rates, the extent to which the stock recommendations of each of the 25 individuals considered generated returns that departed from those available concurrently from the general run of comparable risk securities in the market. A tabulation of these values, for the cases in which the differences in observed mean return were statistically significant at either the .05 or .01 confidence level, is presented for the period of the six pre-recommendation months, for the recommendation month $(t=0)$ alone, and for the six post-recommendation months combined. The analysts are ranked according to the size of the recommendation-month return residuals (where significant) on their particular stock selections. The number of recommendations issued by each and the average betas of the stocks involved are indicated as well.

By way of interpretation, take the figure of 53.08% shown for analyst A. The 34 purchase recommendations authored by that individual had mean returns *during* the respective months in which those advisories appeared that surpassed by 4.42 percentage points (53.08/12) the same months' mean returns on the mass of NYSE/ASE listed equities having corresponding betas. This analyst led the sample in that respect.

The data have several striking features. First, of course, there are in fact distinct differences among individuals with regard to the market performance of the securities each suggested. The sample splits virtually down the middle by that test: the stocks selected by thirteen of the group had significantly positive excess returns in the month recommended; the corresponding selections of the other twelve were indistinguishable from the market as a whole. Moreover, even within the "good" analyst subset, there is a wide range of performances, running from 15 to fully 53% annualized excess return levels. Thus, it would appear that the researcher one chooses to listen to could well have some real impact on one's investment results.

RECOGNITION LAGS

A second attribute of the tabulation is the intriguing evidence that the securities analyzed and recommended by the successful analysts displayed, in all but two instances, positive and statistically significant return differentials during the six months *prior* to their recommendation. This is similar to the finding that emerged from our original investigation of the aggregate array of the firm's recommendations, and it suggests a sort of "visibility threshold" phenomenon at work. That is, it may often require several months of superior market performance by a security — occasioned, presumably, by a succession of favorable new items of information about the enterprise involved — before it catches the attention of an analyst. He or she then engages in additional research, discovers more good information, packages all this in a research report, and disseminates it to the investment community — whereupon rapid digestion takes place and a quick price response occurs.

Note that the month t=0 annualized mean excess returns are noticeably higher, for all thirteen ranked analysts, than are those of the preceding six months: this is consistent with this attention-discovery-comprehension hypothesis. For four other analysts (designated N through Q), on the other hand, the pre-recommendation return differentials are positive and significant but the recommendation-month ones are not, implying that these individuals picked up the favorable signs too late to generate any really new insights. The party, it seems — whatever its duration may have been — was over by the time they arrived.[14]

We can find confirmation of such a characterization of the process in the behavior of the recommended securities *following* the initial appearance of the recommendations. There are only scattered indications of positive excess returns occurring after month t=0, which is what would be expected if the analysts had done a skillful job of uncovering the bulk of all previously unrecognized favorable information about the studied securities in their research reports.[15] An immediate revision in market attitudes, yielding sizable short-run superior profits, followed by a return to normal market relationships, would be the logical — and is the apparent typical — stock price scenario.

In that view, the competent securities analyst performs a worthwhile information-improving and information-accelerating function which contributes to an accurate reappraisal of security values. Given that we find no visible overreaction in the data — i.e., prices do not appear to rise too far initially and then have to be corrected by significant negative return differentials in the months subsequent to recommendation — it does seem legitimate to term the reappraisal "accurate," and thereby to applaud the quality of the ranked analysts' research reports.

Even within the latter contingent, there exist clear differences in quality. A comparison of the stock selections of the top, middle, and bottom thirds of that group, for example — analysts A through D, E through H, and I through M, respectively — reveals a statistically significant disparity between the recommendation-month mean excess returns of the three subsets' collective securities recommendations, each at well beyond the .01 confidence level.[16] While all thirteen were apparently competent researchers, therefore, some were especially so, and the rankings are not without content.

EFFORT AND REWARD

Certain other aspects of the cross-sectional pattern of observed investment outcomes are of potential interest as well. Among these is the matter of a relationship between the *quality* and the *volume* of the recommendations involved: are the more successful analysts those with the larger number of released stock selections?

The answer, as it happens, is both yes and no — for what seem to us logical reasons. Thus, the difference between the mean number of recommendations made by the upper-thirteen and lower-twelve analyst subgroups depicted (respectively, 215 and 97) is easily significant at the .01 level, indicating that the "good" analysts in fact generated a larger volume of research reports.[17] Within the top-thirteen array, on the other hand, the Spearman rank correlation coefficient between the listed analyst quality rankings, and a corresponding ranking by number of recommendations, turns out to be -0.54 and also comfortably surpasses the 1% confidence level threshold.[18] For that group, then, volume and stock selection performance are *inversely* related.

The rationale for these apparently conflicting

findings is straight-forward and is buttressed by a supplementary piece of evidence. The recommendation volume disparity between the top and bottom analyst groupings can be attributed almost entirely to a difference in their average *employment tenure* with the brokerage house in question. As judged by the time span observed between the first and last recorded recommendations of each of the individuals studied,[19] the upper-thirteen analysts had a mean research-activity experience of 55 months, whereas for the lower-twelve, the counterpart figure was just 34 months. The larger volume, then, is primarily a duration phenomenon — and its origin admits of reasonable surmise. Presumably, the brokerage firm tends to weed out the unsuccessful analyst (whose stock selections merely match the market) after a respectable trial period[20] and retains for an extended interval in a research role only those who do demonstrate some consistent competence. In the latter group, however, it would appear that the more painstaking craftsmen — i.e., those who spend more time on each recommendation and thereby issue fewer — are the particularly strong performers. While admittedly this explanation is inferential, the underlying scenario hypothesized is plausible.

No corresponding linkages to the risk level of the securities recommended could be discerned. The average β of the stocks advocated by the top-thirteen analysts is not distinguishable from that of the selections of the bottom-twelve, nor is there a significant relationship between the respective mean-β and quality rankings of the top-thirteen themselves.[21] To believers in market efficiency, such a result should be generally reassuring, suggestive as it is of no systematic pattern of latent excess returns or information vacuums across the risk spectrum of available common stocks. It is reinforced by a similar finding elsewhere that securities betas and recommendations quality are unrelated for the mass of the cooperating firm's research output, arrayed without regard to analyst authorship.[22]

TRADING OPPORTUNITIES

Even given these indications that certain securities analysts seem able regularly to identify stocks that offer attractive return possibilities, the extent to which those suggestions can be translated by many of the firm's customers into actual profitable trading outcomes is, of course, still problematical. The evidence on the 1964-70 realized investment return experiences of a large sample of those customers, wherein very impressive results on short-term (under one month) stock purchase-and-resale cycles were manifest, would support the notion that the opportunity may well exist.[23] Indeed, it was those findings that in large measure prompted the current investigation — as an inquiry into one possible source of the observed trading success. Although this success may not necessarily have been associated with the specific securities that were the subject of the brokerage house's research reports, the data here and those cited previously[24] unquestionably raise that possibility.

The issues involved are the obvious ones of timing and transactions costs. While we do not have available *daily* price data in the vicinity of the various recommendation release dates to allow us to examine the first of these directly, the responding investor/client would presumably have to act very quickly in a sensitive marketplace to realize any worthwhile trading gain from a recommended security, and it would not require very many such responses to attain the proper new equilibrium valuation level. Hence, relatively few investors would be able to exploit any particular investment suggestion.

In addition, the realizable gains would have to be sufficient to overcome the attendant burden of commission charges and assorted fees in order to elicit investor interest in the first place. As we found elsewhere,[25] that burden is not trivial, consuming nearly two thirds of the gross returns realized on the less than thirty-day investment cycles engaged in by the customer sample studied between 1964 and 1970.[26] Yet, the average net outcome of those trades *was* distinctly positive, and the potential for taking useful advantage of a capable security analyst's advice cannot be ruled out.

Parenthetically, since our appraisal of the market performances of the recommended securities treats only month-end-to-month-end price changes, a detection of recommendation-related excess returns may be difficult in many instances where they do exist — and would show up if daily prices *were* available for scrutiny. In effect, a number of such events will simply get submerged in the noise of an entire month's stock price movements; the full extent even of those which do get identified may similarly often be diluted. For this reason, the figures in Table 1 almost certainly understate both the frequency and magnitude of the relevant superior-return occurrences and tell a milder story than the underlying evidence would justify.[27] Combining, as we have, "weak buy" and "hold" suggestions with outright "buy" recommendations in the array of considered research reports, would tend to have an added dampening influence on the findings.

SUMMARY

These barriers notwithstanding, the data provide clear indications of substantial differences across the investigated analyst sample in security selection talents — at least as measured by the observed return experiences of the securities involved, in and around the particular months of their selection and recommendation. The separate analyst track records, which emerge from an examination here of a body of some 4,000 investment suggestions made by one of the major retail brokerage houses over a seven-year period, offer quite respectable documentation for the propositions (1) that consistently good research abilities do exist, and (2) that distinctions in this regard among individuals can indeed be drawn. The former finding is not at odds with characterizations of market "efficiency" in that the issue is one of information discovery and acceleration rather than an incorrectness of prices, given extant information. The latter conclusion, of course, would support the contention that a meaningful differentiation among firms acting as brokers and advisors, in the quality of their respective research "products," is not a totally outrageous notion.

[1] See, for example: I. Friend and M. Blume, "Measurement of Portfolio Performance Under Uncertainty," *American Economic Review,* Vol. 60, No. 4, September, 1970, pp. 561-575; M. Jensen, "The Performance of Mutual Funds in the Period 1945-1964," *Journal of Finance,* Vol. 23, No. 2, May, 1968, pp. 389-416; M. Jensen, "Risk, the Pricing of Capital Assets, and the Evaluation of Investment Portfolios," *Journal of Business,* Vol. 42, No. 2, April, 1969, pp. 167-247; M. Jensen (editor), *Studies in the Theory of Capital Markets,* New York: Praeger, 1972; J. Lorie, et. al., *Measuring the Investment Performance of Pension Funds,* Park Ridge, Illinois: Bank Administration Institute, 1968; W. Sharpe, "Mutual Fund Performance," *Journal of Business,* Vol. 39, No. 1, January, 1966, pp. 119-138; J. Treynor and K. Mazuy, "Can Mutual Funds Outguess the Market?", *Harvard Business Review,* Vol. 44, No. 4, July-August, 1966, pp. 131-136.

[2] H. Cheney, "How Good Are Investment Advisory Services?", *Financial Executive,* Vol. 37, No. 11, November, 1969, pp. 30-35; S. Colker, "An Analysis of Security Recommendations by Brokerage Houses," *Quarterly Review of Economics and Business,* Vol. 3, No. 2, Summer, 1963, pp. 19-28; A. Cowles, "Can Stock Market Forecasters Forecast?", *Econometrica,* Vol. 1, No. 3, July, 1933, pp. 309-324; R. Diefenback, "How Good is Institutional Brokerage Research?", *Financial Analysts Journal,* Vol. 28, No. 1, January-February, 1972, pp. 54-60; D. Logue and D. Tuttle, "Brokerage House Investment Advice," *Financial Review,* 1973, pp. 38-54.

[3] F. Black, "Yes, Virginia, There is Hope: Tests of the Value Line Ranking System," *Financial Analysts Journal,* Vol. 29, No. 5, September-October, 1973, pp. 10-14; H. Cheney, *op. cit.*

[4] J. Groth, W. Lewellen, G. Schlarbaum, and R. Lease, "An Empirical Analysis of Brokerage House Securities Recommendations," *Financial Analysts Journal,* forthcoming.

[5] Which include the formal recommendation categories of "buy," "weak buy," and "hold."

[6] Or, in about 3% of the cases, dealt with securities for which market price and dividend information was not available in the supplementary common stock data file assembled for the larger research project that gave rise to the present investigation. See the following discussion.

[7] As developed in: J. Lintner, "Security Prices, Risk, and Maximal Gains from Diversification," *Journal of Finance*, Vol. 20, No. 5, December, 1965, pp. 587-615; J. Mossin, *Theory of Financial Markets*, Englewood Cliffs, N.J.: Prentice-Hall, 1973; W. Sharpe, *Portfolio Theory and Capital Markets*, New York: McGraw-Hill, 1970.

[8] See: R. Ball, "Risk, Return, and Disequilibrium: An application to Changes in Accounting Techniques," *Journal of Finance*, Vol. 27, No. 2, May, 1972, pp. 343-363; F. Black, M. Jensen, and M. Scholes, "The Capital Asset Pricing Model: Some Empirical Tests," in: M. Jensen (ed.), *op. cit.*, pp. 79-121; M. Blume, "On the Assessment of Risk," *Journal of Finance*, Vol. 26, No. 1, March, 1971, pp. 1-10; M. Blume and I. Friend, "A New Look at the Capital Asset Pricing Model," *Journal of Finance*, Vol. 28, No. 1, March, 1973, pp. 19-33; E. Fama and J. MacBeth, "Risk, Return, and Equilibrium: Some Empirical Tests," *Journal of Political Economy*, Vol. 81, No. 3, May-June, 1973, pp. 607-636.

[9] J. Groth, W. Lewellen, G. Schlarbaum, and R. Lease, *op. cit.*

[10] But where, consistent with received doctrine, the twenty benchmark subportfolios were formed on the basis of individual-security betas estimated from data of an earlier (pre-1964) period.

[11] *Ibid.*

[12] For a full description, see: R. Lease, W. Lewellen, and G. Schlarbaum, "The Individual Investor: Attributes and Attitudes," *Journal of Finance*, Vol. 29, No. 2, May, 1974, pp. 413-433; R. Lease, W. Lewellen, and G. Schlarbaum, "Market Segmentation: Evidence on the Individual Investor," *Financial Analysts Journal*, Vol. 32, No. 5, September-October, 1976, pp. 53-60; G. Schlarbaum, W. Lewellen, and R. Lease, "Realized Returns on Common Stock Investments: The Experience of Individual Investors," *Journal of Business*, Vol. 50, No. 4, October, 1977.

[13] J. Groth, W. Lewellen, G. Schlarbaum, and R. Lease, *op cit.*

[14] Six months prior to recommendation was as far back as our examination was carried. It is not impossible, therefore, that excess returns on the securities existed even before that point.

[15] Return residuals were computed for *each* of these six months for each analyst, and equally sparse signs of significant values for individual months showed up therein.

[16] The computed t values for the significance tests ranged upward from 33.6, whereas the critical t's are in the vicinity of 2.5 for the .01 level. Alternative breakdowns of the ranked analysts — into two and four groups — produced similar results.

[17] The computed t statistic was 3.071, and the required $t(23, .01)$ is 2.807.

[18] Pursuant to a computed t of 8.343, in comparison with a critical $t(11, .01)$ of 3.106.

[19] For lack of direct information on specific research-employment starting and termination dates, it was necessary to use this proxy.

[20] Obviously, one long enough to allow the generation of at least the thirty recommendations chosen here as the cutoff point for inclusion in the sample. The difference between the research-experience figures of 55 and 34 months for the two groups *was* significant at the .01 level.

[21] Which is not to say, however, that there are not differences among analysts in the risk characteristics of the securities they research. When the group was arrayed in descending order according to the mean β figures in Table 1, and then divided into thirds, there did turn out to be a significant difference (at beyond the .01 level) between the three subsets in the β's of the respective securities recommended. A division into quartiles and quintiles produced the same results. Thus, analysts do tend to specialize in stocks with distinctive risk features.

[22] *Ibid.*

[23] G. Schlarbaum, W. Lewellen, and R. Lease, *op. cit.*

[24] J. Groth, W. Lewellen, G. Schlarbaum, and R. Lease, *op. cit.*

[25] G. Schlarbaum, W. Lewellen, and R. Lease, *op. cit.*

[26] Specifically, post-transactions-cost mean rates of return thereon were equal to 37% of the mean pre-cost rates.

[27] A replication of the analysis, using instead an *equal*-weighted version of the NYSE/ASE market index as the basis for estimating the bench-mark cross-sectional risk/return parameters as well as individual-security betas, did not alter that story.

How good is institutional brokerage research?*

Not very, judging from the results of this study of the track records of eleven leaders in the field.

Clinton M. Bidwell, III

Government securities and shares in selected banks were first publicly traded in America under a buttonwood tree in New York on May 17, 1792. Since that date common stocks have become a popular medium of investment and speculation. But the small simplistic market of that era has evolved into a large complex institution, abetted by a massive international communications network and increasingly sophisticated operating techniques.

Throughout this evolution one element has remained constant and always has been the central fascination of the stock market: it is the belief of one's ability to predict the future price movement of a particular common stock. A vast array of individual investors, of numerous occupations, and stockbrokers, ana-

* The author is indebted to Doctor Edward Benson, his Doctoral Committee Chairman, now a Vice-President and Director of Bristol & Gallagher, San Antonio, Texas.

lyst, investment managers, and assorted observers attempt to make correct predictions daily, buying or selling stocks based upon their judgments.

The most highly paid and elite group of stock price predictors are the Wall Street-based institutional analysts. By education, experience, and talent, these analysts have risen to the highest paid, most prestigious pinnacle of the analytical hierarchy. The ability of this group of analysts to select stocks of future superior performance potential is the subject of this inquiry.

This study covers a random sample of institutional brokerage research reports published between 1970 and 1973 inclusive. Since that time, a major structural change has occurred in the business of institutional brokerage with the advent of fully negotiable commission rates on March 1, 1975. The research expenditures of brokerage firms since that date have been undermined in that they are no longer shielded by a fixed commission rate income schedule. Furthermore, the institutional investor is now under increasing fiduciary obligation that impels execution of orders through brokerage firms offering the lowest execution cost. Thus, it is not surprising that several prominent research firms have disappeared from the scene as independent entities: Auerbach, Pollak, Coleman Company, William D. Witter, and Baker, Weeks, just to name the most prominent ones. Viewed in this light, the time period of this study, 1970-1973, contains a period of relative institutional research proliferation because of: (1) the then existent fixed commission structure, and (2) the incredible relative growth of institutional commission volume.[1]

Insofar as negotiated rates have altered the quantity and quality of institutional research output, perhaps logically in a negative fashion, the relevance of the conclusions to today's institutional research may be subject to qualification.

1. Footnotes appear at end of the article.

BACKGROUND

The academic's view and practitioner's view as to the nature of the stock market and the value of stock selectivity are diametrically opposed.

The academic view depicts an efficient stock market[2] in which new information is immediately available at minimal cost to the investment community. Coupled with negligible transaction costs, stock prices will immediately adjust to reflect new information. Thus, each common stock at any instant of time is priced fairly with respect to its value (i.e., it is neither underpriced nor overpriced but is equal to the mean expected value of the distribution of the next period return minus a factor allowing for a holding period return commensurate to the risk of the security).

In the efficient stock market model, no investor can consistently achieve abnormally high returns and the "benefits from security analysis cannot be expected to exceed the cost of trading."[3] The prime function of the portfolio manager, to this view, is to offer a combination of the market portfolio (full diversification) and a riskless asset investment (treasury bills), the relative proportions depending upon the investor's risk utility curve. Any deviation from this balanced, full diversification will result in a distinctly inferior investment (higher risk with no increase in return potential).

The practitioner or traditional view is that security markets are not perfect: actual price will not always equal value. Portfolio managers and analysts can attain consistently superior returns, per units of risk accepted, by stock selectivity resulting in a non-diversified portfolio; "these intentionally prominent features will regularly be rebuilt to new designs as investment opportunities change. If there are no plot and no leading character roles, the individual security holdings are no more a portfolio than talk is drama."[4]

Analysts utilize a number of fundamental and technical approaches to isolate stocks whose prices and values are divergent. By discovering a change in a company's future earning stream, or a change in the probability distribution of that stream, the analyst can, in an imperfect market, preempt the market adjustment process and thereby profit.

Implicit in this view of the market is that stock prices do not instantaneously adjust to new information and that knowledge and analysis are important and can lead to stock selections yielding above average performance.

PRIOR RESEARCH

To date, research on practitioner performance has mainly focused on the portfolio returns (including risk-adjusted analysis) of institutional investors, due in part to various public disclosure requirements permitting external scrutiny. These portfolio forms include mutual funds, common trust funds, corporate pension and profit sharing funds, insurance companies, state and local pension funds, investment counseling of individual portfolios, mutual saving banks, and the investments of non-profit institutions. Most of these studies of money management results conclude that there is no superiority over random portfolio selections,[5] therefore lending support to the academic view of the stock market.

By implication, therefore, the security analysis provided by brokerage firm research as an input into the portfolio decision making process has also been declared ineffectual.

The output of institutional brokerage research is shielded by the lack of disclosure requirements and the select receiving audience of institutional investors. Because of this difficulty in obtaining data, few published articles deal with the return performance of research recommendations.

Possibly the strongest supporting evidence of the ability of the selections of institutional analysts to outperform the market return is found in the Chase Manhattan portfolio selection game.[6] From early 1970 to mid-1972, 34 competing brokerage firms submitted recommendations whose average performance was about double that of the Standard & Poor's 500 Stock Average.[7]

The most comprehensive testing of institutional brokerage research was done by R. E. Diefenbach[8] over the November, 1967-May, 1969 period. His conclusion was essentially that "this group of investment recommendations did not in the aggregate provide a useful universe from which to select investment ideas."[9]

RESEARCH DESIGN

Based on a variety of sources,[10] eleven institutional research firms were chosen for this study based upon their reputation for research excellence:

> Loeb, Rhoades
> Drexel Burnham
> Faulkner, Dawkins, & Sullivan
> White, Weld
> Baker, Weeks
> Mitchell, Hutchins
> Smith, Barney
> Donaldson, Lufkin & Jenrette
> G. H. Walker, Laird
> Oppenheimer
> William D. Witter

In part, the selection technique creates an ex-post bias in that indications of research firm preference and reputation are taken from sources published during and after the period of the study. Such a bias would naturally prejudice the results in favor of the research firms thus chosen for inclusion.

Indices of research output were obtained from the firms cited covering the four-year period 1970-1973. From these indices a random sample of 122 reports was selected,[11] each of three pages or greater in length and explicitly advising the purchase or sale of a specific common stock. Industry reports, informational or follow-up reports, and short reports were excluded, so that the focus was on the in-depth efforts explicitly offering the promise of selectivity.

The reports were divided into purchase recommendations (115) and sell recommendations (7)[12] and the return performance was measured as to the absolute returns, market-relative returns, and risk-adjusted market-relative returns. Two holding periods were selected: one year and a multi-period study of returns from the date of the report to May 31, 1974. The data allowed a sample of 99 for the one-year study and 112 for the multi-period study of purchase recommendation performance. The terminal date for the multi-period study of May 31, 1974 is somewhat capricious; however, it provides a second time framework for investigation.

MEASUREMENT OF RETURN

The holding period returns for the stock observations and the indices will be computed by the following formula:

$$\overline{K} = \frac{\overline{D} + \overline{A}}{\overline{P} - \frac{1}{2}\overline{A}}$$

$\overline{K}$ = the annualized holding period return for the observation, including capital appreciation (or depreciation) and dividends received during the period. This measure is an accurate approximation of the internal rate of return.

$\overline{D}$ = the average annual dividend, computed by summing the total cash dividends received during the particular holding period and dividing by the length of the holding period. This latter variable is expressed in years or in decimals of years (i.e., 2.43 years) which measure the holding period.

$\overline{A}$ = the average annual appreciation (or depreciation) in the market value of the stock or index. Expressed mathematically, the formula for $\overline{A}$ is $P_n - P_o/N$, where P_n is the market price at the end of the period, P_o the market price at the beginning of the period, and N the length of the holding period. The price of the security observations are adjusted to reflect all stock dividends and stock splits during the period.

$\overline{P}$ = the average market price: expressed

mathematically, $P_n + P_o/2$.

The ($-\frac{1}{2}\overline{A}$) part of the divisor is an adjustment computation allowing this formula to produce returns closely approximating the internal rate of return of the stock or index. Interest is in comparative analysis of these returns, not as absolute values. Hence, this formula is useful in producing internally consistent returns for both the stock and the index observation for both the one-year and the multi-period study. It contains both the key aspects of return: capital changes and dividends, and produces annualized results so that comparisons can be made between the one-year study and the multi-period study.

To combine individual return observations over multi-periods, we sum the weighted return component of each asset over all time periods giving the total contribution of each asset to the total portfolio return for each sub-period. Homogeneity of holding periods, using this methodology, is both unnecessary and unassumed.

RISK/ADJUSTMENT PROCESS

The return of each security observation is adjusted by the security's beta, or volatility as measured by the security's co-movement with the Standard & Poor's 500 Stock Index. The adjustment provides a risk-adjusted return to the security which can then be compared to its actual return to note any positive or negative residual return.[13]

Mathematically, the risk-adjustment process is as follows:

$$\Sigma = (R_s - R_f) - \beta (R_m - R_f)$$

Σ = the residual return of the stock. That is, the return of the stock not explainable by its co-movement with the market index.

R_s = the holding period return of the stock, the computation of which is explained in the previous section.

R_f = the risk-free rate of return during that period as measured by Treasury Bill yields. This rate must be subtracted from the stock and the market index return to keep results consistent with capital market theory, and also because the betas are computed by risk premiums, after the risk-free rate has been subtracted from both the stock and the market.

β = the beta of the security, as previously explained.

R_m = the holding period return of the Standard & Poor's 500 Stock Index.

The residual return may be either positive or negative: positive indicating some level of superior risk-adjusted performance; negative, the reverse. As a hypothetical example, stock X produces an 11% return, while the index shows an 8% return. The beta of stock X is 1.3, and the risk-free rate during the holding period is 4%:

$$\Sigma = (11\% - 4\%) - 1.3\,(8\% - 4\%) \qquad (1)$$
$$\Sigma = +1.8\% \qquad (2)$$

Expressed somewhat differently, stock X returns 11% or 7 percentage points above the risk-free rate of return. Given the stock's beta and the market return of 8%, the expected risk-adjusted return of stock X is 5.2 percentage points about the risk-free rate. The attainment of a risk premium return of 7% versus the expected 5.2% results in positive residual return, or performance above that expected given the market movement and the beta (volatility) of the stock.

Presented graphically:

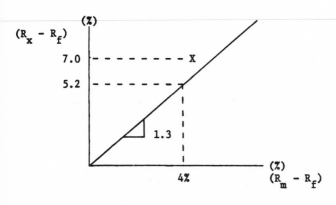

The return premium of 5.2% is expected, a return of 7.0% actually occurs; the difference, or 1.8% return premium, is a positive return bias which could have been obtained through stock selectivity should stock X have been purchased.

STATEMENT OF HYPOTHESIS

There are four major null hypothesis (H_0) and corresponding alternative hypothesis (H_1):

H_0: The mean return of the recommended stock is the same as the mean return of the Standard & Poor's 500 Stock Indices for a one-year holding period.

H_1: The mean return of the recommended stock is different (higher or lower) from the mean return of the Standard & Poor's 500 Stock Indices for a one-year holding period.

H_0: The mean return of the recommended stocks is the same as the mean return of the Standard & Poor's 500 Stock Indices for variable holding periods, beginning with the date of the report and terminating May 31, 1974.

H_1: The mean return of the recommended stocks is different (higher or lower) from the mean return of the Standard & Poor's 500 Stock Indices for variable holding periods.

H_0: The mean return of the recommended stocks less the appropriate risk-free rate of return for each holding period is the same as the mean expected excess return of the recommended stocks for a one-year holding period.

H_1: The mean return of the recommended stocks less the appropriate risk-free rate of return for each holding period is different (higher or lower) from the mean expected excess return of the recommended stocks for a one-year holding period.

H_0: The mean excess return of the recommended stocks is the same as the mean expected excess return of the recommended stocks for variable holding periods, beginning with the date of the report and terminating May 31, 1974.

H_1: The mean excess return of the recommended stocks is different (higher or lower) from the mean expected excess return of the recommended stocks for variable holding periods.

SECURITY
SELECTION
AND ACTIVE
PORTFOLIO
MANAGEMENT

ONE-YEAR NON-RISK-ADJUSTED

Of the 115 purchase recommendations selected, sixteen were written after June 1, 1973. These sixteen can be included in the multi-period study, but not in the one-year study as they are not outstanding for a full year as of the cutoff date for this study, May 31, 1974.

The 99 observations that were included in this sample produced a mean excess return above their Standard & Poor's counterparts of 2.63% with a computed standard deviation of 43.86%. These figures are calculated by computing the differences in return between each of the 99 stock observations and the Standard & Poor's 500 Stock Indices for the same periods.

A mean return difference of zero or one not significantly different from zero is expected if there is no selectivity superiority. It is further expected that about one half of the stocks recommended would outperform the index and about one-half would not. In fact, 45 of the stocks produced higher returns over one year than the corresponding Standard & Poor's returns, while 53 produced a return inferior to the corresponding Standard & Poor's returns. However, a few of the superior performing stocks, notably Levitz Furniture and Rapidata, attained such extremely high differential returns that the overall mean return of the stocks is 2.63% greater than the Standard & Poor's returns.

For the one-year study period of performance, the stock observations attained a mean annual return of 8.83% as compared to the mean performance of the matching Standard & Poor's 500 Stock Index of 6.20%. This difference, however, is inconclusive because of the large standard deviation associated with the mean difference in returns. Although the difference is not statistically reliable, it appears sufficiently significant to warrant further testing.

MULTI-PERIOD NON-RISK-ADJUSTED

A total of 112 observations are included in this time framework. Three of the 115 purchase recommendations selected pertain to companies existing for one year after the report issuance date, but then acquired by other companies prior to May 31, 1974. The mean holding period from the date of the research recommendation to May 31, 1974, is 2.13 years, with a range of from 0.44 years to 4.22 years. The sample stocks produced a mean return 10.96 percentage points lower than the mean return of the 112 matching Standard & Poor's 500 Indices. Moreover, only 30 stocks outperformed their index counterpart, while 82 stocks exhibited relatively inferior returns. The actual mean return of the stocks is − 18.44%, as compared to the mean return of the matching indices of − 7.88%.

The mean return differential of negative 10.96% and a standard deviation of differences in return between the stocks and the indices of 26.48%, given the sample size, yield a Z value of − 4.38. As this value lies outside of the .05 tolerance level (± 1.96), the second null hypothesis is rejected and its alternative hypothesis adopted:

> The mean return of the recommended stocks is lower than the mean return of the Standard & Poor's 500 Stock Indices for variable holding periods (each terminating May 31, 1974).

ONE-YEAR RISK-ADJUSTED

The 99 stock observations produced a mean residual return premium 1.79% above their expected mean return premium. The mean beta of these observations was 1.44, indicating a sample of relatively volatile (risky) securities. The mean difference of 1.79% and the standard deviation of 40.35% yields a Z value of 0.44. Therefore, the results are inconclusive, and the third major null hypothesis is not rejected. Although lacking statistical reliability, the positive return residual may be sufficiently significant to warrant further investigation.

Of the 99 observations, 43 yielded return premiums above that expected, while 56 had return premiums below the expected. As is true in the non-risk-adjusted one-year study, the extraordinary returns of

SECURITY
SELECTION
AND ACTIVE
PORTFOLIO
MANAGEMENT

MGIC, Levitz, and Ryder Systems brought the mean return premium difference above zero in spite of the inferior measured performance by the majority of the stocks.

MULTI-PERIOD RISK-ADJUSTED

The 112 stock sample in this holding period produced a mean residual annualized return premium 4.95 percentage points lower than anticipated. This negative residual, with a sample standard deviation of 25.85%, gives a Z value of -2.03. This value, being below 1.96, the critical value for the .05 significance level for a two-tailed test, rejects the fourth null hypothesis. With the statistical significance as described, the alternative hypothesis is adopted:

> The mean excess return of the recommended stocks is lower than the mean expected excess return of the recommended stocks for variable holding periods (each terminating May 31, 1974).

In this holding period, 40 of the stocks exhibited performance superior to an unbiased estimate of their performance, but 72 stocks did not match or exceed their estimated performance.

THE BAD NEWS

In all four of the study subsections, the clear majority of research recommendations offered inferior returns when measured against the Standard & Poor's Index returns or against an unbiased estimate of the return based on the stock's beta, the market return, and the risk-free return. An examination of performance by individual firms shows that Mitchell, Hutchins, Smith, Barney, and William D. Witter were above average in all aspects measured, with Mitchell, Hutchins perhaps producing the best overall record.

The test results are surprising in a number of respects: the significantly inferior performance of research for the variable period studies, terminating May 31, 1974; the preponderance of negative performance comparisons in the return of the stocks recommended with their expected returns or with the returns of the Standard & Poor's Indices; and the ability of only one firm, during only the one-year study period, to obtain significantly superior return results.

Institutional investors who give up large amounts of commission dollars to receive this research must continually question its value. This study implies that the research reports may well be valueless, or even of negative value, in abetting security selections leading to superior institutional portfolio returns. Further, portfolio turnover based on these research suggestions may cost needless commission dollars and thus impair portfolio return.

The findings indicate a lack of ability on the part of the most qualified analysts to isolate and recommend undervalued securities. The negative performance over the multi-period can possibly be explained by: (1) the juxtaposition of security price changes in the first five months of 1974, during which the "glamour stocks" performed worse than the market; (2) a lack of analytical visibility beyond one year; and/or (3) a sort of bandwagon effect following a recommendation, followed by a period of significantly inferior returns.

[1] New York Stock Exchange, Research Department, "Institutional Holdings of NYSE-Listed Stocks — 1971" (New York Stock Exchange, February, 1971), p. 2.

[2] See James H. Lorie and Mary T. Hamilton, *The Stock Market: Theories and Evidence* (Homewood, Illinois: Richard D. Irwin, 1973); William F. Sharpe, "Mutual Fund Performance," *Journal of Business,* Vol. 39, No. 1 (January, 1966), pp. 119-139.

[3] Oldrich A. Vasicek and John A. McQuown, "The Efficiency Model," *Financial Analysts Journal,* Vol. XXVII (September-October, 1972), p. 76.

[4] Charles D. Ellis, *Institutional Investing* (Dow Jones-Irwin, Inc., Homewood, Illinois, 1971), p. 27.

[5] Wharton School of Finance and Commerce, University of Pennsylvania, *Study of Mutual Funds* (Washington, D.C.: Government Printing Office, 1962).
Minturn R. Sedgwick, "The Record of Conventional In-

SECURITY
SELECTION
AND ACTIVE
PORTFOLIO
MANAGEMENT

vestment Management: Is There Not a Better Way?" *Financial Analysts Journal*, Vol. 29, No. 4 (July-August, 1973), pp. 41-46.

Edward Malca, "Characteristics and Performance of Bank-Administered Commingled Equity Funds for Employee Benefit Plans: 1962-1970," a forthcoming Ph.D. dissertation, The City University of New York, 1973.

Peter J. Williamson, "Measurement and Forecasting of Mutual Fund Performance: Choosing an Investment Strategy," *Financial Analysts Journal*, Vol. 28, No. 6 (November-December, 1972), pp. 78-92.

Michael C. Jensen, "Problems in Selection of Security Portfolios: The Performance of Mutual Funds in the Period 1945-1964," *Journal of Finance*, Vol. 23, No. 2 (May, 1968), pp. 389-416.

[6] "Best Paper Portfolio Has Appreciated 90% in Chase Bank's Game," *The Wall Street Journal*, New York, ed. (October 6, 1972), p. 17.

[7] *Ibid.*

[8] R. E. Diefenbach, "How Good Is Institutional Research," *Financial Analysts Journal*, Vol. 28, No. 1 (January-February, 1972), pp. 54-60.

[9] *Ibid.*, p. 56.

[10] Muller & Company survey, as partially reproduced in *Business Week*, September 15, 1973, p. 200.

"The Search for Analytical Excellence," *Institutional Investor*, Vol. 6, No. 10 (October, 1972), pp. 49-69.

"The Best Research Report I've Read: A Survey," *Institutional Investor*, Vol. 5, No. 3 (March, 1971), pp. 34-37.

"Institutional Research: End of an Era?" *Institutional Investor*, Vol. 6, No. 6 (February, 1972), pp. 27-34.

"If Member Firms Went Public Now, What Multiples Would Their Stock Command?" *Institutional Investor*, Vol. 4, No. 2 (February, 1970), pp. 48-49.

[11] A two-stage random sampling technique was employed, such that the joint probabilities of any observation being selected were equal. At the first stage a random number identified from which firm the report was to be drawn. A second random number selected the exact report for possible inclusion. A table of random numbers was employed and sampling was without replacement so that an observation could not be chosen twice.

[12] Because of the small size of the sell recommendation samples, this area of analysis will be ignored in this paper.

[13] The historical beta calculations were basically provided by O'Brien Associates, Inc., Santa Monica, California.

A NEW LOOK

AT AN OLD TRADITION

Corporate and investor returns:
A guide to strategy

Different forces determine the company's reinvestment rate and the stockholder's return, but their inextricable linkage is an aid to portfolio decisions.

John D. Connolly

The purpose of any investment is a return commensurate with risk, provided, of course, that the return is competitive with existing alternatives. This competitive aspect of investing ensures that capital will flow to those concerns with the most promising direct investments. It also tends to flatten out the returns from indirect investments, stocks and bonds, for a given stratum of risk. For the return on capital to the investor is the cost of capital to the company. The higher the company's return on its incremental investment, the lower the cost can be while still providing an adequate return to the investor. But if a company invests poorly, security holders will not be afforded a competitive return unless the company pays more for investable funds, for example, by selling equity at less than book value. To the extent that capital is perfectly allocated, investor returns will be homogenous and our capital markets will be efficient.

While our system does lean in this direction,

perfection is only an ideal. More importantly, everything is in a state of flux, and the markets must react. Companies change internally or change is thrust upon them from their environment, alternatives are constantly shifting, and even the value of money is not fixed. An understanding of the mechanism that adjusts security values to compensate for change in corporate or stockholders' returns is the scientific side of portfolio management. The art lies in identifying those changes in advance.

THE RETURN TO THE INVESTOR

Investor returns for various strata of risk will vary with the psychology of the moment. The yield spread between high and low grade corporate bonds has a predictable behavior pattern as the future course of the economy brightens or clouds up. But the common component of investor return at all levels of risk is the cost of money. Where the investment instrument fixes the nominal return, as in a bond, the market will protect the real return by adjusting for perceived levels of inflation through price changes. The thesis that equity represents a hedge against inflation derives from the possibility of a company including the rate of inflation in its own return on investment through changes in the prices of the products it sells, thus maintaining the investor's real return without a capital loss.

In severe inflationary periods, such as the one we have just come through, this thesis has proved unworkable. The rate of return demanded from common stocks has evidenced a volatility similar to that of the short-term debt market, generating severe stock price attrition. Interest rates are surely not the only reason for stock price movements, but that a general link exists between equities and fixed income securities, whether long or short, seems incontrovertible. The stock market therefore will respond to changes in the discount factor much as the bond market will.

CORPORATE
AND
INVESTOR
RETURNS: A
GUIDE TO
STRATEGY

This suggests that some of the strategies used in the bond market to ride the yield curve can be employed to adjust the "term structure" of an equity portfolio. Since the discount rate is applied to future return, a change in the discount rate will have the most pronounced effect on those equities whose total return is more dependent upon future earnings growth than on current yield. In a period when the discount rate rises, as is likely when alternate returns in the fixed income market climb sharply, growth stocks will be under pressure. The reverse is, of course, true when rates fall. Only in a quiescent inflation and interest rate environment can growth and yield stocks be considered to be on equal footing.

WHY HIGH P/E'S?

A graphic example of the varying reactions of yield and growth investment vehicles to changes in the environment for stockholder return is shown in Table I. We have taken two companies with the same level of profitability, a 15% return on equity, but with differing opportunities or proclivities for reinvestment. A slow growth company, for example GM, has limited investment outlets with a resulting high payout. A similarly profitable company in an expanding environment may end up with an identical total return of 12.5%, but the method of delivery will emphasize growth rather than yield. The faster growth company will also carry a somewhat higher P/E.

It is essential to understand that the premium P/E is not created by a higher level of growth, per se, but by the fact that the company can earn a higher return on incremental investment than the shareholder. The wider the spread between the company's return (return on equity) and the stockholder's return (market discount factor), the more pronounced the premium P/E will be, or, viewed another way, the premium over book at which the stock will sell. In short, if a company with a higher return than its stockholders reinvests a larger portion of its earnings, the increment

SECURITY
SELECTION
AND ACTIVE
PORTFOLIO
MANAGEMENT

TABLE I

Impact of a Decline in Total Demanded Return
on Companies with Varying Growth Rates

First Case

	Yield	+	Earnings Growth	=	Total Stockholder Return
Slow-Growth Company	7.5%	+	5.0%	=	12.5%
Faster Growth Company	5.0%	+	7.5%	=	12.5%
	(Payout ÷ P/E)	+	(ROE x Earnings Retention Rate)	=	Total Stockholder Return
Slow-Growth Company	(66.7% ÷ 8.9X)	+	(15% x 33.3%)	=	12.5%
Faster Growth Company	(50.0% ÷ 10.0X)	+	(15% x 50.0%)	=	12.5%

Second Case

	Yield	+	Growth	=	Total Stockholder Return
Slow-Growth Company	6.5%	+	5.0%	=	11.5%
Faster Growth Company	4.0%	+	7.5%	=	11.5%
	(Payout ÷ P/E)	+	(ROE x Earnings Retention Rate)	=	Total Stockholder Return
Slow-Growth Company	(66.7% ÷ 10.3X)	+	(15% x 33.3%)	=	11.5%
Faster Growth Company	(50.0% ÷ 12.5X)	+	(15% x 50.0%)	=	11.5%

Percentage Decline in Demanded Stockholder Return = 8.0%
Percentage Increase in Slow-Growth Company = 15.7%
Percentage Increase in Faster Growth Company = 25.0%

to the company's growth rate will exceed the decrement to yield caused by a lower payout ratio. If the market is to keep the total return of the stock in line with current alternatives, the yield must be further depressed through a rise in the multiple.

Our interest is in the intensity of the reaction of various classes of stocks to a change in the market environment. The second half of Table I assumes that the return provided by alternative investments, such as the short-term money market, has declined either because of supply-demand conditions or a moderation in the perceived rate of inflation, which in turn has lowered stockholder demands in the equity markets from 12.5% to 11.5%. With both companies still earning 15% on equity, the spread between the company's return and the stockholder's return has widened. The wider the spread, the more valuable the portion retained by the company becomes. Growth becomes more important. The P/E's of both companies rise, but the growth company reacts more strongly and its premium expands. Growth stock volatility is, however, a two-edged sword.

A bond market analogy can be useful here. Volatility rises with longer maturity and lower coupon bonds. The reason is that yield to maturity (total return in the bond market) becomes more dependent upon the repayment of principal than upon the current coupon. This promised future return is greatly affected by changes in the discount factor. In the stock market, a growth stock is more highly dependent upon promised future return as opposed to current yield and is therefore more sensitive to changes in demanded stockholder return (the discount factor).

Implicit in this analysis is a strong argument for growth stocks if one believes that inflation is indeed on the wane. This is apart from the effects of inflation on an individual company's operations. To the extent that an industry dependent upon discretionary income, such as the autos, is severely impacted by inflation's effective reduction of real income, an easing of inflation will have a further benefit. In addition, weaker

TABLE II

Impact of an Increase in Corporate Return
on Companies with Similar Growth Rates

First Case

	Yield	+	Growth	=	Total Stockholder Return
GM	6.5%	+	5.0%	=	11.5%
Ford	6.5%	+	5.0%	=	11.5%

	(Payout ÷ P/E)	+	(ROE x Earnings Retention Rate)	=	Total Stockholder Return
GM	(66.7% ÷ 10.3X)	+	(15.0 x 33.3%)	=	11.5%
Ford	(50.0% ÷ 7.7X)	+	(10.0 x 50.0%)	=	11.5%

Second Case

	Yield	+	Growth	=	Total Stockholder Return
GM	6.5%	+	5.0%	=	11.5%
Ford	6.5%	+	5.0%	=	11.5%

	(Payout ÷ P/E)	+	(ROE x Earnings Retention Rate)	=	Total Stockholder Return
GM	(72.2% ÷ 11.1X)	+	(18.0% x 27.8%)	=	11.5%
Ford	(58.3% ÷ 9.0X)	+	(12.0% x 41.7%)	=	11.5%

Percentage Increase in Company Return = 20.0%
Percentage Increase in High Return Company (GM) = 7.8%
Percentage Increase in Low Return Company (Ford) = 16.9%

companies will be aided by an easing of the financial distortions caused by inflation. The point, however, is that, as a general rule, deep discount bonds and growth stocks are the place to be in a falling interest rate environment.

COMPANY RETURN

The spread between stockholder and corporate rates of return can be as affected by company strategy as by market conditions. If, for example, a company finds the secret of investing its cash flow at a significantly higher rate of return, either higher growth will result from the same level of earnings retention or the same growth will be possible with a higher dividend payout. In either case, the stock price will be forced up in order to keep the total stockholder return consistent with that available in the market as a whole. Quite often cyclical changes in return on equity are misinterpreted as signaling permanent alterations in earning power or growth rates. If such misjudgments become the conventional wisdom, true opportunity is presented to the portfolio manager who focuses on inherent or normalized profitability.

Table II contrasts the impact of a rise in profitability on a high and on a low return company. Ford and GM can be used as examples. We have assumed that GM increases its return on equity from 15% to 18%, or by 20%, and that Ford has a similar percentage increase which raises its return from 10.0% to 12.0%. Both companies are assumed to share in the 5% industry growth rate. We realize that this is a debatable point, just as we realize that the quality difference between these two companies would prompt investors to demand a higher return from Ford as compensation for the added risk. Nevertheless, we have kept the stockholder return constant for both companies at 11.5% in order to illustrate how the pressure on stock price operates.

It is clear that an improvement in profitability is more beneficial for the low return company. While the increased spread between corporate and stockholder return should make GM more valuable to investors, Ford, with the same percentage increase in profitability, moves from a negative to a positive spread. The leverage is actually on the dividend. A greater increase in payout is possible with no diminution of growth. It is also interesting to note the behavior of stock price versus book value. When Ford is capable of investing its cash at a higher return than generally available in the marketplace, its stock will be bid to a premium over book. The reverse is true when market returns are better than corporate returns.

An intriguing paradox is sometimes created. The more determined to grow that some low return companies become, the deeper the share price should be discounted from book. This discount can effectively limit a company's ability to finance as well as provide a negative reward for management. The market has its own discipline for those who ignore the marginal return on capital.

Rising corporate returns tend to bias stock performance in favor of low return companies given equal opportunities to grow. This rule of thumb can be added to our first conclusion — falling market alternatives work in favor of growth companies given the same level of profitability. Very often these two forces are acting in opposite directions, particularly in the early stages of an economic recovery when rising business activity creates the appearance of better corporate profitability but has not yet put upward pressure on money rates. Both low return and high growth companies may then simultaneously act well.

SENSITIVITY — THE ROLE OF TIME AND RISK

The total return formula that we have used is a conceptually simpler and yet more elaborate way of stating the valuation truism contained in the discounted dividend stream theories of valuation. Table III shows how the two concepts are reconciled.

Reconciliation with the traditional valuation

CORPORATE
AND
INVESTOR
RETURNS: A
GUIDE TO
STRATEGY

model exposes total return to the same criticism, namely the inability to deal with high growth companies. Indeed, as the growth rate begins to approach

TABLE III

Reconciliation of Traditional Valuation Model with
Total Return Formula

$$P = \frac{D}{k - G}$$

$$k - G = \frac{D}{P}$$

$$k = \frac{D}{P} + G$$

$$k = Y + G$$

$$\text{Total Return} = Y + G$$

$$\text{Total Return} = (\text{Payout} \div \text{P/E}) + (\text{ROE} \times \text{Earnings Retention Rate})$$

the demanded stockholder return, P/E sensitivity expands rapidly. Finally, when a growth rate above the stockholder return is achieved, a negative yield is required to balance the equation. Any static approach deteriorates in a dynamic world.

The core concept in approaching high growth companies is that exceptional growth is transitory and that every industry either attracts competition or eventually reaches some degree of saturation. What distinguishes great companies is the unusual duration of both their profitability and growth, but even the greatest company will eventually slow down to sustainable levels for these key variables from which a P/E can be calculated. The current price then will be shaped by this eventually stable P/E, by the current high growth rate, and by the longevity of the growth phase. In effect the current P/E premium above the future stable P/E is subject to decay over the time span of exceptional growth at a rate equal to the difference between the market's demanded return and the stock's apparent total return measured by current growth and yield.

On the one hand, the portfolio manager can calculate a current P/E from his impression of the duration of the growth interval and the profitability and reinvestment parameters that will apply in the stable phase. Or, alternatively, he could start with the current P/E and calculate the time needed to amortize it down to the stable P/E level, using what might be called a Multiple Attrition Rate (MAR), or the difference between the currently apparent total return and the market's demand rate of return. The total return equation could then be balanced as follows:

$$\text{Yield} + \text{Growth} - \text{MAR} = \text{Total Return}$$
$$(\text{Payout} \div \text{P/E}) + (\text{ROE} \times \text{ERR}) - \text{MAR} = \text{Total Return}$$

AN EXAMPLE WORKED OUT

The fundamental risk in growth stock investing lies not merely in mistaking profitability levels but also in misjudging the duration of growth. With risk so inextricably linked to time, it is useful to examine how both these concepts may be altered by changing market alternatives as they affect the discount factor. We will use Kresge as an example as it is not only a superior profit and growth company but also one where eventual saturation is clearly a major issue. In addition, Kresge also represents a company that has fully utilized the pricing mechanism used by the market to allocate capital by repeatedly injecting equity into the company at prices far higher than book.

We estimate Kresge's earnings in 1976 at $1.70 per share for a P/E on the current price ($34) of twenty times. The S&P 425 (108.00) has an eleven multiple, based on a 1976 earnings estimate of $9.50. Even if we assume that the company's growth will slow down, Kresge's premium to the S&P might be justified by a combination of higher return on equity and higher reinvestment rate, providing we have a long enough interval of high growth. The time interval is approximated by amortizing the P/E premium at a rate determined by the difference between Kresge's total return and the market's total return. We should interject here

CORPORATE
AND
INVESTOR
RETURNS: A
GUIDE TO
STRATEGY

that we expect Kresge eventually to maintain a return on equity and reinvestment rate above those of the market in general because of management strength and, thus, we expect its multiple to stabilize somewhere above that of the market as a whole. It is the multiple premium of the current, high growth Kresge above that of the future, stable Kresge with which we are concerned.

Table IV shows three equations of total return. The first is for the S&P and is based on our estimates of 1976 earnings of $9.50, a dividend of $4.12, average equity per share of $75.54, and the current index of 108.00. These figures result in a return on equity of 12.6%, an earnings retention rate of 56.7%, internally generated growth of 7.1%, a payout ratio of 43.3%, a yield of 3.8%, a P/E of 11.4 times, and total return of 10.9%. The S&P average total return of approximately 11% coincides well with our estimate of the median return which leads us to believe that it is representative of the rate around which the market is currently arbitraging opportunities. (In late 1974, however, the market return was over 13%. The decline in the inflation rate, evidenced by the action of interest rates, resulted in this easing of demanded returns. If the trend continues, the general stock market outlook could continue to be pleasant.)

The second total return equation is our estimate of what Kresge might look like in the future. We have labeled it Kresge (80's) after the British fashion of dating companies like Rolls Royce (1971). We assume that the company's return will decline somewhat from the current level of roughly 16% but will remain above that of the S&P average simply because the average contains so many clearly inferior companies. A 14% return seems reasonable. We are, however, assuming that the company will eventually raise its payout to the S&P level of 43% as expansion opportunities in an increasingly saturated market become limited. The resulting earnings retention of 57% produced 8% growth, only slightly above the S&P. Investors can accept a lower 3% yield and still arrive at an 11% total

TABLE IV

Total Return Equations

S&P 425	Yield	3.8%	+	Growth	=	Total Return
S&P 425			+	7.1%	=	10.9%
S&P 425	(Payout ÷ P/E)		+	(ROE X Earnings Retention Rate)	=	Total Return
S&P 425	(43.3% ÷ 11.4X)		+	(12.6% X 56.7%)	=	10.9%
Kresge (80's)	Yield	3.0%	+	Growth	=	Total Return
Kresge (80's)			+	8.0%	=	11.0%
Kresge (80's)	(Payout ÷ P/E)		+	(ROE X Earnings Retention Rate)	=	Total Return
Kresge (80's)	(43.0% ÷ 14.3X)		+	(14.0% X 57.0%)	=	11.0%
Kresge (70's)	Yield	0.7%	+	Growth − Growth in Shares	=	Total Return
Kresge (70's)			+	20.0% − 2.9%	=	17.8%
Kresge (70's)	(Payout ÷ P/E)		+	(ROE X Earnings Retention Rate) − Growth in Shares	=	17.8%
Kresge (70's)	(14.0% ÷ 20.0X)		+	(16.0% X 125.0%) − 2.9%	=	17.8%

CORPORATE
AND
INVESTOR
RETURNS: A
GUIDE TO
STRATEGY

return. The P/E will decline to fourteen times but not all the way to the S&P level.

The final total return equation is Kresge today, labeled Kresge (70's). Of particular importance are the high apparent total return, the extraordinary earnings retention ratio (due to the sales of stock), and the growth of shares outstanding, which deducts from the shareholder's return.

Kresge has been able to show growth in sales and assets above its reinvestment rate because of the company's ability to raise equity on attractive terms. (Over the last five years, the equity account has increased 25% more than the cumulative earnings during that period, despite a modest payout ratio.) The stock sells at a multiple of book because the company's return is above that of the equity market in general. As long as this relationship continues, the company will be able to increase its equity account faster than shares outstanding and positively affect its total return. The next injection of equity will occur through the conversion of the $200 million debentures sold in 1974. The conversion price of $35.50 is far more visible now than a few months ago, and we expect the company to call this issue within two years, assuming a feasible stock price. Such a conversion would continue an adjusted earnings retention rate at over 100%.

Since Kresge (70's) offers a far higher total return than the market, it would appear to be attractive. But since we expect it to evolve into Kresge (80's) with a lower P/E, the stock should be bid up only high enough to offset the amortization of the P/E differential by above average near-term earnings growth. The risk lies in growth slowing sooner than expected. We can judge this risk by calculating a break-even number of years for which the current high total return must be maintained to justify the investment.

Currently, Kresge's P/E premium is 39.9% above the eventually sustainable level, the difference between the current total return and the market return is 6.8%, and the break-even time is five years. If the market return were higher than the current 11%, the difference between the market's return and Kresge's total return would be diminished, and either the time needed to break even would expand or the P/E premium would shrink. Six months ago, when the market was demanding a total return of 13%, a 39.9% P/E premium could only be justified if we assumed that Kresge's current total return could be maintained for seven years. The alternative would be for a shrinkage in the P/E premium over Kresge (80's).

The portfolio manager's quandary can now be concisely stated. How likely is it that Kresge will show outstanding growth for more than five years? Or is it possible that market rates could continue to slide, justifying an even higher premium?

STOCK SELECTION VS. RISK SELECTION

While the artistic world of the stock market defies a fully structured approach, the mathematical relationship between company and stockholder returns, payout and plow-back strategies may be useful indicators of the market's potential response to change. In addition, risk can be more fully appreciated. The specific company risk of ebbing profitability can be divorced from the risk of capital loss resulting from higher rates in the debt market. Portfolio strategies can be devised which minimize, ignore, or even seek certain types of risks depending on the investing environment. Finally, the growth stock problem can be reduced to one of time with the investment decision hinging on a rational analysis of the probable alternatives.

CORPORATE
AND
INVESTOR
RETURNS: A
GUIDE TO
STRATEGY

Remembering Benjamin Graham — teacher and friend

A touching memoir, and an incisive and rigorous system for investment success.

James B. Rea

Benjamin Graham died at his home in France on September 21, 1976. He was creative and brilliant to the end. He had recently completed research going back fifty years (from 1925 to 1975) showing that if one had used just a *few* of his simple investment criteria during that period, he would have outperformed the Dow by a factor of over two to one. Ben's last message to me was, "Invest in financially sound companies whose earnings and dividend yields are high." By his criteria, a company is financially sound when it owes less than its net worth; and its earnings and dividend yields are high when they are twice and two-thirds, respectively, the average Triple-A bond yield.

    Ben and I met about three years ago. At that time, I was a consultant with a number of corporations, and most of my work was associated with corporate acquisition search. These companies were interested in acquiring *all* of the stock, rather than just *some* of the stock as in an investment search. We observed that the principles of acquisition search and investment search are similar.

It was about the time that Ben wrote his article called "Renaissance of Value" in *Barron's* and copies of this article were sent to me by a number of my clients, and each in his nice way said, "You know, this article is something that you should really read. Mr. Graham's thinking is similar to yours, but he's way ahead of you. He's been doing it for fifty years, and maybe if you got to know him you'd learn a lot."

So, I read the article and agreed completely. Then I tried to get in touch with him and I found that none of my clients knew him; and I didn't know where he lived, so I sent a copy of my computer print-out (which was then used only for acquisition search) to him at *Barron's,* hoping they would forward it on to him.

APOLOGY AND MEETING

But when I didn't hear from him in a month or two, I bolstered my ego by rationalizing that, well, that world-famous fellow, he couldn't be expected to answer all of the letters that came from strangers, so I forgot about it. And then I got a call from Connecticut where Ben was staying with his oldest daughter, Marjorie, and he asked if I was the Jim Rea that sent him this "great big volume called Radix." Defensively, I said yes. He thanked me and apologized; and said that he usually answered his mail quite promptly, but that he had had a stroke while in France and that he was forced to go to a hospital, and he said that the only thing really worth reading was what I had sent him through *Barron's.* (I found out later that's about all he had to read.) But I enjoyed the compliment, and he said that I didn't have to go to New York as I had promised in my letter, but "just come on down to La Jolla. I'll be there in another week or so; bring your wife, and we'll all get together."

So, we made a plan to meet in La Jolla a few weeks after he had called and one of the questions before he hung up was, he wondered how come I was generating *his* kind of stocks in my computer. He asked was I using his criteria, and I said I wasn't sure but I didn't think so, because I was not familiar with his criteria. I told him that my computer measured reward and measured risk and printed out in the order of highest reward-to-risk ratio. He said yes, and with some patience he reminded me that he had read the literature that I had sent him and that he agreed with my concepts of reward. But he had some questions that he'd like to talk to me about regarding my concepts of risk.

Subsequently, we met in La Jolla with our ladies. We had tea and cookies, and then he started out. He said, "Dr. Rea, I'd like to have you explain the theory of Radix to me, but please don't use your mathematics." He said, "Can't you explain it in a way that our ladies can understand it as well?" (I, incidentally, found out later that he was well trained in mathematics).

I wasn't quite prepared for that, but I suggested that maybe if Ben would allow me I'd use my corny "milk cow" analogy. His eyes twinkled and he smiled and said, "Go right ahead."

COW SELECTION

So, I suggested we assume that all four of us were on our way out to look for the best milk cow we could find, and that we were going to invest in a herd of milk cows. The first thing, of course, we would want to find a cow that gave lots of milk, and we'd want that cow to give more milk the next year, and we'd like stability in its milk growth. We wouldn't want the cow to be giving a lot of milk this month and then not so much the next month. In other words, we'd want stability in that growth of milk. But then Ben said, "Dr. Rea, how about the cheese?" (He was always ahead of me). And I said,

> "Well, the cheese is the dividend that you get from the milk and you give back to the customer.

110
SECURITY
SELECTION
AND ACTIVE
PORTFOLIO
MANAGEMENT

"Being a good Scotsman, I'd like all of this at a very low price. In other words, I'd like high milk production — that's high earnings. I'd like lots of growth in the milk — that's growth in the earnings — and I'd like lots of stability in that growth. And I'd like lots of cheese — high in dividend yield.

"To get a high reward you have got to have lots of milk, lots of growth in the milk, lots of stability in that growth, and lots of cheese from the milk. And, above all, the price must be low.

"Now, let's remember that we are buying this cow primarily for its milk, growth, stability, and cheese, and we assume that we are able to get it at a low price. But what happens if the milk dries up after we bought the cow? It would be safer if what we paid for that cow was no more than what we could get for the 'meat on its bones.' We wouldn't get much for the fixed assets — that's the bones of the cow. We might get a little bit for the hide. But, the 'meat on its bones' is what we could get if we quickly liquidated the cow.

"Now, to the extent that the price we would pay for the cow was higher than what we could get if we liquidated the cow, we could consider that a higher risk. Of course, it's true that is just one component of total risk, because there are many other risk components.

"But if we measured reward by the things we originally bought the cow for, namely, milk, growth, stability, and the cheese; and we measured risk by what we paid for it relative to what we could get in case the cow's milk dried up — in other words, for the meat on its bones; and if we divided reward by risk to get the reward-to-risk ratio, then we could get a *relative* measure of 'how good' that cow was (relative to other cows). And in the same way, Radix could get a measure of 'how good' a stock was relative to other stocks.

"At least Radix could be used for *macro-screening*, because in the New York and American exchanges and the OTC, as covered in the Standard and Poor's Data Base, there are over 4,000 stocks and it would be very difficult to manually compute the reward-to-risk ratio for all of these companies and then to sort them in the order of highest reward-to-risk ratio."

I had originally thought that we might have just one meeting in La Jolla, but we liked each other and so we started working together. I learned so much that every chance I could get when Ben was willing and feeling okay, I would drive to La Jolla to work with him. And it seems that our ladies liked each other, too, and so we spent quite a bit of time, at least once a month, going over some of the basic investment criteria which we used in our research.

Ben and I in the months to follow decided to use at least ten basic criteria in our research. Five of the ten were very sensitive to price and earnings changes, whereas the other five were not. Seven were Ben's and three were mine.

THE FIRST FIVE CRITERIA

I'll begin with the first five. One criterion is that we would like the earnings yield to be at least twice the average Triple-A bond yield. For example, if the average Triple-A bond yield were 8%, as it is close to that today, twice that would be sixteen. This means we'd want a price-to-earnings ratio (100 divided by 16) of 6¼ or less.

The second criterion is that we'd like the price-to-earnings ratio to be down to at least 4/10 of its previous average high.

Ben had originally used his criterion that the price *itself* should be down to one-half of its previous high. But I argued that it would not be logical to ask that a company's price be down to half its high if during that period its earnings had, say, tripled.

He said, "Well, then what do you think we should use instead?"

And I said, "Originally, the price-to-earnings ratio, say at the end of 1972, was as high as eighteen as an average P/E high. And then towards the end of 1974, it had dropped down by, say, two-thirds — in other words, dropped down to one-third of its high value, or to about six." So, I was thinking about one-third of the P/E high and Ben had been talking about one-half of the price high — and so we compromised and decided to use 4/10, and to use the P/E ratio rather than price alone. We carried it a step further by thinking in terms of the average P/E, which we defined as the average price in a given year divided by the year-end earnings. There is a print-out in Value Line that gives the average P/E for each year for each stock covered. So, we decided to use 4/10 of the average P/E high.

The third of these first five criteria is that we'd like the price to be equal to or less than two-thirds of the tangible book value.

The fourth criterion is that we'd like the dividend yield to be equal to or greater than two-thirds of the average Triple-A bond yield.

The fifth criterion is that we would like the price to be down to what Ben called his "net current asset value" (sometimes referred to as "net working capital"). Ben originally defined his net current asset value to me as the current assets minus the current liabilities, which is working capital, and minus the long-term debt. He defined this as "net working capital" or "net current asset value."

On the other hand, I proceeded further, especially since it was usually available in the computer, to define "Net Quick," using corporate acquisition jargon, as the current assets minus current liabilities, minus long-term debt, but also minus minority interest, minus deferred taxes, minus any leasehold liabilities, minus pension liabilities, and even minus any preferred which is really an equity.

In other words, the corporate acquisition concept of "Net Quick" was the *quick* liquidation value of the company: you gave no value to the fixed assets, or to any other long-term assets. Thus, if you started with the short-term assets (current assets) only, and paid off *all* debt, and in fact paid off the preferred also, you would then end up with the so-called quick liquidation value (which I had been calling the "Net Quick" in the common in Radix because it had been developed initially for corporate acquisition search). This is the common stockholder's "Net Quick" value as defined for acquisitions. It is what you would get if you were the last man in the liquidation line. We agreed that Ben's Net-Net-Net Current Asset Value was the same as my "Net Quick."

SCORING

We knew that it would be very rare to find a company that met all five of these rather stringent criteria. So, we agreed that if, for the New York Stock Exchange, we could find stocks with at least a "three and a half" rating out of the five, and for the American and OTC we could find at least four out of five, we would consider them "buys." Yes, I hear your question: You say, "What's three and one-half? How can you get a half point?"

Each one of our ten rating criteria has a half point and a whole point. For example, we said the dividend yield ought to be two-thirds of the Triple-A bond yield or higher. Well, if the Triple-A bond, for talking purposes, were nine, and two-thirds of that is six, then we would want a dividend yield of six or higher. But suppose that it's 5.9 — a little bit less than six. We decided that if it were equal to or greater than 4.5, which is *half* the nine Triple-A bond yield, then between 4.5 and six we'd give it a *half* a point, and at six or above we'd give it a *whole* point in our rating system.

THE SECOND FIVE

I'd now like to talk about the second set of five criteria; those which do *not* change rapidly with changes in price and earnings. The first one is that we would like a current ratio (current assets divided by current liabilities) of at least two or higher (Ben had previously used 1.9).

The second of these five is that we would like the total debt to be less than the company's tangible

SECURITY
SELECTION
AND ACTIVE
PORTFOLIO
MANAGEMENT

net worth; in other words, less than the equity (a debt-to-equity ratio of one or less).

The third criterion of that second set of five requires the total debt to be less than twice the net, net, net current asset value, as described in the first set of five.

Now, these last three that I've just been talking about, namely, current ratio, total debt to equity, and total debt relative to twice the net, net, net current asset value — these are criteria for financial soundness, and we agreed that we would like at least two out of three of these for an entity to qualify as a financially sound company. Our research showed that *total debt* (relative to equity and twice the net, net, net current asset value) was the most important factor affecting financial soundness. The current ratio criterion was not as important and much easier to meet.

As the fourth criterion in this last five, we'd like the growth rate over the last ten years to be at least 7% *compounded*, which means that, as a first approximation, we would like the company to have doubled its earnings in the last ten years.

And the last of the five of the second set of five criteria says that we would like no more than two declines in year-end earnings (relative to the preceding year) in the last ten years. Now, if it had three declines, we'd give it a half point; but if it had only two declines or fewer, we'd give it a whole point, which is another example of our half point/whole point criteria. A decline was defined as a drop of 5% or greater.

Our research also showed that financial soundness was relatively much more important than earnings growth and stability in that growth.

We again found it hard to find very many companies that met all five of these last criteria. So here again, we agreed that for a "buy," three and one-half out of five would be okay for the New York Stock Exchange, and four out of five would be okay for the American and OTC.

Actually, we would not even consider the first five unless a company met the requirements of the second five. We decided to use Radix as it existed for "*macro*screening" from the 4,000-some stocks in Standard and Poor's Stock Guide, using IMS (which is Investors Management Sciences in Denver, a wholly-owned subsidiary of Standard and Poor's). Using IMS each month we find those companies that come closest to meeting the highest reward-to-risk ratio as previously explained. And to those companies that survived that screening, we would then apply our ten criteria.

In other words, *macro*screening normally gets us down to a more manageable number of stocks; then we use our manual search technique to identify those companies that not only come close to meeting these ten criteria that we have just talked about, but also very *clearly* meet the three criteria that I would like to tell you about subsequently in this paper.

THE CRUCIAL ROLE OF DIVERSIFICATION

But before I do so, let me say that there is one other criterion that is seldom mentioned with emphasis, but that I feel is worth a lot of emphasis: the criterion of *diversity*. Even though one could find a number of stocks which meet our "buy" requirements using our ten criteria, Ben always suggested that we "just buy a little bit of each, really not trusting it too much, because there may be many other reasons, that you don't know about, as to why the company might not do as well in the future." And "to buy only a little bit of it so as not to emphasize any one, and to buy the stocks of *other* companies, again just a little bit, which *also* meet our criteria."

The criteria themselves are quite stringent, as you can see. But although they are, they certainly are not fool-proof; for that reason, we don't want to invest in any fewer than thirty companies. In fact, Ben said that his best performance record in the past was when the market was low enough to allow him to invest in over a hundred companies, buying just a few hundred shares in each company and so not "loading up" on any one.

I remember the first time Ben asked me the question, "How do you do your *research* in deciding on which companies you ought to buy?" And I pulled out my list of many things that I checked on. These were the same things that I had considered in "corporate acquisition search," in trying to buy *all* of the stock. And it involved not only looking at items similar to those criteria that we just talked about, but it meant looking at the management, looking at the company's competition, making sure we knew about all their products and services, and by the time we did in-depth research using this complete list, it would take a lot of time.

So, after I got through "bragging" about my list, Ben said, "Well, then how many companies do you think you could invest in?" And I said, "If I worked very hard, say twelve hours a day, and also took a trip and visited each company and found out a lot about everything on my list, maybe I could invest in seven or eight companies . . . to keep 'up-to-date' on each one of these companies." Without saying that I was wrong, he just said, "Well, I never found that to be very important."

He said, "So often when I went to the trouble to get all this information on any one company, I found it was not always right. And even the presidents and vice presidents of the companies were not consistent in what they told me." And he said, "I think we are doing really *enough* research if we make sure that these companies meet our ten criteria, so why don't we just buy a little bit in each company? Don't trust it. And diversify by buying just a little bit of another company that also meets our criteria." He said, "I think our performance will be much better if we do that rather than trying to do so much in-depth research." What he really was saying was that he had found that *diversity* was more important than *in-depth research*.

WHICH CRITERION COUNTS MOST?

I'd like now to talk to you about the subject of "weighting factors." Each one of our ten criteria had been considered of equal weight in our rating system. And we knew that wasn't quite right, but we had no evidence of what else to do. We intuitively knew that one criterion could have a higher weight than another, so Ben suggested that we do research by looking back fifty years, from 1925 to 1975, to determine the relative importance of each of these criteria, by checking just one at a time, and comparing our results with the Dow.

We agreed that it was important, in looking back fifty years, to include only four of those first set of five criteria, because the last of the first five, which was that the price should be equal to or less than the net, net, net current asset value of the company, had already been researched by Ben's own personal life experience over fifty years. So, we would *not* take our time researching *that* one.

To summarize some of Ben's very recent research work, he found that if you used just the earnings criterion, the average compound growth in price going back fifty years was 19.9% as compared to the Dow of 7.5%. In other words, if you had just used the criterion for earnings yield alone, you would have more than doubled the Dow in the fifty-year period. Also, he found out that the dividend yield criterion — that dividends shall be equal to or greater than two-thirds of the Triple-A bond — was almost as important, namely, 19.5% as compared to the Dow of 7.5%. The tangible book value criterion, that the price be equal to or less than two-thirds of the tangible book value, gave him 14.2%; and his old favorite, price "high-low," only came out with 9.5%. He actually had not had time to check the price-to-earnings ratio "high-low," which we had agreed to, and discussed previously in this paper.

Ben and I both knew that using all ten criteria was a bit too complex. And, sure enough, Ben found that if you used only *two* of those first set of five, earnings yield and dividend yield, those two criteria were by far the most important performance criteria of the first five.

SECURITY
SELECTION
AND ACTIVE
PORTFOLIO
MANAGEMENT

SURPRISING THE STUDENTS

As most of you know, Ben had originally taught a course in investments (as well as many other subjects) at Columbia University in New York. After he retired and moved to Beverly Hills, he taught a class in investments at UCLA. He again retired from teaching, at UCLA, and moved down to La Jolla where he decided to concentrate his efforts in the investment research field and in writing about the results of his research. In fact, UCLA had contacted him to see if he would assist in a series of investment seminars, and Ben told me that he was the one who recommended that they contact me to see if I'd give a course in the subject of investment analysis at their Graduate School of Management.

I accepted the appointment and taught the class with emphasis on Ben's fundamentals. He agreed to give the last lecture of the class. I think there was a little bit of a "ham" in Ben. He liked to come up with the unexpected, or the unknown, and to keep the students "on their toes." First of all, he pointed out that they were to be commended on the fact that they had learned a lot about our ten criteria, the half point and whole point system, and all the details. In fact, three of the students were especially commended because they had taken the ten criteria, and using UCLA's computer, had programmed it, and with the Compustat tape, had found that, going back over ten years based on our ten criteria, they could more than double the Dow in the performance during that period.

But when Ben got through congratulating them, he pointed out that had they used only two of those ten criteria, they would have done almost as well; and besides they would have had *many more* stocks to choose from, and, therefore, better safety through higher diversity, and really they would not have had to have a computer in picking the stocks when only two criteria were used.

Of course, this really did shock the students, and the three men who had done the original work based on the ten criteria decided that they would check on Ben. And so they took his two criteria and went back over the same ten-year period to see what the performance would have been.

Those two, by the way, were that the total debt be less than the equity, and that the earnings yield be at least twice the average Triple-A bond yield. The results were quite rewarding. When they used just his two criteria instead of all ten, they came out with a performance nearly double the Dow.

Ben, however, conceded that when the market was very low, as it was at the end of 1974, it might be preferable to use more of the ten criteria to reduce the number of stocks to choose from.

PUTTING THEORY INTO PRACTISE

Ben was actually so excited about the results of his research that he really wanted to apply the results by starting a new fund — and to prove that these simpler criteria, rather than the complex ones, would work even better (especially through more diversity).

Ben and I and our ladies were driving back from Mexico where we'd spent the weekend together, and he said, "You know, Jim, we should start a new private investment fund based on the results of our recent research."

Although the Fund initially started just using his *two* criteria, and by also picking those companies that came closest to meeting our ten criteria, later on, after we got together in France, I added the *third* criterion as a result of Ben's latest work done in France, where he confirmed that *dividend* yield was almost as important as earnings yield. So, we now actually use *three* basic criteria in the Fund, namely: that the debt-to-equity be less than one; the dividend yield be at least two-thirds the average Triple-A bond yield; and the earnings yield be at least twice the average Triple-A bond yield. This means that we currently look for a P/E of seven or less for New York Stock Exchange companies and six or less for American and OTC companies, and we insist on a dividend yield of more than 5%, because the average Triple-A bond yield is close to 8%. And, of course, we don't even look at a company unless its total debt is less than its equity.

Just before Ben left for France last June, he came up from La Jolla to Los Angeles to spend some time with us in our home and, incidentally, to leave his favorite cat, Minet, with us. But at breakfast, just before he caught the plane for France, he suggested that we agree upon a 1/3-1/3-1/3 policy for the Fund. At that time the Dow was hovering around 1,000. And for many months since then it continued to hover around 1,000. By 1/3-1/3-1/3, he meant one-third of the entire Fund ought to be in high-grade U.S. government securities; actually, we invested in 8% U.S. government notes, due 15 February 1983.

He recommended that the next one-third be in his net current asset type of companies — that is, where the price is preferably down to two-thirds of the net current asset value, but for sure less than the net current asset value. He admitted that we might not be able to find enough stocks to invest one-third of the Fund in that category and still limit each investment to just a few hundred shares, because when the market grows higher, the first ones that seem to disappear are the ones whose prices are down equal to or less than their net, net, net current asset value. But to the extent that we could find these stocks, we should try to invest one-third of the Fund in that area.

And the last one-third ought to be in what we called "performance companies," where we originally started with the ten criteria and then finally contracted it to the three criteria (where we invested in companies with high earnings and dividend yields, and when the total debt was less than the equity).

WHAT ABOUT "THE MARKET"?

We agreed that the most we'd invest in common would be 75%, as when the market was lowest in 1974, and when at least 25% would be in high-grade government bonds. We further agreed that when the market was high, we should not be higher than 75% in

U.S. government securities, and preferably not less than 25% in common stock.

Ben said that he didn't see how anyone could be sure as to what the market as a whole was going to do — it might go higher, or it might go lower. My own rationale was in agreement on that point, especially since I felt that most human decisions are made on *emotions, feelings,* and *desires,* rather than logic; besides, I couldn't see how anyone could foresee all future events, and further they couldn't foresee what the mass psychology and buy-sell feelings and reactions would be in response to those future events.

So, rather than there being an "intelligent" or "efficient" market, we agreed that there rather was an *emotional and irrational* market. We would really be put out of business if the public as a whole followed *our* kind of reasoning, because then the market would not go much too high relative to Ben's "central" value, nor would it go much too low. We just would be put out of business.

In fact, we agreed that we were really grateful that we could capitalize on the fact that the market was as *emotional and irrational* as it was and *did* go much too high and much too low; *when* we didn't know, and *why* we didn't know, and we certainly couldn't do any predicting as to what it would do. When the market went too high, we were "kicked out" only because fewer and fewer stocks met our buy criteria. Incidentally, our sell criterion was 50% improvement from buy price, or two years, whichever occurred first. And finally, we agreed that the market was *not* efficient, intelligent, nor logical.

Ben was always looking ahead. He asked me just before he left for France, "What are we going to do, Jim, when the market eventually does go too high, and when we sell at 50% improvement in price and we can't find very many stocks meeting our criteria to invest in and, therefore, we're forced to invest more and more in high-grade government securities; so, what are we going to do for an alternative?"

He said that some of his money that he made in

SECURITY
SELECTION
AND ACTIVE
PORTFOLIO
MANAGEMENT

those periods of time with the Graham-Newman Fund was made through special situations, such as arbitrages. He said that his investment in GEICO was an example of a special situation which did *not* meet his criteria. He also said that they had paid out each year, as an average, 26% if they *included* GEICO. But if they *excluded* GEICO in their calculations, they paid out at least 22%. But he pointed out that all of that 22% was not made by just buying stock in performance companies, nor by buying stock in net current asset companies, which he said was his primary investment strategy at the time. He said that he always had to invest in something else when squeezed out of the market because the market was too high, and arbitrages were his favorites.

PLAYING IT THE OTHER WAY

So, just before he left for France, he said, "Why don't you consider something I've been thinking about? Do your research on it first, but here is my thought: You have the computer print-out, Radix, and we've been looking at the top side of the print-out, namely, the companies with highest reward-to-risk ratio. Well, how about the bottom side? What if we were to write options *naked*, in other words, to sell call options (or buy puts) in companies' stock which we *don't* own. But only for those companies that are on the bottom side of the print-out, which are the ones that are the most popular in that their price-to-earnings ratios are extremely high, they don't pay much dividend yield, and they haven't had that much growth recently, nor stability in that growth, and their balance sheet is highly leveraged where their net current asset value is negative, their debt is much greater than their equity, and, in other words, they don't have much financial soundness. There are a lot of those companies, popular companies, that have the *lowest* reward-to-risk ratio and have the poorest rating using our ten criteria, so we wouldn't want to own those stocks, but maybe we could write options on those stocks naked."

"So, do your research on that and see how it would come out if a certain portion of the Fund were applied in that direction . . . a fairly small portion until we've tested it out. How about that as a special situation?

"Never stop your research, Jim. Keep your research up and keep looking for new areas of investment."

This was Ben's last word to me before he left. And while he was in France, he did quite a bit of research in options, and especially the concept of writing naked options.

IT ALSO WORKS FOR LARGE COMPANIES

As a further incidental subject, while Ben was in France I did some research on the application of his simple criteria, two originally and now three, to only *large* companies. Many investment advisors have a minimum of, say, $50 million in total tangible book value . . . others $100 million. I know of one large investment advisor who even uses $500 million as a minimum in total tangible book as to size. My research has shown that there are quite a few companies available, mostly on the New York Stock Exchange, of course, that *do* meet those three criteria, and there's no reason why applying these three criteria to large companies could not be quite profitable to many investment advisors who handle very large sums of money.

There have been arguments by some investment advisors that Ben Graham's criteria are fine if one only had a small amount of money to manage and was willing to invest in very small unknown companies, but that his criteria are limited to that. I have evidence to prove, but I did not have a chance to discuss it with him while I was in France with him, that if one did use his simple three criteria applying them only to larger companies, one would still do very much better than the Dow. One wouldn't do quite as well as with the smaller companies alone, but one would do sufficiently better than the Dow that it would certainly pay one to do so. Also, I recall that Ben's research done with Bob Fargo about a year ago showed very good results compared to the Dow when applying his criteria to the Fortune 500 companies.

AND SO, FAREWELL . . .

I want to end this paper by pointing out that I was very fortunate in being able to work with Benjamin Graham for the last three years of his life. I learned a lot from him, not only in the field of investment analysis, but in many other areas, and I miss him very much. Since he now has put the entire responsibility of our Fund on me, I'm somewhat angry "that he could desert me"; but when I think of all the good things he did for me, I'm sure it's only my indication of *anxiety* in having him leave me so soon when we were working so well together.

In our last meeting together — that was on a Monday, September 20 — I gave him a big hug and kiss; and he did me. He knew he was leaving, and I told him at the time that I was sure he was going on the greatest journey of his whole life, and that he would explore the entire universe. I don't know what made me say that, but I felt that very strongly, and I thought to myself after his death: "You know, if you can beat your lady at Scrabble on a Sunday night, in French and in Spanish, and walk from your bed to the television set, and then accomplish an hour's research work, all of that on Sunday, and meet with your partner and family on Monday, and then leave on Tuesday, well, 'What a way to go.'"

So, I'm very fortunate to have had a chance to work with him. It would be too heavy a load to try to carry the mantle that he left. I know I can pick up a piece of it, and although I may now have some of Ben Graham's "stripes" on me, I know they'll fade pretty rapidly unless I perform well with the new Fund that we started. So, I intend to continue my efforts on research and see to it that the Fund really does perform well, and that it follows Ben's criteria very carefully and precisely. I hope I will have fulfilled my promise to Ben in writing this paper summarizing my experiences with him and the results of his recent research.

Relative stock valuation made simple

Growth and P/E's should bear some systematic relationship to each other. Here's how to systematize without hardly trying.

Joseph A. Lavely

Although most of us would rather forget it, most of us well remember the two-tier market of 1973. The fifty or so institutional favorites, the "Vestal Virgins" of the time, enjoyed price/earnings ratios many times greater than those of the vast majority of stocks. By the end of 1974, hardly a virgin survived; most had been badly tarnished by the ensuing bear market.

When the two-tier market was at its zenith, the relationship between high P/E and low P/E stocks did not appear to be all that abnormal, since the one-decision concept seemed valid to many investors. Proven growth stocks need be purchased only; the decision concerning when to sell these stocks would never have to be faced. In retrospect, we wonder how values could have been so factitious. But, of course, hindsight always transcends foresight.

The purpose of this paper is to present a tool that can help investors and analysts maintain a prudent perspective in assessing the comparative value of stocks. The tool is a set of mathematical equations that were derived as a method of analyzing the market's relative appraisal of the tiers. The equations have helped quantify the extent to which the upper-tier stocks were overpriced then, and they have proven to be of considerable utility in comparing the propriety of relative P/E ratios since then. The primary usage of the equations is as an aid in estimating whether the price of a particular stock is out of balance with the prices of other stocks.

Derivation of the equations requires an elementary understanding of the application of logarithms of numbers. Application of the equations, however, is very simple; almost anyone can employ them.

P/E VS. GROWTH

The price of a share of stock reflects the market's evaluation of the future benefits which the stock is expected to produce and the risk associated with this expectation. These future benefits flow from the stock's future earnings per share (EPS). The stock's current P/E ratio depends upon the prospective growth and riskiness of EPS. The faster EPS is anticipated to increase and/or the less risky is the stock, the higher is the P/E ratio which the market currently awards the stock.

In order to earn an above average rate of return, the analyst searches for stocks with P/E ratios that are either too high or too low in relation to those of other stocks. Typically, the higher the P/E ratio, the greater the future of growth of EPS which the market contemplates. When the P/E ratio is "too high" or "too low" relative to other P/E ratios, the market's expectations are unrealistic and will be brought back into balance. The correction process entails a relatively declining stock price when the ratio is "too high" and a relatively increasing stock price when the ratio is "too low." The following equations constitute a tool that helps the analyst discern whether a current P/E ratio is out of line.

PRICE VS. GROWTH

Understanding is enhanced by using earnings/price (E/P) ratios in the equations rather than P/E ratios. The E/P ratio is the inverse of the P/E ratio; it is calculated by dividing 1.0 by the P/E ratio. The E/P ratio indicates EPS per dollar of stock price. The higher the P/E ratio, the lower the E/P ratio and the less EPS which is purchased per dollar of stock price. Investors pay more per dollar of current EPS because they expect it to appreciate more rapidly than the EPS of other stocks.

In virtually all cases, investors expect EPS to advance over time. Thus, the ratio of earnings per dollar of current price will also rise over time, at the compound annual rate of, say, g. Symbolically, this expectation can be expressed as $(E/P)(1 + g)^n$, where n is the number of years over which the growth occurs. To illustrate, the EPS of a stock with a P/E of 25 might be expected to accumulate at a compound annual rate of 20%. Consequently, earnings per dollar of current price, E/P, would improve to $(\$.04)(1 + .20)^1 = \$.048$ in one year or $(\$.04)(1 + .20)^5 = \$.100$ in five years. The EPS of a stock with a P/E of four might be expected to increase at a compound annual rate of only 5% (hence, the low P/E ratio). The earnings per dollar of current price of this second stock would rise to $(\$.25)(1 + .05)^1 = \$.263$ in one year or $(\$.25)(1 + .05)^5 = \$.319$ in five years.

A number of pertinent questions arise. How long will it take for the E/P of the first stock to equal that of the second? What if the analyst is unwilling to project the growth rate of EPS more than a limited period into the future? How fast must the E/P of the first stock expand if it is to equal that of the second in five years? What would be the answers to these questions if EPS develops at some other rate? The answers to all of these questions can be computed very simply and very quickly with the equations that are to follow.

LOGARITHMS MADE EASY

If the analyst is to believe his calculations, he

should understand them. It is desirable, then, to explain the derivation of the equations rather than merely present them. To explain their derivation, however, first requires a few comments on the application of logarithms.

The logarithm of a number is the power to which 10 must be raised in order to equal that number. The logarithm of 100 is 2.0 because 10 to the second power, $(10)^2$, equals 100. The great advantage of logarithms is that their usage reduces the complexity of mathematical manipulations; adding logarithms is analogous to multiplying the numbers, and multiplying logarithms is analogous to raising a number to a power. For example, to raise a number, say 1.14, to its 17th power, simply multiply the logarithm of 1.14 by 17 and find the antilogarithm of the product: $\log(1.14) \times 17 = .0569 \times 17 = .9673$; antilog$(.9673) = 9.277$. That is, $(1.14)^{17} = 9.277$. Whereas in the past the benefits of using logarithms were limited to rather few people, nowadays, anyone with an appropriate calculator can use them.

HOW LONG TO EQUIVALENCE?

With the aid of logarithms, it is easy to answer the question of how long it will take for the E/P of one stock to equal that of a second stock. Take two stocks with respective ratios of E_1/P_1 and E_2/P_2. If their EPS grow at respective rates of g_1 and g_2, then in n years in the following equation their future EPS per dollar of current price will be equal:

$$(E_1/P_1)(1 + g_1)^n = (E_2/P_2)(1 + g_2)^n \qquad (1)$$

Beginning with Equation (1), Exhibit 1 shows the derivation of two extremely useful equations, Equations (2) and (3). Although these equations appear imposing to anyone but a mathematician, in fact, they are very simple to use. Equation (2) states that n is equal to the quotient of two differences. Using the data in the previous example, an electronic calculator provides the answer in seconds. It will take about 13.7 years for EPS per dollar of current price of the faster growing stock to reach the same level as that of the slow-growth stock.

$$n = [\log(E_2/P_2) - \log(E_1/P_1)]/$$
$$[\log(1 + g_1) - \log(1 + g_2)] \qquad (2)$$

$$n = [\log(.25) - \log(.04)]/$$
$$[\log(1.20) - \log(1.05)]$$

$$n = [(-0.6021) - (-1.3979)]/[(0.0792) - (0.0212)]$$

$$n = (.7958)/(.0580)$$

$$n = 13.72$$

THE NECESSARY GROWTH RATE

Alternatively, Equation (1) can be solved for g_1 (or g_2). Suppose an analyst concludes that projections beyond five years into the future entail too much risk. He can specify that $n = 5$ and solve Equation (1) for g_1 to determine the growth rate of EPS for the faster growing stock which makes it as good a purchase as the slow-growth stock. The necessary growth rate is calculated by solving Equation (3) and subtracting 100% from the antilogarithm of the left side of the equation.

Again using the data previously cited, EPS of the first stock would have to appreciate at a compound annual rate of 51.5% in order for the EPS per dollar of current price of the first stock to equal that of the second stock in five years.

$$\log(1 + g_1) = [[\log(E_2/P_2) - \log(E_1/P_1)]/(n)]$$
$$+ \log(1 + g_2)$$

$$\log(1 + g_1) = [[\log(.25) - \log(.04)]/(5)] \qquad (3)$$
$$+ \log(1.05)$$

$$\log(1 + g_1) = [[(-0.6021) - (-1.3979)]/(5)]$$
$$+ (0.0212)$$

$$\log(1 + g_1) = [(.7958)/(5)] + (.0212)$$

$$\log(1 + g_1) = (.1592) + (.0212)$$

$$\log(1 + g_1) = .1804$$

$$\text{antilog}(.1804) = 1.515$$

$$g_1 = 1.515 - 1.000$$

$$g_1 = 51.5\%$$

130

SECURITY
SELECTION
AND ACTIVE
PORTFOLIO
MANAGEMENT

CHECKING THE INPUTS

Implementation of Equation (2) requires only two bits of information on each stock: its current E/P ratio and its expected growth rate of earnings. The E/P ratio can be calculated from the P/E ratio listed with the stock quotations in most major newspapers. Estimates of the expected rates of growth of earnings can be obtained from many stock advisory services. The advantage of both Equations (2) and (3) lies in examining the plausibility of these assumptions which are used as inputs. The analyst can plug in the E/P ratios and the assumed growth rates and judge the credibility of the answer. If he believes that the answer is unrealistic, he can decide which of the two stocks is mispriced and act accordingly.

STANDARD OIL: AN ILLUSTRATION

To illustrate how easy it is to apply these equations, the following three stocks are considered: Standard Oil of California, Standard Oil of Indiana, and Standard Oil of Ohio. For convenience, these firms are referred to here as California, Indiana, and Ohio. The E/P ratios, growth rates of EPS, and logarithms of these values for each of the three companies are presented in Exhibit 2.

The January 7, 1975 issue of the *Wall Street Journal* gives the P/E ratios of California, Indiana, and Ohio as 3, 7, and 21, respectively. The October 25, 1974 issue of The Value Line Investment Survey, a highly respected and widely used advisory service, estimates the growth rates of EPS of these firms during the period from 1971-1973 to 1977-1979 at 9.5%, 14.0%, and 29.0%, respectively. In the following calculations these growth rates are assumed to persist past 1979.

With Equation (2), the time period required for EPS per dollar of current price of Ohio to become equivalent to that of Indiana is 8.9 years; the period required for equivalency with California is 11.9 years. The period required for EPS per dollar of current price of Indiana to equal that of California is 21.0 years.

If the analyst is willing to allow only five

years until equivalence is reached, Equation (3) provides the framework for computing the necessary growth rate of EPS for the stock with the lower E/P ratio. The EPS per dollar of current price of Indiana would have to expand at a compound annual rate of 29.7% to equal that of California within five years. Similarly, the EPS of Ohio would have to grow at 42.0% to catch that of Indiana and at 61.6% to equal that of California in five years.

BUT ROMANCE REMAINS!

The two equations presented here provide the analyst with a tool which aids him in retaining perspective concerning the relative values of stocks. In a two-stock comparison, the information obtained from using the equations provides insight in judging the sensibility of the projected growth rates of EPS which are inherent in the stock's P/E ratios and in determining which of the stocks is the better buy. The analyst's judgment remains of paramount significance. Unfortunately (or fortunately), the equations remove none of the romance of stock analysis.

SECURITY
SELECTION
AND ACTIVE
PORTFOLIO
MANAGEMENT

EXHIBIT 1
DERIVATION OF EQUATIONS

$$(E_1/P_1)(1 + g_1)^n = (E_2/P_2)(1 + g_2)^n \qquad (1)$$

Multiplying the logarithm of $(1 + g_1)$ by n is analogous to raising $(1 + g_1)$ to the nth power.

$$(E_1/P_1)(n) \log(1 + g_1) = (E_2/P_2)(n) \log(1 + g_2)$$

Similarly, adding the logarithms of (E_1/P_1) and $(1 + g_1)$ is analogous to multiplying the actual numbers.

$$\log(E_1/P_1) + (n) \log(1 + g_1)$$
$$= \log(E_2/P_2) + (n) \log(1 + g_2)$$

By simple algebra,

$$(n) \log(1 + g_1)$$
$$= [\log(E_2/P_2) - \log(E_1/P_1)] + (n) \log(1 + g_2) \qquad (1a)$$

$$(n) \log(1 + g_1) - (n) \log(1 + g_2)$$
$$= \log(E_2/P_2) - \log(E_1/P_1)$$

$$(n) [\log(1 + g_1) - \log(1 + g_2)]$$
$$= \log(E_2/P_2) - \log(E_1/P_1)$$

$$n = [\log E_2/P_2) - \log(E_1/P_1)]/$$
$$[\log(1 + g_1) - \log(1 + g_2)] \qquad (2)$$

Dividing both sides of Equation (1a) by n yields Equation (3)

$$(n) \log(1 + g_1)$$
$$= [\log(E_2/P_2) - \log(E_1/P_1)] + (n) \log(1 + g_2) \qquad (1a)$$

$$\log(1 + g_1)$$
$$= [\ [\log(E_2/P_2) - \log(E_1/P_1)]/(n)] + \log(1 + g_2) \qquad (3)$$

EXHIBIT 2

	California	Standard Oil of Indiana	Ohio
E/P Ratio	.3333	.1428	.0476
log (E/P)	−.4771	−.8451	−1.3222
g	9.5%	14.0%	29.0%
log (1 + g)	.0394	.0569	.1106

P/E ratios from the Wall Street Journal, November 18, 1974.
Growth rates (g) from Value Line, October 25, 1974.

Are financial ratios worth the effort?

Security analysts are NOT wasting their time: some financial statistics do have predictive value.

Donald M. Peterson

I n the study of stock price behavior of individual companies, financial ratios have too often been treated as the unwanted and neglected stepchild. The reasons for this are twofold. First, it's always more fun to tell a story than to calculate ratios. Second, with the advent of the random walk hypothesis, we have been told that the marketplace is highly efficient and that financial ratios calculated from historic information have no predictive value. So why should we use financial ratio analysis?

A recent study[1] indicates that financial ratios, the neglected stepchild, are indeed linked to investment results and should be used in both security analysis and portfolio management. Let's go back to basics.

RANDOM WALK OR FUNDAMENTAL ANALYSIS?

Two schools of thought have emerged in recent years concerning common stock valuation. At one ex-

134

SECURITY
SELECTION
AND ACTIVE
PORTFOLIO
MANAGEMENT

1. Footnotes appear at the end of the article.

treme are proponents of the broad form of the random walk hypothesis who argue that historic data have no relevance in predicting stock prices. Their rationale is that only future events are relevant to future prices and that all past information has been fully discounted in the current price of the stock. At the other extreme are financial analysts who rely entirely on historical data and financial ratios in appraising the value of a particular common stock. They argue that the existence of principles or rules of thumb in investment analysis leads to investment performance superior to that of a random selection. In between these two approaches is the majority of analysts who rely on financial ratios and historical data to obtain an overall impression of the worth of a company and then use other subjective valuation techniques, including intuition, in deciding whether or not to recommend the purchase or sale of its common stock.

The dilemma then is which approach should be followed to attain superior investment performance. Should the analyst spend his time interpreting financial ratios calculated from historical data and try to develop meaningful rules of thumb or should he accept the implications of the random walk hypothesis, ignore historical data, and look only to the future? Or are both approaches necessary? While it is tempting to resolve the dilemma by accepting both approaches, evidence to date has not supported the superiority of such a compromise.

WHICH IS SUPERIOR?

There are essentially two ways of testing the superiority of one approach over the other. First, one can examine the investment performance of security analysts who rely entirely on publicly available financial information for their investment decisions. Their performance can then be compared with that of security analysts who spend their time predicting events and estimating the impact of these events on future prices. Unfortunately, analyzing the performance of these two groups of security analysts is not possible because very few analysts practice one approach to the exclusion of the other.

Second, one can examine the historical relations between changes in common stock prices and various financial ratios commonly used by security analysts. If no relation exists, then either isolated financial ratios are not useful by themselves in predicting changes in common stock prices, or the wrong financial ratios were used in the test.

This second approach, although deficient in some ways, is quite popular with researchers. The main disadvantage is its ex post character in that what may have been true in the past may not be true in the future. However, most analysts, except those of "contrary opinion," would be more comfortable using a particular rule of thumb which has been successful in the past rather than one which has not been successful.

But much progress has been made in the academic community regarding the nature of security prices. This progress is most evident by the identification and classification of the random walk hypothesis. First, there is the *weak* form, which merely states that the current price of a stock fully reflects all information found in its historical price movements. Therefore, according to this weak form, analyzing past prices — as practiced by technicians — is not a profitable approach to security analysis. Second, there is the *broad* or *semistrong* form — the concern of this article — which suggests that all public information is reflected in the current price of the stock. According to the semistrong form, analyzing public knowledge such as that extracted from annual reports, including dividend increases, historic earnings, debt/equity ratios, and so forth, will not lead to superior investment results. And, third, there is the *strong* form of the random walk hypothesis which suggests that not even analysts with information above and beyond that which is publicly known are capable of attaining superior investment results. This strong form has been tested using the performance of mutual funds and other professional investors who might have this special information and analytical ability.

THE EVIDENCE: SEMISTRONG FORM

Studies using twenty years of financial data on companies comprising the S&P 425 index, with 25 companies in a homogeneous group, suggest that links exist between financial ratios and investment results, perhaps not with the degree of certainty a statistician would require but good enough for use by many financial analysts. This evidence does not fully support the semistrong form of the random walk hypothesis in terms of risk, returns, and risk-adjusted returns. The evidence shows that:

Superior risk-adjusted returns (Alpha) are associated with:

1. Average and slightly above average earnings growth, with significantly inferior results found in the low-growth groups.
2. "Undervalued" situations, as defined by a modification of Graham's P/E versus growth criterion.[2] For P/E ratios alone, the results were inconclusive.
3. Average and slightly above average dividend yields.
4. Average payout ratios.
5. Moderate dividend increases.
6. Smaller companies, as measured by total invested capital.
7. High rates of return on total capital.
8. Low debt/capital ratios.

High market risk (Beta) is associated with the following indicators:

1. Low P/E ratios.
2. Extremely high earnings growth and extremely low or negative earnings growth.
3. Extremely "undervalued" and extremely "overvalued" situations, as defined by a modification of Graham's P/E versus growth criterion.
4. Very low dividend yields.

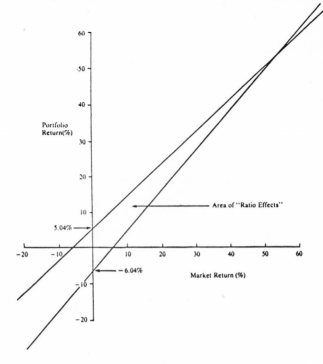

FIGURE 1   RANGE OF RISK-ADJUSTED RETURNS (ALPHA)

5. Low payout ratios.
6. Substantial changes, either increasing or decreasing, in a company's dividend rate.
7. Relatively small total invested capital.
8. Low rates of return on total invested capital.
9. High debt/capital ratios.

High one- and two-year returns are associated with:

1. Low P/E ratios.
2. Very high one- and four-year earnings growth rates.
3. "Undervalued" stocks, as defined by a modification of Graham's P/E versus growth criterion.
4. Very low dividend yields.
5. Low payout ratios.
6. Dividend increases.
7. Relatively small total invested capital.
8. Both low and extremely high rates of return on total invested capital.
9. High debt/capital ratios.

"RATIO EFFECTS"

By plotting portfolio returns of each homogeneous group of 25 companies against one market return, one finds an area of "ratio effects" for alpha [Figure 1]. The characteristic line on top, indicating superior risk-adjusted performance, shows the results of an investment in the stocks of a homogeneous group of 25 companies having a rather low debt/capital ratio. In contrast, the characteristic line on the bottom reflects the inferior risk-adjusted performance of an investment in companies which have a very high payout ratio. As shown in the diagram, favoring or disfavoring a particular ratio can make a difference of about +5% to −6% per year in risk-adjusted return.

Now let's consider the effect of financial ratios on market risk, beta. Figure 2 shows that the area of ratio effects for beta lies between .77 for companies which have slightly above average payout ratios to

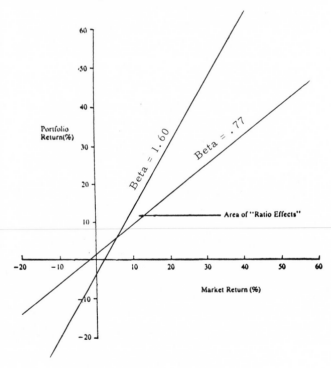

FIGURE 2.   RANGE OF MARKET RISK (BETA)

1.60 for companies which have little or no dividend. Again, these betas are for an equal dollar investment in the common stocks of 25 homogeneous companies grouped according to the aforementioned ratios. Such a range of ratio effects on beta certainly implies that financial ratios are indeed important with regard to market risk.

Finally, with regard to total return unadjusted for risk, the group of stocks showing the best performance is linked to very low total invested capital and very low payout ratios. In the first case, the group of 25 stocks of companies with the smallest total invested capital was up 8.0% per year more than the average stock in the S&P 425, and the corresponding figure for the group with low payout ratios was 7.0%. In contrast, the worst performance was turned in by companies showing slightly above average P/E ratios (−5.8%). Next in line were those having very high payout ratios (−5.4%).

SOME IMPLICATIONS — STRATEGY BEFORE SELECTION

If the evidence indicates that the values of certain financial ratios are linked to risks, returns, and risk-adjusted returns from common stocks, it follows that to achieve superior performance a portfolio manager must choose the proper strategies to use at the proper time. This task is not easy, and it requires inputs from specialists in economics as well as security analysis. But the point here is that knowing the risk/return relation of different groups of stocks, and given a market forecast, the portfolio manager is in a position to discuss the appropriateness of a stock in a portfolio.

For a portfolio manager, then, *Strategy Before Selection* simply means that decision rules regarding the purchase or sale of a particular issue should be made first. While this procedure appears obvious to many practitioners, in fact very few use such a procedure.

An overview of a proposed procedure implementing the concept of *Strategy Before Selection* is found in Figure 3. Consider the following steps:

Step 1. Analysts and portfolio managers suggest different strategies to be tested in terms of risks, returns, and risk-adjusted returns. These strategies are based on the values of various financial ratios or combinations thereof. Should a portfolio be structured toward a low P/E? a high growth rate? a low debt/capital ratio?

Step 2. The strategies are tested using historic information.

Step 3. Depending on a particular portfolio's risk/ return objectives, the portfolio manager chooses a strategy.

Step 4. Stocks which meet the specifications of the strategy are listed.

Step 5. From the list of stocks in Step 4, research analysts eliminate (subjectively) the less desireable issues.

Step 6. The portfolio manager selects stocks on the final list, since these stocks now meet both the risk/return constraints of the portfolio as well as the approval of the analysts.

As shown by the feedback loops in the diagram, the role of the portfolio manager is most important, for he is responsible for choosing both a strategy and the stock of a company which meets the specifications of the strategy; but this strategy must be consistent with market policy. If market policy is positive, then ratios linked with high betas are preferred; if it is negative, then low betas are preferred. If no market policy is in effect, then ratios linked with high alphas should be considered.

Second, the security analyst should be concerned with selecting stocks which will outperform the market on a risk-adjusted basis, i.e., those issues most favored to give a positive alpha. Therefore, he should consider companies exhibiting ratios identified with superior risk-adjusted returns. For example, perhaps the favorite among these strategies is

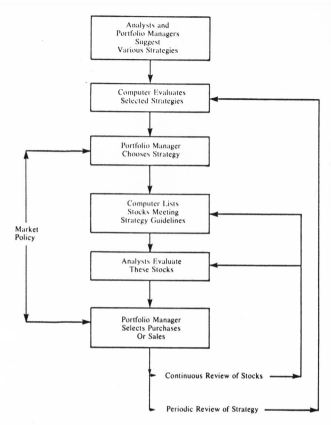

FIGURE 3. FLOWCHART PROCEDURE FOR IMPLEMENTING THE
PRINCIPLE OF STRATEGY BEFORE SELECTION

Graham's low P/E and high stable growth criterion. If
the security analyst wishes to recommend issues that
will do well in a market upswing or downturn, then he
should so qualify his opinion.

A FINAL NOTE

The evidence indicates that financial ratios are
useful in explaining the risks and rewards from stock
market investments. Users of these ratios will reply to
this apparently simplistic conclusion that such a
statement is obvious. In contrast, some observers will
reply that markets are efficient and that by the time
any generally available financial information is

SECURITY
SELECTION
AND ACTIVE
PORTFOLIO
MANAGEMENT

known, this information has already been discounted in the price of the stock. They conclude that financial ratios calculated from historical data generally known to the financial community are not useful.

In summary, then, the answers are really not as obvious as one would wish, but much of the evidence sides with the users of financial ratios.

[1] Donald M. Peterson, *Financial Ratios and Investment Results,* Lexington Books, D.C. Heath & Co. (Lexington, Mass., 1974).

[2] See Benjamin Graham, David Dodd, Sidney Cottle, and Charles Tatham, *Security Analysis, Principles and Techniques,* McGraw-Hill Book Co. (New York, 1972), p. 537.

A new guide to superior stock selection

Stocks making long-term new highs show remarkable tendencies to outperform the market, especially when earnings follow suit.

Charles F. O'Hay and Charles T. Casazza

T he old adage — buy stocks making new highs because they have many friends and few enemies — is well-known throughout the investment community. Despite the widespread acceptance of this oft-stated thesis, however, how do these new highs perform after their breakouts relative to the rest of the market? Can this thesis be utilized in the current market cycle?

In this report, we have examined the performance, sustainability, and durability of both new all-time highs and new ten-year highs nine months into the 1966/1968 and 1970/1973 bull markets. We chose nine months in order to achieve an optimum number of candidates while still allowing sufficient time for the group of new highs to come to fruition from a capital gains point of view.

In analyzing, at the minimum, new ten-year highs made in the first nine months of the 1966/1968 and 1970/1973 periods, we found the following:

- *Performance* — As a group, the list of new high issues outperformed the popular market averages by a significant margin. The performance premium exists at three junctures: The first intermediate market top, at the trough of the first intermediate market correction, and at the final market peak. Relative strength of the new ten-year highs list was superior in all three periods including periods of intermediate-term market correction.

- *Sustainability* — Approximately 70% of the issues achieving a new ten-year high are able from these new high prices to have a percentage gain in excess of the total bull market move from the trough of the cycle.

- *Durability* — In the 1966/1968 and the 1970/1973 bull markets, the percentage of issues which had at least a six-month differential between their new high prices and their final cycle tops was 81% and 90%, respectively. Also, approximately one third of the issues make their final tops after the popular averages have already peaked.

The implication of these conclusions is that many issues making a new ten-year high nine months into the market cycle could significantly outperform the popular averages. The most intriguing point, though, is that this outperformance can be anticipated even after a significant market move on the upside has occurred — for this is when the new high issues begin to appear.

Historically, the initial move of a bull market is quite dynamic and the difficulty of becoming fully invested, reducing large cash positions, is well-known. The proponents of the new high list concept would suggest that being unable to become fully invested in such a short period of time may not be so crucial for three reasons:

- Any missed portion of the market move is more than offset by the future performance of the new high issues.

- As the bull market progresses on the upside, the

new high list would be representative of the leadership in the remainder of the move.

- It reduces the likelihood of being invested in sterile issues.

BUILDING THE SAMPLE

Even if an investor subscribes to these points, however, it has never been all that clear which new high list to utilize — the daily list in The Wall Street Journal, the weekly list in Barron's, etc. — which are essentially new highs in the current year only.

In our opinion, neither the Journal nor Barron's list is appropriate. We chose to use a new ten-year high as a minimum requirement. The rationale is twofold: selectivity and psychological impact. Significantly fewer issues appear on a ten-year new high list than on one based upon a shorter timeframe. On the one hand, the breadth of the list is not so large as to become unwieldy. On the other hand, the list is not so selective as to include too few names. In essence, this approach lends itself to a workable number of names.

In terms of psychological impact, the overhead supply concept of technical analysis is considered. Using a shorter timeframe, it is possible for an issue to establish a new high into the midst of a significant congestion zone, an area where considerable past trading has taken place. This could hamper future performance. A new ten-year high avoids this possible negative impact.

Another decision that had to be made: How many months into each bull market should be used to construct a new high list? The nine-month cutoff point was chosen because it too yielded a workable number of names. But more importantly, the issues that achieve a new high early in the cycle are assumed to be higher priority stocks to be owned by the investment community for the remainder of the bull market.

In deriving the new high list, we scanned more than 1,000 charts, a rather large sampling. We do not purport to have found every issue making a new high in these periods. The charts we looked at, though, were considered representative of institutional grade common stocks or stocks with a wide investor following.

THE RESULTS:
THE 1966/1968 BULL MARKET

Using our criteria after the October, 1966 Dow low, 135 issues made — at the minimum — a new ten-year high prior to the nine-month cutoff point of July, 1967.*

The DJIA registered a 35% advance from the October, 1966 low of 736 to its final 995 peak in December, 1968. In computing the individual gains for the 135 issues, we found that 94, or 70% of the issues, had a greater percentage move from their new high price to their final cycle top than did the Dow from its actual low to its final top.

As shown in Chart 1, the Dow's 35% gain came

CHART 1

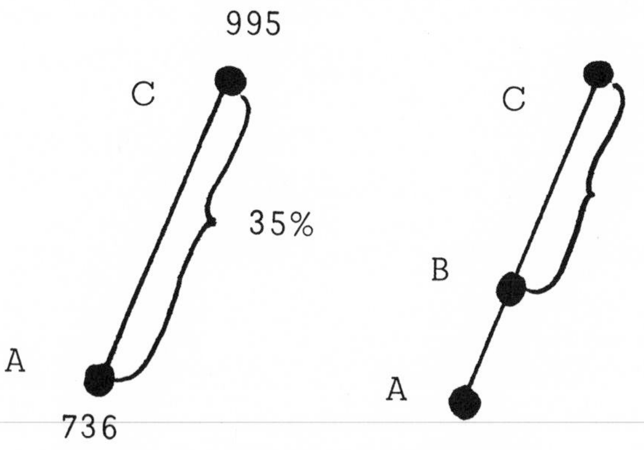

94 out of 135 issues exceeded
the 35% Dow move

from its absolute low, A, to its final peak, C. An issue's percentage rise was computed from its new high, B, to its final peak, C. The percentage move from A to B was not computed for the 135 issues.

* Complete and detailed data, with names of all companies on these new high lists, are available on request from the authors.

Not only was the magnitude of these price moves significant, but a majority of the issues were able to qualify as long-term capital gain candidates. Over 80% of the issues had at least a six-month differential between their new high prices and their final cycle tops.

TABLE 1

Monthly Distribution of New 10 yr. Highs at Cycle Tops 1966/1970

	1967	1968	1969	1970
January	—	5	2	4
February	—	—	2	2
March	2	—	1	4
April	1	2	4	1
May	9	1	6	—
June	1	11	2	—
July	7	5	1	—
August	6	—	—	—
September	3	—	1	—
October	4	6	4	—
November	1	4	6	—
December	3	21[a]	3	—
Total	37	55	32	11

Note: (a) Market Peak

In Table 1, we determined when each of the 135 issues made their final cycle tops. Even after the bear market had begun in January, 1969, 32% of the issues made their final peaks during the primary downtrend, some as late as March/April, 1970. The ability of these stocks to continue attracting investor attention well into the bear market seems to indicate that their dependence on market direction may be far less than many studies show. In the same vein, the type of resiliency exhibited could also argue that an investor may have much more time to decide upon the future market direction than would normally be the case.

SECURITY
SELECTION
AND ACTIVE
PORTFOLIO
MANAGEMENT

PERFORMANCE

In order to assess how well these 135 issues performed during the 1966/1968 bull market, we priced

all the issues' individual highs at three market junctures:

- September, 1967 — The month of the intermediate-
  term peak.
- March, 1968 — The month terminating the intermediate-term correction.
- December, 1968 — The final market top.

After completing this, we examined means for
ascertaining the most representative Dow Jones figure
for comparative performance results. We decided the
most consistent approach would be to find the number
of new highs made in each of the nine months and
multiply these by the Dow Jones high for that month
(Table 2).

TABLE 2

Dow Jones Average Cost of the 135 Issues
(Number of New Highs Each Month X DJIA High)

1966

November	11 × 827 =	9,097
December	9 × 827 =	7,443

1967

January	20 × 857 =	17,140
February	16 × 872 =	13,952
March	25 × 883 =	22,075
April	15 × 903 =	13,545
May	12 × 915 =	10,980
June	10 × 892 =	8,920
July	17 × 919 =	15,623
	135	118,775

118,775 ÷ 135 = 880

This type of calculation provides a representative (although hypothetical) Dow Jones figure
weighted by the number of new highs at the Dow
Jones price level where they occurred. The figure we
derived was 880 — the effective Dow Jones cost of the
135 issues.

The intermediate-term peak in the market occurred in September, 1967, and despite the fact that
this was only two months after our July, 1967 nine-

month cutoff date, the new high issues were ahead by 22.7% from the time they made their new highs to this September peak (Table 3). The Dow Jones rose by only 8.1% from our representative DJIA figure.

The Averages then declined from September, 1967 to March, 1968, the month that ended the intermediate-term correction. In March, 1968, the DJIA high was down by 2.9% from our representative price, yet the new high issues remained in plus ground, up by 11.0%.

TABLE 3

Performance Statistics

	Month of Intermediate-Term Peak September, 1967	Month of Intermediate-Term Low March, 1968	Final Market Top December, 1968
Representative DJIA 880	952	854	995
	+8.1%	(2.9)%	+13.0%
New High Stocks	+22.7%	+11.0 %	+37.2%

Finally, at the ultimate market peak, the new high issues had appreciated by 37.2% compared with a 13.0% gain for the DJIA. Despite the fact that a significant portion of the new highs occurred in the high 800/low 900 Dow area, these issues still approached the market trough-to-peak move of 35%.

THE RESULTS:
THE 1970/1973 BULL MARKET

With the 1970/1973 bull market beginning in May, 1970, the nine-month cutoff date for the new high list was February, 1971. Again, in looking over the 1,000 charts, we found 89 issues that met the criteria.

In computing the Dow Jones representative figure for performance comparisons (Table 4), we again multiplied the number of new highs made in each month by the Dow Jones high for that month to arrive at the effective Dow Jones cost of 844. Proceeding with the calculations, we found that the distribution of new highs in this nine-month period is dis-

150

SECURITY
SELECTION
AND ACTIVE
PORTFOLIO
MANAGEMENT

similar to the 1966/1968 experience. In 1970/1971, nearly one half of the issues qualified in the last two months of the nine-month period. In 1966/1968, only about 20% of the issues qualified in the last two months of the nine-month period.

TABLE 4

Dow Jones Average Cost of the 89 Issues
(Number of New Highs Each Month X DJIA High)

1970

July	$2 \times 743 =$	1,486
August	$4 \times 772 =$	3,088
September	$9 \times 778 =$	7,002
October	$2 \times 791 =$	1,582
November	$10 \times 789 =$	7,890
December	$20 \times 848 =$	16,960

1971

January	$25 \times 873 =$	21,825
February	$17 \times 898 =$	15,266
	89	75,099

$$75,099 \div 89 = 844$$

This had a large impact on the DJIA computation. The 844 representative Dow Jones price was an increase of 33% from the DJIA May, 1970 low of 636. The 880 representative figure arrived at in 1966/1967 was only a 19% gain from the October, 1966 low of 736. Yet, despite having a greater number of issues qualifying after a greater percentage market move, the April, 1971 intermediate-term peak performance results still show a significant outperformance by the new high issues (Table 5). The new high issues were ahead by 24.4% compared with 13.5% for the DJIA.

TABLE 5

Performance Statistics

	Month of Intermediate-Term Peak April, 1971	Month of Intermediate-Term Low November, 1971	Final Market Top January, 1973
Representative DJIA 844	958	855	1067
	+13.5%	+1.4%	+26.4%
New High Stocks	+24.4%	+26.9%	+73.6%

The market then gave up most of its gain during the April/November, 1971 intermediate-term correction. From our representative Dow Jones price of 844, the market was up by only 1.4% to the November, 1971 high at DJIA 855. In comparison, the new high issues were up by an astonishing 26.9% from their new high prices to their November, 1971 highs.

At the final market peak in January, 1973, the DJIA was up by 26.4% from our representative DJIA number. The new high issues gained by 73.6%. Considering that the broader-based market indices (such as Indicator Digest and Value Line) peaked in April, 1972, the performance of the new high list is even more startling.

From the May, 1970 low of 636 to the final January, 1973 peak, the DJIA appreciated by 67%. As shown in Chart 2, of the 89 new high issues, 63, or 71%, exceeded the DJIA move from their new high prices to their individual cycle tops.

As was the case in the 1966/1968 cycle, these significant price movements were coupled with the outstanding ability to qualify as long-term capital gain candidates. The percentage of issues which had at least a six-month differential between their new high prices and their final cycle tops was 90%.

Lastly, Table 6, which shows the months in which the 89 issues achieved their final tops, is presented. Even after the January, 1973 market peak, 37% of the new high issues made their cycle tops well into the ensuing bear market — some as late as March/April, 1974.

DO EARNINGS MATTER? — A FUNDAMENTAL APPROACH TO THE NEW TEN-YEAR HIGH LIST

In the new ten-year high screening format, as in any selection process, there were issues that exhibited outstanding price performance while others showed more modest capital appreciation.

There are many determinants of the price of a common stock, but all fall under two broad categories — earnings considerations and price/earnings ratios.

CHART 2

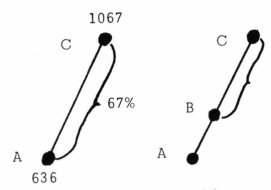

63 out of 89 issues exceeded
the 67% Dow move

TABLE 6

Monthly Distribution of New 10 yr. Highs at Cycle Tops
1971/1974

	1971	1972	1973	1974
January	—	—	13[a]	3
February	—	4	1	—
March	3	4	6	3
April	7	6	—	1
May	—	4	—	—
June	1	2	—	—
July	1	—	4	—
August	—	3	—	—
September	1	—	2	—
October	—	—	12	—
November	—	3	—	—
December	1	3	1	—
Total	14	29	39	7

Note: (a) Market Peak

In working with the more quantifiable variable, earnings, we found the probability of an issue's becoming an outstanding market performer appears dependent upon its relative earnings progression over the length of the market upcycle. (Relative earnings is defined as the ability of an issue's earnings either to match, or

A NEW GUIDE
TO SUPERIOR
STOCK
SELECTION

to exceed, the DJIA earnings gains over the length of the market move.) The degree of lackluster price performance for some of the new high issues seems hinged upon how poorly relative earnings fared over the life of the bull market.

Although the new ten-year high list does represent a group of issues that significantly outperforms the market, it does not appear to represent in so clear-cut fashion a body of names that will exhibit superior earnings growth as well. Our findings are that the list is initially composed of issues that are anticipated to have above average earnings potential, and as time progresses, if earnings do not come through, it reduces the likelihood of superior price performance.

In order to expand our understanding of why these issues performed so well, we decided to initiate a second, and fundamental, screen — how the earnings of each new high issue performed over the course of both past market cycles.

Leaving aside price/earnings considerations, we assumed that the price performance of any group of common stocks, including the new ten-year high list, is a function of earnings. Knowing the price performance of the new high list was already outstanding, in other words, could the performance be improved by determining the earnings characteristics of the individual issues qualifying? In this vein, we constructed a scattergram plotting the stocks on the new ten-year high list nine months into the 1966/1968 (Chart 3) and 1970/1973 (Chart 4) market cycles at the intersection of the points indicated by earnings change and price change. As anticipated, the distribution of the points demonstrates a positive correlation. In addition, we inserted a grid defining the earnings growth of the DJIA unit (vertical line) over the market cycle and the price appreciation of the DJIA (horizontal line) from our representative Dow Jones cost of the new high issues over the life of the market cycle. This forms four quadrants, defined as follows:

Quadrant I — New ten-year high issues achieving above average price performance but

154

SECURITY
SELECTION
AND ACTIVE
PORTFOLIO
MANAGEMENT

CHART 3

DISTRIBUTION OF NEW TEN YEAR HIGHS
NINE MONTHS INTO THE BULL MARKET
1966/1968

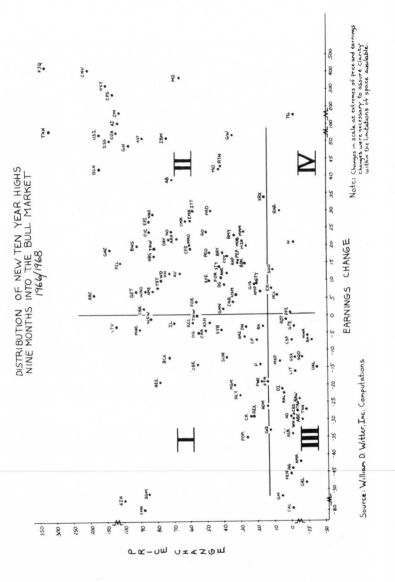

Source: William D. Witter, Inc. Computations

156

SECURITY
SELECTION
AND ACTIVE
PORTFOLIO
MANAGEMENT

CHART 4

DISTRIBUTION OF NEW TEN YEAR HIGHS
NINE MONTHS INTO THE BULL MARKET
1970/1973

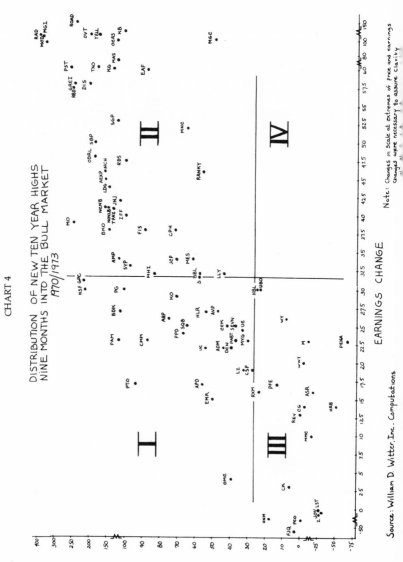

Note: Changes in scale at extremes of price and earnings
changes were necessary to assure clarity

EARNINGS CHANGE

Source: William D. Witter, Inc. Computations

below average relative earnings comparison.

Quadrant II — New ten-year high issues achieving above average price performance and above average relative earnings comparison.

Quadrant III — New ten-year high issues having below average price performance and below average relative earnings comparison.

Quadrant IV — New ten-year high issues having below average price performance but above average relative earnings comparison.

DISTRIBUTION OF THE NEW TEN-YEAR HIGHS
NINE MONTHS INTO THE BULL MARKET — 1966/1968

The year-end 1966 Dow Jones earnings were $57.68. When the bull market terminated in December, 1968, the earnings for the Dow unit were $57.89, or virtually flat. The DJIA appreciated by 13% from our representative DJIA cost of the 135 new high issues. In terms of price performance alone, 99 out of the 133 issues[1] outperformed the market (Quadrants I and II). In viewing earnings solely, only 76 of the 133 issues outperformed the DJIA earnings unit (Quadrants II and IV). Of the 76 issues with better relative earnings, 69, or 91%, outperformed also in terms of price performance.

In retrospect, if a relative earnings screen were initiated, all the new high issues in Quadrants I and III would have been dropped for not meeting the relative earnings criteria. More importantly, the performance of this smaller group would have been significantly better than the performance of the new ten-year high issues as a whole.

---

[1] There were actually 135 issues; however, two issues recorded deficit earnings over the period covered and could not be plotted.

DISTRIBUTION OF THE NEW TEN-YEAR HIGHS
NINE MONTHS INTO THE BULL MARKET — 1970/1973

The year-end 1970 Dow Jones earnings were $51.02. In January, 1973, the month terminating the bull market, the year-end 1972 earnings were $67.11, or ahead by 31%. The DJIA appreciated by 26.4% from our representative cost of the 89 issues over this period. In terms of performance alone, 69 of the 89 issues outperformed the market (Quadrants I and II). On the other hand, only 43 issues, or 48% of the issues' earnings, outperformed the DJIA unit's earnings (Quadrants II and IV). Once again, in retrospect, with a relative earnings screen, all 43 of the issues achieving above average relative earnings outperformed the market.

QUADRANT I VERSUS QUADRANT III —
THE EARNINGS UNDERPERFORMERS

With both of these quadrants containing the new ten-year high issues that posted inferior relative earnings, we find only about one half of them outperformed the market (30 out of 57 in 1966/1968 and 26 out of 46 in 1970/1973), certainly not overwhelming probabilities for success. Stocks appearing in Quadrant I, above average price performance but below average relative earnings comparisons, may have outperformed the market because:

- Period selected was a bull market and stocks in general appreciated in price.
- These issues may have enjoyed a better markup in price/earnings ratios than the issues in Quadrant III because of low variability of earnings, no decline in earnings in the prior economic/market slump, etc.

The relative earnings screen alone certainly does not represent the only criterion for explaining stock price action. However, with only a 50% chance for market outperformance with below average relative earnings, we feel the relative earnings screen performed its function. In other words, the less the dependence upon multiple improvement, the better.

THE CURRENT NEW HIGH LIST —
THE 1974/1975 NEW TEN-YEAR
HIGH ISSUES NINE MONTHS
INTO THE BULL MARKET

In Table 7, the new ten-year high issues nine months into the 1974/197? bull market are presented. Again, after scanning over 1,000 charts, we arrived at 79 issues that, at a minimum, achieved a new ten-year high during the November, 1974/July, 1975 timeframe. If past performance of the past new high lists is indicative of what we should expect from this list, these

TABLE 7   1974/1975 New Ten-Year High Issues

Nine Months into the Bull Market

Stock	New High Price	Stock	New High Price
AMAX	53	MAPCO	25 7/8
Air Products	57	McDermott	53 5/8
Albertson's	19 5/8	MCA	53 3/8
Amalgamated Sugar	41 1/8	Moore McCormack	17 1/4
Amsted Industries	32 1/2	National Chemsearch	51 1/8
Anderson Clayton	29 5/8	National Semiconductor	36 3/8
Archer-Daniels-Midland	15 1/2	Northern Natural Gas	32 7/8
Baker Oil Tool	44 3/8	Northwestern Steel & Wire	40 3/8
Bates Manufacturing	27 7/8	NVF	7 1/2
Big Three Industries	38 3/4	Orange-co	13 7/8
Bucyrus-Erie	23 3/8	Parker Pen	12 3/8
Cleveland-Cliffs Iron	41 3/4	Petrolite	69 1/8
Continental Oil	58 5/8	Pillsbury	34 3/4
Crane	33 1/2	Pittsburgh Forgings	17 3/8
Daniel Industries	12 1/4	Pittston	23
Dentsply	36 1/2	Proler	26 3/8
Diamond Shamrock	49	Raytheon	58 5/8
Dillon Companies	24	Revlon	80 7/8
Dow Chemical	70 1/8	Rival Manufacturing	9 7/8
Eastern Gas & Fuel	31 1/2	Roadway Express	41 7/8
Falcon Seaboard	26 5/8	Rosario Resources	36 5/8
Fluor	40 1/8	Safeway	44 3/8
Franklin Mint	25 3/4	St. Joe Minerals	22 1/8
Gearhart-Owen	20 3/8	Smith International	29 1/4
Getty Oil	175 1/8	Southland Royalty	49 5/8
Glatfelter (P.H.)	33 7/8	Staley (A.E.)	13 1/4
Heinz	52 3/8	Standard Brands	28 1/2
Hewlett Packard	100 3/4	Stauffer Chemical	56
Houston Natural Gas	34 1/8	Texas Pacific Land Trust	15 1/2
Hughes Tool	45 1/4	Trinity Industries	28
Inland Container	33 7/8	Union Camp	63 1/8
International Minerals	43 1/4	U.S. Steel	56
Jorgenson (Earl M.)	28 1/4	Univar	8 3/8
Joy Manufacturing	36 1/4	Universal Leaf	20
Kaneb Services	21 1/2	Utah International	57 1/8
Kellogg	18 3/8	Vetco	36
Koppers	27 1/2	Vulcan Materials	31 5/8
Lubrizol	56 5/8	Western Co. of N.A.	15 1/8
Mallinckrodt	49 3/8	Westmoreland Coal	25 1/4
		Yellow Freight System	28

issues should outperform the popular averages for the remainder of the bull market.

In trying to ascertain how well these new high stocks have performed so far in this bull market environment, we once again calculated the Dow Jones

Average Cost of these issues by multiplying the number of new highs made in each of the nine months by the Dow Jones high for that respective month (Table 8).

The representative (although hypothetical) Dow Jones cost of the 79 new high issues was 830. In 1966/1967, the representative Dow Jones cost of the

TABLE 8

Dow Jones Average Cost of the 79 Issues
(Number of New Highs Each Month X DJIA High)

1974

November	1 × 692 =	692
December	— ——	——

1975

January	6 × 717 =	4,302
February	7 × 757 =	5,299
March	11 × 797 =	8,767
April	21 × 835 =	17,535
May	18 × 869 =	15,642
June	10 × 885 =	8,850
July	5 × 889 =	4,445
	79	65,552

$$65,552 \div 79 = 830$$

new high issues was an increase of 19% from the actual low. In 1970/1971 the representative Dow Jones cost was 33% above the actual low. In 1974/1975, the representative Dow Jones cost of the 79 new high issues was 46% above the actual 1974 market low.

Assuming that July 15, 1975 represented an intermediate-term peak in the Dow Jones Industrial Average, it is possible to calculate performance statistics for the first leg up in the current bull market.

Even though almost 70% of the new high issues qualified with the DJIA already in the mid-high 800s, these stocks still showed above average performance comparisons at the July 15, 1975 market peak, being up by 18.8% compared to a 7.1% move by the DJIA from our representative DJIA cost figure (Table 9).

SECURITY
SELECTION
AND ACTIVE
PORTFOLIO
MANAGEMENT

TABLE 9

	Intermediate- Term Peak July 15, 1975
Representative DJIA 830	889 +7.1%
New High Stocks	+18.8%

1974/197? EARNINGS MODEL

In dealing with the past, hindsight presents utopian results, for we know which issues did post below or above average relative earnings. Projecting the future certainly brings about far more uncertainty. Nevertheless, the stocks that made new ten-year highs in 1974/1975 are quite revealing as to investors' expectations of the relative (and absolute) earnings gains anticipated over the life of this market cycle. Which of these issues can be expected to show better relative earnings?

As of mid-January, 1976, investors' expectations of both relative (and absolute) earnings gains for the issues on the new high list have been good. Of the 79 new high issues, over 90% have posted better relative earnings than the Dow from the year-end 1974 level to the third quarter of 1975. While the Dow Jones Industrial Average's earnings have declined 24% over that time period, two thirds of the issues have posted earnings gains. In total, the new high issues earnings are up 11% compared to the 24% decline in earnings for the Dow Jones Industrial Average.

The question remains, though, how many of these issues can be anticipated to show better relative earnings for the remainder of the bull market cycle? This is where the element of forecasting comes to the forefront in developing an earnings model.

The first exercise would be to estimate the year the bull market would be completed and then forecast what the DJIA unit's earnings would be in that year.

Our forecast is for the bull market cycle to end

in 1977 with the DJIA earnings unchanged from 1974
year-end levels.

ESTIMATE OF DJIA EARNINGS

1974	$99 (actual)
1975	81
1976	99
1977	99

%

The current situation strikingly resembles the
1966/1968 period when earnings were also essentially
flat. In addition, both periods contained many relatively unfamiliar names from an institutional point of
view.

Having made a forecast of earnings for the DJIA
unit, and calculated the percentage earnings change
over the life of the expected market cycle, the next
step involves determining the expected percentage
earnings change over the expected market cycle for
each of the stocks on the new ten-year high list, nine
months into the bull market. The greater the relative
earnings performance for a stock versus the earnings
performance of the DJIA unit, the higher the probability of the stock's outperforming both the market and
the new ten-year high list as a whole.

Keep profits: The true discount factor *

The dividend discount model breaks down because of inadequacies in identifying the discount rate; here is a whole new approach.

Arnold X. Moskowitz and George A. Harben

There has been rapid progress in the development of capital asset pricing models that minimize variance for given expected returns through efficient allocation of funds. But there has been no comparable progress in an area that is critical to these models, namely, stock evaluation theory. The profession remains enthralled by the "present value of future expected returns" hypothesis. What follows breaks cleanly with that hypothesis. Instead of the usual direction of influence from bonds through some discount rate to an evaluation of stocks, Keep profits theory reverses the direction of the flow of influence. It moves from earnings to bonds and from earnings through a variable dividend-based discount rate to stocks.

* We are indebted to Monica D. Spicker for research and her assistance in the statistical analysis underlying this report.

1. Footnotes appear at the end of the article.

Pre-growth theory or "classical" stock valuation models took stocks to be less reliable versions of British consols. Like bonds, they provided income, but they had no maturity. According to this scheme, stocks could be evaluated as a perpetual stream of the current level of dividends or the average level of past dividends. The whole was then discounted back to present value according to some fixed rate which was usually taken to be the then-current long-term interest rate plus some risk premium.

This scheme seemed unsatisfactory, however, because (at least in prosperous periods) dividends grew in line with earnings. One growth model therefore assumes a fixed rate of dividend increase — some past rate of increase being taken to be a fair proxy for the future. But the constant discount rate is assumed to be greater than the dividend growth rate, which allows this growth model to be evaluated at a limit.

A second growth model makes no requirement that the discount rate must be greater or less than the dividend or earnings growth rate. But so that the model can be evaluated at a limit, dividends are assumed to stop growing after a specified period with payments from that point evaluated as a perpetuity — in short, no "decay" rate is hypothesized, but growth is assumed to halt. Alternatively, an estimated selling price may be introduced based on a low no-growth multiple, but in either case the value of the perpetuity (or the proceeds of the sale) is discounted to present value over the intervening years at some fixed rate.

Standard stock valuation models that discount future dividend flows are based on borrowed logic from capital budgeting theory, where such flows determine the optimal selection of alternative investments using net present values or internal rates of return.

For capital budgeting the formulations are quite correct, since corporations can calculate initial project cost, forecast expected cash flows, and, most importantly, if the project is debt financed, funds can be raised at some current market rate which is known and fixed for that particular investment.

This formulation breaks down when it is transferred to stock valuation, however. Although investors purchase securities at a certain cost and receive expected cash flows in the form of dividends in the future, they do not have a fixed interest rate or a fixed discount rate to determine net present value, because interest rates vary substantially over the term of the investment. Furthermore, in our previous article in this *Journal,* we showed that negative yield curve regimes are not infrequent historically, and during such periods, the short rate had the most influence on stock prices — yet clearly it is inappropriate to use a short rate to discount distant expected future returns to present value.

Because the discounted future flow concept breaks down over the issue of the discount rate, we have developed an alternative formulation with a discount rate that is independent of interest rates. It simply is the recent pattern of profitability, reflecting management's privileged information about long- and short-term earnings prospects as measured by adjusted retained earnings corrected for inventory profits — that is, Keep profits — divided by dividends. This ratio is significant because in general managements will raise the dividend only if an increase in Keep profits is expected to be permanent. Thus this discount rate reflects not a market rate of interest but an interim view of inherent profitability that is tailored for each enterprise.

THE NEW LOOK

As an alternative to the standard growth model, therefore, and to the classical "stocks-valued as a perpetuity" models, we will propose a fourth model that may be described as classical since it does not depend on a growing stream of future earnings or dividends. Instead, for stock evaluation purposes, the present-profitability-depreciated value of past investments provides an alternative stream. On the other hand it is neo-classical, because it does not assume a fixed discount rate, and it discounts profits rather than dividends.

We have been using Keep profits models to forecast the stock market since 1974 with some success. In this paper, we test the Keep profits stock valuation model in log form from 1938-77 for validation purposes. We also show log regression results of S&P 500 prices versus Keep profits, together with one-plus-the-ratio-of-Keep-profits-to-dividends, for three sub-periods using quarterly data (1949-1977, 1960-1977, and 1968-1977). Toward the end of this report, there is a simulation of the model over the last ten-year period (1968-1977). This simulation is ex ante: that is, we provide the model with data from 1949 through 1968 only, estimating coefficients for that time frame. We then forecast the period from 1968 through 1978.

This test "loads the dice" against the model, since the period from 1949 to 1968 is one in which our variables, stock prices, and the economy are rising with only brief interruptions. Since we terminate the coefficient estimation procedure at the peak, we are forcing the model to forecast over the following ten years in which stock prices move over wide bull market/bear market ranges in a consolidation pattern, apparently in response to a series of spectacular events: the 1970 recession, the dollar's fall after the link with gold is cut, the wage/price freeze and subsequent controls, the end of the Vietnam War, a President's resignation and replacement, and another recession. Through all of this, a simple model of two variables, Keep profits and a discount factor for Keep profits that measures the dividend coverage in terms of Keep profits, is able to move in a non-extrapolative snake-like pattern, tracing the 1970 decline, the subsequent recovery, a second decline in 1974.

Needless to say, the model received information on dividends and Keep profits only. In fact, a strong point of the model is that estimates of dividends and earnings are commonly considered to be the major variables that determine stock prices. Information about dividends is plentiful and can be readily used by market participants as one element of a discount factor, as hypothesized by the Keep profits model. Information about Keep profits is less readily available, but reported profits less dividends approximates Keep profits (or corporate savings) with an adjustment for inventory profits.

The model also conforms to the efficient market hypothesis, but does not depend on it, since it uses current data for its discount variable. In addition, we perform several other tests: 1) Keep profits and reported profits are compared over various time periods to show that Keep profits has provided more reliable forecasts; 2) Keep profits with a CCA (an adjustment for underdepreciation of fixed assets) is shown to be not significant for stock valuation purposes. On the other hand, the international value of the dollar is shown to be a critical variable affecting stock prices; and 3) Volatile changes in food prices have also affected Keep profits by causing exaggerated inventory profit swings in particular quarters. The construction of a durables-based Keep profit series has been useful for interpreting results. But the new series does not significantly improve forecasts over longer periods.

KEEP PROFITS STOCK MARKET MODEL

We take issue with the fundamental proposition of classical and growth models that the value of an asset is the discounted value of its expected returns, since it involves a discount rate fixed in the future. In terms of equities, for example, we argue that the discount rate varies according to the degree of coverage of dividends by Keep profits. Furthermore, Keep profits are a major determinant of market interest rates, so that the evaluation moves, not from fixed-income market rates as discount rates to stocks, but in the other direction. The level of Keep profits determines the degree of both dividend and interest coverage and is thus a major determinant of stock and bond prices. Moreover, we would argue that the primary Gordon Model in particular calculates the discount rate "k" after the fact, and "k" is not a piece of information that is available to most investors (See Appendix I for a detailed discussion). Furthermore, are investors discounting dividends or profits?

Keep theory starts from a different premise. We argue that *stocks are not bonds and the discount factor is not an interest rate and it is not fixed in the future.* Instead, the Keep profits discount rate varies daily, if not hourly, as information is received in the marketplace, and we argue that *investors are discounting not dividends but profits* — in particular Keep profits. A variable discount rate that is not fixed in the future accords well with the manner in which stock prices are continuously changing, often rapidly, in reaction to all kinds of good and bad news. Indeed, the stock market evaluates an enormous number of events, including such intellectual events as the "efficient market" theory itself and its antecedent, random walk.

The definition of our earnings variable is pretax operating income minus taxes paid minus pretax inventory profit minus dividends, which we call Keep profits: the profits that corporations keep at the bottom line to grow. We view dividends in the aggregate to be a proxy for normalized earnings or the earnings the managements feel are clearly sustainable with adequate provision for continued growth.

If we wished to put the Keep profit model in a neo-classical form, without specifying the character of the variable discount rate, present stock prices could equal the future flow of Keep profits (KE) in different periods with each item divided by an appropriate discount rate (k_N).

$$P = \sum_{N=1}^{\infty} \frac{KE_1}{1 + k_1} + \frac{KE_2}{1 + k_2} + \frac{KE_3}{1 + k_3} + \ldots + \frac{KE_N}{1 + k_N}$$

168
SECURITY
SELECTION
AND ACTIVE
PORTFOLIO
MANAGEMENT

According to the adaptive expectations hypothesis, we could use as a proxy for this sequence of future Keep earnings (with variable discount factors) the sequence of *past* Keep earnings with the variable past discount rates that were presumably applied to them, namely, the long-term bond rates in each period plus some risk premium.

As previously indicated, however, we do not believe that stocks' earnings are discounted by any interest rate past or present, fixed or variable. Rather, we believe that earnings are a major determinant of long-term rates — in short, that the influence flows in the other direction.

Before we create a statistical alchemy based on the ratio of Keep profits to dividends as a measure of present profitability, we should seek some justification for this procedure in the real marketplace.

BEHAVIORAL ASSUMPTIONS OF THE KEEP PROFITS STOCK MARKET MODEL

As a guide to investor behavior, why not assume that competition in the marketplace has led to a format for most stock market reports that is responsive to investors' primary concerns? Brokerage research comments usually include a few years' past earnings and dividends, plus one forecast — earnings for the coming year. No serious effort is made to quantify long-term earnings trends, but much is made of comparative P/E ratios over time.

P/E's — perhaps with some adjustment for average P/E's in the marketplace — are assumed to persist for certain companies on the basis of past prices for its stock and average past earnings and dividends. Indeed, this is the one element of most brokerage reports that summarizes a considerable amount of past information. When current P/E's are high compared to past P/E's on a market-adjusted basis, stocks are considered overvalued, and when they are low (and no obvious reasons can be advanced for this situation), stocks are often rated "Buy."

Thus, in research reports, the emphasis falls on very recent past earnings and present earnings estimates — and especially on the latter when they extrapolate an earlier trend. And when they use P/E ratios to justify purchase, research reports emphasize the significance of *average* past earnings levels with respect to estimated current earnings and stock prices, which is the equivalent of the constant term in a regression equation. But if stock buyers give serious credence to hypothetical future growth rates over extended time horizons in accord with the assumptions of classical and growth evaluation models, brokerage reports fail to reflect this fact — yet long horizons are needed for this approach, since an extended series of "expected" returns discounted to present value must be summed according to these models.

On the basis of simple observation, therefore, the assumptions of both classical and growth models do not appear to be justified. *Fixed rates discounting expected future returns to present value are enshrined in the textbooks — and in many major models — but not in the marketplace,* although such rates are properly used to justify specific real capital projects *for which interest costs are known.*

Are growth models therefore holdovers from the days when faith in future growth was stronger? Arguably, yes. Forecasts with each item in the proper sequence over long periods were occasionally produced to engender a sense of euphoria (or to assuage the sense of risk) that might otherwise have been implicit in the purchase of particular growth stocks. But such forecasts are markedly absent from the marketplace today.

In the main, therefore, we do not believe that stock buyers give credence to long-term estimates of growth, while also making equally tenuous assumptions about future interest rates. The nebulous is not discounted by the hypothetical. Instead we believe that investors rely primarily on the *recent pattern* of past earnings, which are extrapolated to provide estimates of *current earnings* until those earnings are reported. Our regressions support this conclusion. The *recent pattern* includes earnings growth, but also certain standards of dividend coverage in terms of operating earnings that relate to their sustainability and to the possibility of dividend increase.

This leads us to use one-plus-the-ratio-of-present-Keep-profits-to-present-dividends (or the "coverage" factor) as our discount rate — or our "depreciation" rate if the evaluation process is presumed to look backward to the present value of past corporate saving. The rising *average* level of more distant Keep earnings also receives some weight, since (in behavioral terms) purchases are often based on schemes of normalized P/E multiples and the proxy for rising average levels of profits in the Keep equation is the constant term that may be taken to roughly approximate the market level when Keep profits in the current period are zero.

We take a neutral position on the question of taking past earnings discounted according to their present profitability to be a proxy for future returns, or taking them to be the present-profitability-discounted value of past corporate savings that may or may not have been invested. The mathematics of the model are also neutral in this regard.

Belief in a corporation's ability to duplicate past earnings has fluctuated with growth rates and earnings stability, but as faith in the sustainability of past growth trends withers (as at present), there may be a symmetrical tendency to give greater weight to the sum of *past* earnings taken *not as a proxy for the stream of future returns but simply as past investment summed.* Have these "earnings-as-investment" been wisely managed in terms of their allocation between working capital, new plant, human resources, or R + D? If so, such allocations should be throwing off more dividends and earnings *now.* We therefore believe that the stock market evaluates past investments (or expected future returns) according to what present dividend policy tells us about management's estimate of "true" profitability.

THE THEORETICAL ASSUMPTIONS OF THE KEEP PROFITS MODEL

When we leave the world of certainty, we enter a world of variable interest rates. Consequently, we can no longer consider the discount rate "k" as a constant; on the contrary, in the discussion that follows, we will take it as a random variable.

Let us start with the assumption that the present price of a security is a function of the expected price subject to a discount rate (k) that is independent of any market interest rate. In other words, the discount rate will not be a bond rate but simply the external rate of return expected by investors or the difference between the future and present prices divided by the present price.

In addition, efficient market theory would argue that, on average, the external, or market, rate of return earned by investors for various periods should be some function (Ao) that is directly proportional to the corporation's *internal* rate of return. The internal rate of return, furthermore, will be a function of operating earnings as a percentage of assets, with operating earnings defined as pretax profits minus taxes and inventory profits. This variable can also be defined as Keep profits (KE) plus dividends.

If the discount rate "k" is the external rate of return expected by investors, and if that in turn is a function (Bo) of the internal rate of return or the ratio of operating profits to assets, then, of course, "k" will also be a function (Bo) of the asset profitability ratio.

The skeptical reader may wonder how investors in the real world can be making decisions of this type when the size of the corporation's assets seldom seems to play an active role in day-to-day security valuation procedures. Yet few would deny that the efficiency with which the corporation deploys its assets is a significant determinant in the values of equity ownership.

The key to this dilemma lies in the role of dividends, which are both a crucial element in real world security valuation procedures and which also tend to bear a highly consistent relationship to corporate assets. In general, corporate directors will raise dividends only if they are reasonably certain that the current level of reported earnings is likely to be sustainable; they will cut dividends promptly if it becomes clear that the level of earnings previously assumed to

SECURITY
SELECTION
AND ACTIVE
PORTFOLIO
MANAGEMENT

be sustainable turns out to have been overestimated. In other words, dividends are a proxy for management's view of a sustainable rate of asset productivity and will consequently bear a closely proportionate relationship to the value of the assets that produce them.

Here is where the argument now stands. First, the discount rate "k" equals the investor's expected external rate of return, which is a function (B_0) of the corporation's internal rate of return. The corporation's internal rate of return will vary with the relationship between operating profits (Keep profits plus dividends) and assets. And assets in turn will be a function (B_1) of dividends. We can now summarize this set of propositions as follows:

$$k = B_0 \left[\frac{\text{Operating profits}}{\text{Assets}} \right] = B_0 \left[\frac{KE + DIV}{A_1\ DIV} \right]$$

which leads to:

$$k = \frac{B_0}{B_1} \left[\frac{KE}{DIV} + 1 \right]$$

And if we set $\dfrac{B_0}{B_1}$ equal to a new function B_2, we have:

$$k = B_2\ [1 + KE/DIV]$$

namely our discount rate.

The form of the Keep Profits Model is therefore that stock prices are equal to the expected level of Keep profits divided by our variable discount rate, namely, presently profitability or the current rate of return on assets. But present profitability is unknown until profits are reported and results are interpreted according to the anticipations that the recent pattern of Keep profits has generated. In short, the reported profit may reflect the secular or the cyclical trend or episodes that generate a more equivocal response such as weather and strikes. Consequently, we use a weighted average of past Keep profits (as a proxy for anticipations) and reported Keep profits, the composite term being

$$\sum_{m=0}^{M} Wm\ KE_{t-m}$$

where Wm equals the weight to be applied to Keep

profits in several preceding periods and, in the present period, the sum of the weights equalling 1. The stock price model is therefore written:

$$Pt = \sum_{m=0}^{M} \frac{Wm \ KE_{t-m}}{(1 + KE/DIV)_t}$$

We first argued that the average stock market rate of return should be proportional to some function of a corporation's internal rate of return. If we are correct that dividends (with some multiplier) are a proxy for total assets, it remains to be seen what this multiplier is *according to the stock market.* If we are correct in assuming that the average stock market rate of return is proportional to some function of the corporation's

TABLE 1

FORM: $\log \left(\dfrac{\Sigma W_i KE}{P} \right) = a_0 + a_1 \log \left(1 + \dfrac{KE}{DIV} \right)$

DATE	QUARTERLY			ANNUAL	
	1949-77Q	1960-77Q	1968-77Q	1938-76A	1960-76A
a_0	− 2.38	− 2.83	− 2.93	− 3.27	− 3.59
t stat	−13.0	−19.0	−16.7	−18.5	−18.9
a_1	1.47	2.00	2.31	2.91	3.23
t stat	8.97	9.63	8.40	14.5	12.9
$\bar{R}^2$	.923	.877	.878	.915	.887
D.W.	1.46	1.61	1.62	2.06	2.10
P	.9	.7	.6	.7	.6

internal rate of return, then weighted Keep profits discounted by [(1 + KE/Div)] should prove to be a good market forecaster, with both elements of the two-variable model enjoying stable coefficients over various market periods and with both showing high levels of significance with respect to the dependent variable, namely stock prices.

This pushes our theoretical assumptions as far as we wish to go. Indeed there may be no need to go further since with these assumptions we have created a stock market model that "explains" 92% of the movement in stock prices since 1949 with reasonably

SECURITY
SELECTION
AND ACTIVE
PORTFOLIO
MANAGEMENT

stable coefficients over the whole period, which brings us to the statistical results.

TESTS OF THE KEEP PROFIT MODEL

In table 1 we show regression results from testing the discount rate "k" in log form, or more appropriately the discount rate (k) which equals

$$\log k_t = \log \sum \frac{W_m KE}{P} = a_0$$
$$+ a_1 \log (1 + KE/DIV) \quad \text{e.g. \#2}$$

The essential point here is that the discount rate relates to *present* profitability. The log form is superior, since the coefficients do not change much over different time frames, both for the constant and the variable terms. In addition, we show the regression fit for 1949-77 quarterly (chart 1). It shows an excellent fit be-

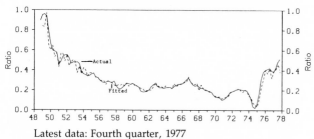

CHART 1

REGRESSION RESULTS FOR THE S&P 500 DISCOUNT RATE
USING THE RATIO OF KEEP PROFITS AND DIVIDENDS

Latest data: Fourth quarter, 1977

tween the actual and the estimated. *Therefore, empirically we have derived a variable discount rate over each period, independent of interest rates.* Using this as our basic formulation, we arrive at a final stock price model, which discounts an average level of Keep profits by the present measure of profitability:

$$\log P = a_0 + a_1 \log \left[\sum_{m=1}^{M} \frac{W_m KE_{t-m}}{(1 + KE/DIV)} \right]$$

TABLE 2

FORM: $\log P = a_0 + a_1 \log \left[\dfrac{\Sigma W_i \, KE}{1 + \dfrac{KE}{DIV}} \right]$

DATA	1949-77Q	1960-77Q	1968-77Q	1938-76A
a_0	3.81	4.16	4.22	2.65
t stat	41.4	49.6	59.1	4.75
a_1	0.18	0.15	0.15	0.34
t stat	5.59	5.73	5.76	2.76
$\bar{R}^2$	.988	.939	.830	.971
D.W.	.746	1.33	1.50	1.36
P	.9	.9	.8	.9

Table 2 shows the statistical results for both regressions over quarterly time frames from 1949 to the present (roughly thirty years) and over annual data (forty years) from 1938 to the present. The fit, as one can see from that table, is 97% since 1938. All the coefficients are significant with high t-statistics; the Durbin Watsons are good and the $\bar{R}^2$'s are roughly 90% over the longer time frame, but drop to roughly 83% over the shortest phase. The results are also impressive in terms of the stability of the coefficients. The Alpha-coefficient ranges around 4.0 (roughly from 3.8 to 4.2) over the quarterly data (thirty years). The a_1 coefficient, which is between 0.18 and 0.15, is again a relatively constant at 0.16. For the annual data, R^2 and the Durbin Watson are good.

We use only recent earnings and dividends for

CHART 2

S&P 500 REGRESSION RESULTS
S&P 500 PRICES vs KEEP PROFITS , DIVIDENDS , AND THEIR RATIO

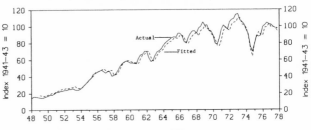

Latest data: Fourth quarter, 1977

176

SECURITY
SELECTION
AND ACTIVE
PORTFOLIO
MANAGEMENT

present stock prices. Therefore, there is no conflict with the efficient market theory, which allows stock prices to adjust to new information in the current period. On the other hand, the Keep profits model does not depend on the efficient markets hypothesis, since our empirical work lends support only to the view that most stock price *change* is explained by current data.

If one were interested in determining what would happen to stock prices if Keep profits were zero, the answer is that, using $(\Sigma W_m \, KE_{t-m})$ for a weighted average of Keep profits, if one period had zero Keep profits, stock prices would fall but not to zero. If several periods went to zero, stock prices should fall to the value of the constant term a_0 which may relate to the liquidation value of assets.

We can also make the following point, since the "a_0" coefficient has risen over time (1949, 1960, 1968) from 45 to 64 to 68, the value of the underlying asset structure is presumed to have risen, and we read these as the probable bottoms of bear markets in terms of the S & P 500. Using the expanded form in table 3, we find the equivalent current (March, 1978) DJIA low to be roughly 625.

TABLE 3

FORM: $\log P = a_0 + a_1 \log \left[\dfrac{\Sigma W_i \, KE}{1 + \dfrac{KE}{DIV}} \right] + a_2 \log \left[\dfrac{CPI \; Ger.}{CPI \; U.S.} \right]$

DATE	1949-77	1960-77	1968-77
a_0	3.91	4.26	4.42
t stat	37.6	45.3	48.6
a_1	0.17	0.14	0.13
t stat	5.22	5.32	5.81
a_2	1.22	1.19	1.91
t stat	2.08	2.15	3.12
$\bar{R}^2$	.988	.942	.862
D.W.	.762	1.32	1.73
P	.9	.9	.8

Keep profits are expressed in U.S. dollars and so is the stock market. Therefore, when the purchasing power of the dollar declines vis-a-vis other currencies that offer comparable investment opportunities, efficient market theory inclines one to the view that U.S. stock prices should fall.

We chose the ratio of the German consumer price index to the U.S. consumer price index to test this proposition, since West Germany offers investment opportunities that are comparable to those in the United States, and West Germany does not control its external prices to the same degree as Japan.

The form of the equation is therefore

$$\log P = a_0 + a_1 \log \left[\left[\frac{W_m \ KE_{t\text{-}m}}{(1 + KE/DIV)} \right] \left[\text{Foreign Index} \right] \right]$$

Table 3 shows the results with the variables rearranged in the following way for analytical purposes:

$$\log P = a_0 + a_1 \log \left[\sum \frac{W_m \ KE_{t\text{-}m}}{(1 + KE/DIV)} \right] + a_2 \log \left[\frac{\text{C.P.I. Germany}}{\text{C.P.I. U.S.}} \right]$$

We made relative prices an independent variable because Germany is not the only alternative investment area, and we wished to determine a separate weighting.

CHART 3

S&P 500 REGRESSION RESULTS
S&P 500 PRICES vs KEEP PROFITS , DIVIDENDS ,
THEIR RATIO , WITH A DEVALUATION FACTOR

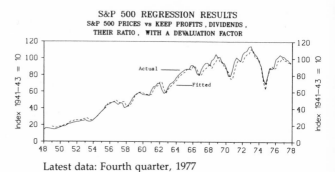

Latest data: Fourth quarter, 1977

178

SECURITY
SELECTION
AND ACTIVE
PORTFOLIO
MANAGEMENT

From Table 3, it is clear that over all time frames, the variable was significant with the proper positive sign, i.e., a German CPI that rises faster than the U.S. CPI should cause U.S. stocks to rise, because U.S. currency will appreciate relative to the D-Mark. (The earnings will be worth more.) The statistics show the price relative (or proxy) currency variable to be significant. R^2's were improved during the last decade by three percentage points from 83% to 86%. (See chart 3 for the fit.)

To make sure that this variable was not acting as a proxy for domestic inflation, we tested the stock price model using the U.S. CPI alone. Over the three time frames this variable changed signs from positive to negative, and in the latest time frame it was insignificant. (To conserve space, these results were not tabulated in this paper.)

TEST #2: CCA INFLATION ACCOUNTING

The next test was to determine whether underdepreciation warrants the inclusion of a capital consumption adjustment (CCA) in the stock price forecasting equation. The theory behind CCA adjustment is that the depreciation rate has not kept pace with the increase in replacement costs. Philosophically, we are opposed to mixing income statement with balance sheet concepts such as the underdepreciation of capital, since we believe the market responds primarily to operating earnings. But the CCA is a two-sided coin in any case. Higher-than-historic costs raise barriers to entry. And it is not the cost of an asset, but the profitability of that investment that matters. Further, if one makes adjustments for underdepreciation, one should also make adjustment for gains on net financial liabilities. Bonds that have been issued at low interest rates in earlier periods will be paid off in cheap dollars, and in the aggregate these far outweigh any overstatement of profits that may accrue from underdepreciation.

For stock market forecasting purposes, however, we only want to find out if the capital consump-

TABLE 4

$$\text{FORM: } \log P = a_0 + a_1 \log \left[\frac{\Sigma W_i \, (\text{KEEP} + \text{CCA})}{1 + \dfrac{\text{KEEP} + \text{CCA}}{\text{DIV}}} \right]$$

$$+ \log \left[\frac{\text{CPI Ger.}}{\text{CPI U.S.}} \right]$$

DATE	1949-77Q	1960-77Q	1968-77Q
a_0	4.10	4.43	4.72
t stat	44.9	51.1	34.6
a_1	.095	.071	.064
t stat	4.00	3.76	3.49
a_2	1.32	1.36	2.78
t stat	2.16	2.27	3.22
$\bar{R}^2$	.987	.932	.818
D.W.	.812	1.37	1.86
P	.9	.9	.9

tion adjustment improves the fit. Table 4 shows that it does not, that over the latest time frame it actually worsens the fit by 4%, and that the Keep profit variable with this adjustment added markedly drops in significance. The form of the equation is:

$$\log P = a_0 + a_1 \log \frac{\Sigma W_m \, (\text{KEEP} + \text{CCA})}{\left(1 + \dfrac{(\text{KEEP} + \text{CCA})}{\text{DIV}}\right)}$$

$$+ a_2 \log \left(\frac{\text{C.P.I. Germany}}{\text{C.P.I. U.S.}} \right)$$

We conclude that those who have found some value in the CCA adjustment may have been picking up the effect of relative international inflation rates. *In short, our tests imply it is the profitability of the investment in an operating sense plus the store of value that is offered by an investment in terms of its denomination in a given currency and not the replacement cost of an asset that is significant.*

TEST #3 KEEP TOTAL VS. KEEP DURABLES

The next test deals with insulating Keep profits from the volatile changes in food prices that turn up in IVA. As we all know, IVA is a function of prices and

180

SECURITY
SELECTION
AND ACTIVE
PORTFOLIO
MANAGEMENT

inventory changes in the economy, including durables and non-durables. Food prices have been extremely volatile in recent years, which has affected inventory profits for the overall economy in far greater proportion than the relative size of the food sector in the economy or in the stock market.

We have therefore developed two series: one for total Keep profits and one for Keep profits in terms of durables that improves the fit of the equation only marginally, probably because there is no significant difference between total IVA and IVA for durables over the longer time frame. But over sub-periods of a year or two, when food prices are erratic, "durable" Keep profits have provided a somewhat better fit, and this has been true in recent periods.

For example, chart 4 shows total Keep profits

CHART 4

KEEP PROFITS
TOTAL vs DURABLES

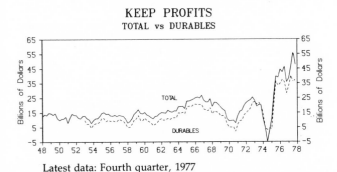

Latest data: Fourth quarter, 1977

and durable Keep profits quarterly from 1953. Notice that in the third quarter of 1977, total Keep profits rose to $56 billion because the IVA adjustment dropped from $20 billion to $6 billion as the result of a drop in food prices. But durable Keep profits in the third quarter were flat. In short, corporate liquidity worsened, and as a result of this factor and the Keep profits to dividend ratio, the stock market dropped. Did this gigantic and, as it turns out, somewhat misleading leap in Keep profits have a great effect in the Keep model? In fact, it did not. The model declined in the period in line with actual stock prices, which underlines the importance of the Keep profits-to-dividend discount factor. (Note: The results of these regressions were not shown to conserve space.)

TEST #4 SIMULATION

The final test is probably the most important. $\bar{R}^2$'s that look good are usually published. But most stock market models hold up over very limited periods, and if their coefficients are not constantly recalculated, they break down, which makes them useless for longer-term forecasting.

In chart 5, we show the results of an ex-ante simulation. We fed in data from 1949 through 1968, estimating the coefficients for that time frame. We then forecasted the period from 1968 through 1978. We view this as a loaded dice simulation — loaded, that is, against the model, because the period from 1959 to 1968 showed economic variables, the market, and the economy heading up very strongly for two decades. Yet we stopped the estimation procedure at the peak and forced the equation to forecast the following ten years of volatile consolidation. During this period, we fed the model only current Keep profits and dividends. Now, obviously, if one were to actually use this

CHART 5

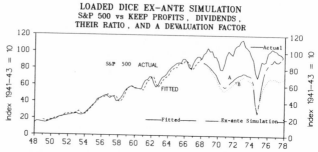

LOADED DICE EX-ANTE SIMULATION
S&P 500 vs KEEP PROFITS, DIVIDENDS,
THEIR RATIO, AND A DEVALUATION FACTOR

Latest data: Fourth quarter, 1977

A) Simulation from second quarter 1968 to fourth quarter 1977 using Keep profits and dividends.

B) Simulation from second quarter 1968 to fourth quarter 1977 with the devaluation factor added.

model as a forecasting tool, the additional piece of information that one would usually add would be the level of stock prices up to the point of forecast. This would adjust the levels component of the equation so that any turns in the stock market that the model would forecast would come from proper levels.

The *result without such adjustments* is shown in chart 5. One can see that the regression follows the turns in the market fairly accurately up to the fitted 1968 period, and then follows it fairly well into the bear market of 1970, through the up markets in 1975-76 and into 1977. This is a very powerful test, and the results are good since, as market participants, we are far more interested in picking turns than in determining levels.

The Keep profits stock market model breaks new ground in terms of valuation theory. In this article, we restrict ourselves to using one version of it for market forecasting purposes. It can also be used to estimate expected future returns from individual equities, however, which will make it a useful adjunct to capital asset pricing models. Perhaps that's an appropriate subject for a future article.

APPENDIX I: THE STANDARD DIVIDEND GROWTH MODEL

Before discussing the Keep profits alternative, we should provide a brief explanation of the standard dividend growth (or Gordon) stock valuation model used by most investing institutions. The fundamental argument of both capital pricing theory and the Gordon model is that the value of an investment is the discounted value of the expected dividends, the discount rate being the rate of profit required for that investment. The Gordon model then adds that future dividends (D_t) equal present dividends times a certain growth rate, i.e., $D_t = do\,(1 + g)^t$. Therefore, present stock prices may be written as:

$$P = \sum_{t=1}^{\infty} \frac{D_t}{(1 + k)^t} = \sum_{t=1}^{\infty} \frac{do\,(1 + g)^{t=1}}{(1 + k)^t}$$

P = Stock prices
D_t = Dividend paid in period t
do = Dividends paid initially
g = Growth rate of dividends
k = Constant discount rate of future dividends

This last equation can be expressed as an infinite geometric progression with the common factor $(1 + g)/(1 + k)$. Summing the progression (assuming $k > g$), the progression yields:

$$P = \frac{do}{k - g}$$

The Gordon model introduces us to some of the problems confronting growth models in general. Many Wall Street observers have assumed that "k" (the discount rate in the Gordon model) is the bond rate with a risk premium added. This is erroneous because, given "k's" construction, it varies independently of interest rates and without regard to the measures that are commonly used to calculate risk premiums. If we rearrange the previous equation in the form of

$$k = \frac{do}{p} + g,$$

an example will also show that the discount rate "k" is calculated as a residual.

In the non-inflationary period 1959-1968, the earnings of Moody's Rail average, the N.Y. Bank average, the Utility average, and an individual stock, IBM, grew by 5.8%, 6.0%, 6.7%, and 17%, respectively. Plugging these values in for "g" in the formula $k = do/p + g$ and adding current dividend yields (d/p), calculated "k" factors for these securities for the year 1968 are 10.7%, 9.4%, 11.3%, and 18%, respectively. This illustrates how "k" factors for individual stocks range widely, although bond rates were approximately 6.7% in 1968. Also, discount rates, "k" in this example, appear to be unrelated to business risk, since investors could hardly have believed that railroads were less risky than IBM. Finally, volatility of earnings certainly was not a factor, and yet "k's" vary from year to year. For example, the "k" for utilities in 1969 rose to 11.7% versus 11.3% in 1968 as data from 1957 was dropped and data for 1969 was added.

Aside from the difficulties posed by "k's" ex post construction and variability and the determination of the growth rate by historical growth rates, a central problem for all growth models is that in the formula

$$P = \frac{do}{k - g}$$

184

SECURITY
SELECTION
AND ACTIVE
PORTFOLIO
MANAGEMENT

the discount rate (k) must be greater than the growth rate (g) or dividends (do) will be divided by zero (if $k = g$) or, worse yet, by minus values when "k" is less than "g."

The dividend growth model as it was first proposed by

Samuel Guild in "Stock Growth and Discount Tables" (1931) has the same problem. In "Growth Yields On Common Stocks" (1961), Soldofsky & Murphy showed Guild's model, which answers the question: What would one dollar of dividends be worth today if it grew at a rate (g) and was discounted by a discount rate (k)? Using Gordon's notation, this expression can be written as:

$$P = \left(\frac{1+g}{1+k}\right)^1 + \left(\frac{1+g}{1+k}\right)^2 + \text{---} + \left(\frac{1+g}{1+k}\right)^N$$

where g = growth rate
       k = discount rate
       P = stock prices for one dollar of dividends
       N = 1, 2, ... ∞

Notice that in this equation (like Gordon's) dividends plus some growth rate are in the numerator and that in the special case that g = 0, we are left with P = 1/k, the value of a perpetuity. But for "g" greater than zero, Soldofsky and Murphy show:

$$P = \frac{1+g}{1+k}\left[1 + \left(\frac{1+g}{1+k}\right) + \left(\frac{1+g}{1+k}\right)^2 + .. + \left(\frac{1+g}{1+k}\right)^{n-1}\right]$$

or

$$P = \frac{1+g}{g-k}\left[\left(\frac{1+g}{1+k}\right)^N - 1\right] \qquad \text{e.g. \#1}$$

Now, for a growth rate of dividends (g) less than the discount rate (k), the term

$$\left(\frac{1+g}{1+k}\right)^N$$

goes to zero, at the limit. It follows that the result of equation (1) for "k" greater than "g" is:

$$P = \frac{1+g^{(-1)}}{g-k}$$

or

$$P = \frac{1+g}{k-g}$$

which is approximately the same as Gordon's:

$$P = \frac{do}{k-g}$$

The crux of the Gordon version of the dividend growth

model is therefore that the growth rate of dividends must be less than the discount rate so that the expression on the right side of the equation can be evaluated at an upper limit — the geometric series must converge.

The alternative growth model, on the other hand, *allows* the discount rate to be higher or lower than the growth rate. This may make it superior to the Gordon Model, since the values on the right side of the equation are more realistically constrained. But when Soldofsky and Murphy opted for the alternative growth model, their flexibility with respect to growth and dividend rates had a price. To provide an upper limit at which to evaluate stocks, they were forced to resort to a zero growth rate (but no subsequent decay rate) for dividends after a specified period to close off what would otherwise be an unending series — the balance being evaluated as a level payment perpetuity.

We should mention that Gordon recognized the primary problem of the growth model, which is that when the discount rate (k) equals the dividend growth rate (g), stock price (P) goes to infinity, without regard to the level of dividends (or earnings). He responded to this problem by creating a secondary formulation of his model:

$$k = g + a_0 (1 + g)^{-a_1}$$

the $1 + g$ term stemming, not from Guild, since it appears in the denominator, but having been developed empirically from regressions of d/p. In sum, a statistical artifact whose numerator a_0 is a constant that can't go to zero and whose denominator $(1 + g)$ is firmly positive is substituted for the troublesome d/p term. But this removed any theoretical justification for the model, in terms of discounted future dividends, although it is argued that it has held up reasonably well empirically.

In this historical rundown, we have tried to show that stock evaluation is by no means in a settled state and that substantial questions can be raised about accepted theories. Our response to many of these problems is to use only current data, *not* because efficient market theory casts doubt on the use of anything else — one may be skeptical about the behavioral assumptions that underlie the efficient market hypothesis — but because current data explain the bulk of stock market change without resort to more complicated formulations.

Certainly the calculation of a discount rate "k" appears to be an exercise in futility. At best it will lead to some "intrinsic" or "central" value theory for stocks, the presumption being that the market is "wrong" and the forecast "right" when the market *remains* below the values indicated by "k." Is the market wrong, or must we wait another ten years before the lagging indicator of growth "g" reflects current reality and nothing else?

BIBLIOGRAPHY

1. Gordon, Myron, "The Savings Investment and Valuation of a Corporation," *Review of Economics and Statistics*, Feb., 1962, pp. 37-51.
2. Gordon, Myron, "Dividends, Earnings, and Stock Prices," *Review of Economics and Statistics*, May, 1959, pp. 99-105.
3. Gordon, Myron, "Security and a Financial Theory of Investment," *The Quarterly Journal of Economics LXXIV* (August, 1960), H72-492.
4. Fama, Fisher, Jensen and Roll, "Adjustment of Stock Prices to New Information," *International Economic Review*, Vol. 10, Feb., 1969, pp. 1-21.
5. Soldolsky, Robert and Murphy, James, *"Growth Yield on Common Stock, Theory and Tables,"* State University of Iowa, 1963.

APPENDIX II: SOME COMMENTS ON METHODOLOGY
Our discount rate is based on dividends because we believe that dividends provide important insights into management's view of inherent profitability. Other people who have viewed dividends as providing important information about profits include S. J. Prais[1] who said that in setting dividend policy "the major short-term question that faces a company is the interpretation of any recent change in its profits. Is it because of some fundamental improvement in the circumstances which can be expected to persist?" The effect on dividends would depend on the board of director confidence on this point. This led Prais to a model for dividends similar to John Lintner's:[2]

$$D = a + b_1P + b_2D\text{-}1 + M$$

where current dividends are D, profits are P, D-1 are dividends lagged by one period, and M is the unexplained error term.

The rationale for Lintner's model is that dividends depend directly on current net income, but also on past dividends, since management is reluctant to cut dividends or to raise them to levels that may not be maintained.

Furthermore, like our stock pricing equation, this model may be viewed ex post: that is, dividends may depend on profits in all previous years according to a distributed lag formulation or the distributed lag may be rationalized according to an "adaptive expectations" framework. This would take dividends to depend *on the expected value of profits on assets currently held rather than on current profits.*

Interestingly, Dobrovolsky[3] found dividends to be *negatively* associated with *changes* in the rate of return on investment since rising returns would lead to a decision to increase corporate saving at the expense of dividends to finance expansion. But this does no more than underline the fact that the *level* of dividends is a sensitive indicator of management's view of current and anticipated profitability *after provision for growth.*

Notice that this also implies an interaction between the level of dividends and the balance of operating earnings, namely Keep profits (KE), which might be a source of multicolinearity in our model if the KE divided by one plus KE/D relationship were not treated *as a single variable.*

On the other hand, Modigliani-Miller's insistence on the theoretical independence of corporate investment and savings decisions[4] would imply no multicolinearity, but they postulated an *informational* link between profits and dividends. In fact, according to these researchers, dividends are an indirect source of information about an otherwise unobservable "noise free" profit potential which they labelled P*.

In effect, therefore, we have simply taken an additional step: We view dividends to be *directly proportional* to the capitalized value of P* subject to minor fluctuations, which in our variable directly benefit KE. In short, if profit potentials rise, corporations may increase their savings (KE) to finance new growth.

But these benefits to KE are directly reflected in our KE divided by KE over dividend variable, with the correct (positive) sign, so that dividends are *free* to fluctuate in line with management's estimate of longer-term profitability including adequate provision for continued growth.

The entire function is therefore a proxy for management's expected *current* return on assets. The rationale for using one plus KE/D to discount KE in the numerator, which is the beneficiary of these short-term fluctuations, is therefore that dividends are directly proportionate to, and hence a proxy for, total assets, so that KE/D in the denominator stands for the long-term expected return on those assets.

188

SECURITY
SELECTION
AND ACTIVE
PORTFOLIO
MANAGEMENT

An internal quote in "Corporate Dividend Policy" by John A.

Brittain, from "Some Problems in the Econometric Analysis of Company Accounts," an unpublished paper presented at the 18th meeting of the Econometric Society in August, 1956.

[2] "Distribution of Incomes of Corporation Among Dividends, Retained Earnings, and Taxes," *American Economic Review,* May, 1956.

[3] "Corporate Income Retention 1915-43," NBER, 1951.

[4] "Cost of Capital, Corporate Finance and the Theory of Investment," *American Economic Review*, June, 1958.

SECURITY SELECTION
AND MODERN
PORTFOLIO THEORY

Whose efficient market?

Institutional investors can still exploit inefficiencies in a market where tax considerations influence the pricing mechanism.

Robert M. Lovell, Jr.

Academic studies of market efficiency have concentrated on ex-post demonstrations that no more than the expected number of publicized participants have been able to obtain risk-adjusted returns in excess of the market over extended periods. If professional investors have apparently been unable to recover management and transaction costs, they attribute their failure to diligent competition among skilled participants utilizing equivalent information. Even the dwindling number of defenders of the value of investment management are now conceding the market's efficient pricing of institutional issues, while contending that market opportunities still exist outside that limited universe of liquid, widely held securities.

Can this institutional market be equally efficient for all participants? A classic investor, interested in the "best," most profitable companies and indifferent as to current yield, sees the market one way. The taxable investor prefers to derive more of his return from appreciation than from dividends which are reduced by his marginal tax rate. Finally, the tax-exempt institution might value the relatively sure return from current dividends more than an equivalent amount reinvested in the company. What return can each of these investors expect, given consistent expectations of future profitability and payout ratios, if, for the sake of argument, we hold essentially unpredictable price/earnings ratios constant?

To provide an answer, we used February, 1976 *Value Line Investment Survey* estimates of three- to five-year future return on equity and payout ratios for the fifty companies in the Standard & Poor's "500" Average having the largest market capitalizations to provide an answer.[1] These companies represent over 60% of the Average's total market value, are widely followed, present almost no problems in acquiring meaningful positions, and have varying degrees of historical volatility. They are certainly a fair sample and, perhaps, a proxy for the institutional market. One might cavil at the estimates, but they are professionally derived by a competent organization. This examination requires only that the estimates are derived in a consistent manner.

A CLASSIC APPROACH (FIGURE I)

All investors wish to own the equities of especially profitable companies. The logic is unassailable, since indefinite maintenance of return in excess of the discount rate (either of the "market" or risk-free alternatives) guarantees long-term performance superior to the standard. In fact, theoretically no price is too high for such an ideal vehicle. During the "two-tier" market of 1971-1972, this approach gained new adherents as more and more managers, attracted by the outstanding price performance of the "best" companies, responded to the exhortations of their clients by increasing their positions at ever-higher prices.

The real world intervened. Some of the most

1. Footnotes appear at the end of the article.

profitable companies ran into problems, the discount period shortened, and new buyers were increasingly difficult to locate as prices dropped, sometimes precipitously. Some market participants, who had imagined they ran diversified portfolios, found themselves concentrated in stocks whose prices were unsustainably high.

On February 29, 1976, the market accorded the multiples shown in Figure I for *Value Line's* estimated returns on equity for our sample. In spite of the intellectual appeal of the approach, it is clear that the market put a finite price on superior return since investors

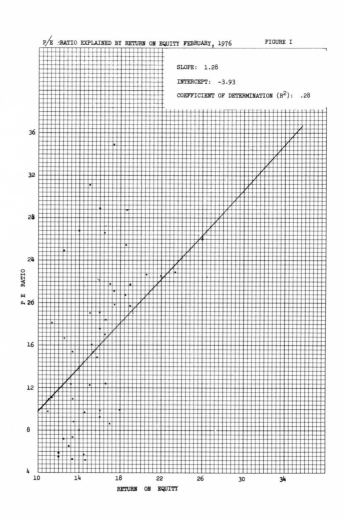

P/E RATIO EXPLAINED BY RETURN ON EQUITY FEBRUARY, 1976   FIGURE I

SLOPE: 1.28

INTERCEPT: -3.93

COEFFICIENT OF DETERMINATION (R^2): .28

SECURITY
SELECTION
AND ACTIVE
PORTFOLIO
MANAGEMENT

were unwilling to pay more than 36 times earnings for any of these companies. Professionals are all too aware that the price for high profitability is less than it was in early 1973.

Estimated future return on equity, however, does not do a very good job of explaining differences in price/earnings ratios. The slope of the regression line (1.28) indicates that the market is willing to pay marginally more for higher incremental returns, but the coefficient of determination (R^2) is rather low at .28 (only 28% of P/E differences were attributable to estimated returns on equity).

GROWTH IS WHAT COUNTS (FIGURE II)

The taxable investor is biased against dividends, since his current return is reduced by his marginal tax rate. Figure II demonstrates the extreme case: a market where dividends are taxed at 100%. This appears to be an indefensible model, but it does a better job of explaining price/earnings ratios than Figure I does (the coefficient of determination is .41 instead of .28).

This was a surprising result.[2] We then ran the estimates against other marginal tax rates to see if there was a level of taxes that better explained price/ earnings ratios.

TABLE I

	ASSUMED TAX RATE		
	100%	70%	30%
Slope	1.83	1.96	1.00
Intercept	−1.70	−5.59	3.42
Coefficient Of Determination	.41	.30	.05

The explanatory relationship between expected returns and price/earnings ratios deteriorates progressively as the marginal tax rate declines. The changes in slope and intercept appear meaningless since the 70 and 30% models describe the market inaccurately.

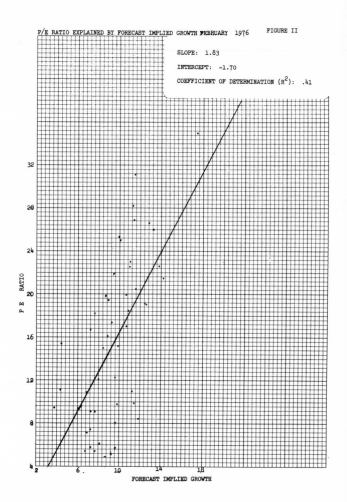

P/E RATIO EXPLAINED BY FORECAST IMPLIED GROWTH FEBRUARY 1976   FIGURE II

SLOPE: 1.83

INTERCEPT: -1.70

COEFFICIENT OF DETERMINATION (R^2): .41

FORECAST IMPLIED GROWTH

TOTAL RETURN (FIGURE III)

The tax-exempt investor should logically value
dividends more highly than retained earnings since
their receipt is a relative certainty. Our final model,
however, assumes that he is indifferent as to whether
his investment pays out earnings or reinvests them in
the company.

Total return (yield + growth) is the current
"operative" doctrine of many professional investors,
but the evidence of Figure III suggests that we are not
putting our tax-exempt clients' money where our

SECURITY
SELECTION
AND ACTIVE
PORTFOLIO
MANAGEMENT

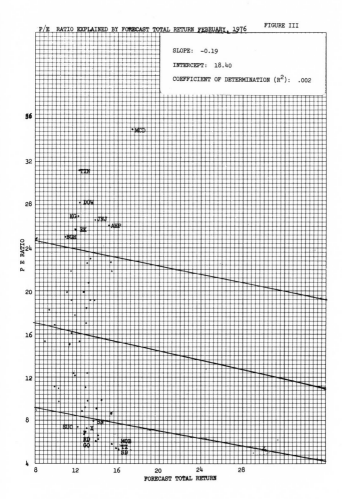

P/E RATIO EXPLAINED BY FORECAST TOTAL RETURN FEBRUARY, 1976   FIGURE III

SLOPE: -0.19

INTERCEPT: 18.40

COEFFICIENT OF DETERMINATION (R^2): .002

mouths are. If dividends are reinvested at a constant ratio of price to book value (or P/E ratio), the total return formula is:

$$\text{Appreciation} = \frac{\text{Estimated Future ROE X \% Future Earnings Retention}}{}$$

$$+ \text{ Yield} = \frac{\text{Estimated Future ROE X \% Future Dividend Payout}}{\text{Price/Book Value}}$$

$$= \text{Total Return}$$

We arrive at our price/earnings ratios in the following manner:

$$\frac{\text{Price/Book Value}}{\text{Estimated Future ROE}}$$

Figure III shows returns and price/earnings ratios when the tax rate is zero. The coefficient of determination is negligible (.002) and the regression line has a negative slope (−0.19). Apparently, the market's capitalization of normalized earnings has virtually nothing to do with expected total return. If this is so, the tax-exempt investor, who apparently represents a growing share of potential equity purchasing power, should be able to exploit these perceived inefficiencies created by the influence of taxpayers.

The two lines outside the central regression line encompass one standard deviation from the mean. Given our estimates, it would appear that the total return investor sees nine "cheap" stocks and eight "dear" stocks in our fifty-company universe. What happens when he and his taxable competitor invest in these issues? We will assume the marginal tax rate of 70% (the maximum Federal rate).

The last column shows that a taxable investor could expect an after-tax return of 12.54% if he purchased the expensive stocks compared with 9.99% realizable from the lower priced portfolio. In order to secure this significant incremental benefit, he undertook the greater risk represented by a higher beta. His willingness to make the bet must reflect his own risk tolerance and ability to forecast maintenance of superior profitability.

The tax-exempt total return investor, however, stood to receive a return 1.07 points higher with less risk from the "cheap" stocks. His choice is clear: the higher yielding portfolio was absolutely and relatively more attractive to him than his taxable competitor. Given these expectations, logic dictates that he not

SECURITY
SELECTION
AND ACTIVE
PORTFOLIO
MANAGEMENT

TABLE II

COMPANY	BETA	GROWTH	YIELD	TOTAL RETURN	TAXABLE INVESTOR TOTAL RETURN
SD	.90	9.28%	6.78%	16.06%	11.31%
TX	.90	6.89	9.06	15.95	9.61
MOB	.95	9.72	5.76	15.48	11.45
GO	.85	7.68	6.45	14.13	9.62
RD	.70	7.44	6.61	14.05	9.42
F	1.05	8.19	6.01	14.20	9.99
X	1.05	7.00	6.04	13.04	8.81
SUO	.95	7.48	4.68	12.16	8.88
SN	.90	9.66	3.88	13.54	10.82
	.92	8.15%	6.14%	14.29%	9.99%
MCD	1.55	17.50%	——	17.50%	17.50%
TXN	1.20	11.55	.74%	12.29	11.77
DOW	1.15	11.36	1.03	12.39	11.67
KG	1.30	11.48	.67	12.15	11.68
JNJ	.90	12.71	.86	13.57	12.97
AHP	1.10	13.26	1.88	15.14	13.82
EK	1.10	9.99	1.80	11.79	10.53
BGH	1.25	10.13	.76	10.89	10.36
	1.19	12.25%	.97%	13.22%	12.54%

play a game whose rules are apparently written to accommodate the very different requirements of the taxpayer.

During the six months subsequent to February 27, the expensive stocks produced a mean total return of minus 5.36% while the "cheap" issues produced average income and price appreciation of 17.56% before taxes. On the surface, it would appear that our

(TOTAL PRE-TAX RETURN: 2/27 — 8/31/76)

"DEAR" STOCKS	% RETURN	"CHEAP" STOCKS	% RETURN
MCD	(13.07)	SUO	40.41
TXN	(8.79)	SN	22.39
DOW	(18.02)	X	(5.69)
KG	8.95	F	12.61
JNJ	5.10	RD	18.25
AHP	3.77	GO	20.67
EK	(11.55)	MOB	10.38
BGH	(9.26)	TX	13.52
MEAN	(5.36)	SD	30.33
		MEAN	17.56

model was extraordinarily powerful in identifying superior performers (albeit weighted heavily to one industry) and laggards *before* the fact.

Clearly, however, performance differences of this magnitude in such a short period are, one, unsustainable and, two, not really related to the investment rationale that underlies the model. The relative price move was essentially a price/earnings ratio adjustment that brought prices more nearly in line with our return expectations.

Given the extent of the move of the tails of our February distribution toward the mean, one would think that August total return expectations would show more correlation with normalized price/earnings ratios. Figure IV shows that this was indeed the case. The coefficient of determination improved to a still insignificant .0378. August's anticipated returns from the "dear" and "cheap" portfolios may be summarized as follows:

| | | ANTICIPATED TOTAL RETURN | |
	BETA	TAX-EXEMPT INVESTOR	TAXABLE INVESTOR
"Cheap" Portfolio	.92	13.90	9.94
"Dear" Portfolio	1.08	13.77	13.05

The tax-exempt investor could still expect a marginally higher return from the lower beta, lower multiple stocks. The taxpayer, however, faces a more attractive prospect than was available in February. Purchase of the "dear" portfolio promises an after-tax return of 13.05% vs. 12.54% six months earlier while portfolio beta has slipped from 1.19 to 1.08. He can expect an internal return 31% higher from the "dear" portfolio while incurring only 17% more risk.

THE ULTIMATE LOGIC

In spite of superior price performance over an extended period, highly liquid companies with above

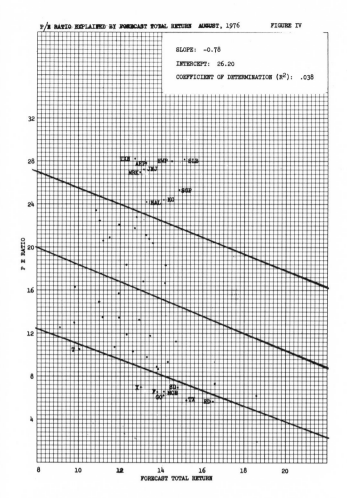

P/E RATIO EXPLAINED BY FORECAST TOTAL RETURN   AUGUST, 1976   FIGURE IV

SLOPE: -0.78

INTERCEPT: 26.20

COEFFICIENT OF DETERMINATION (R²): .038

average payout ratios and below average multiples still offered tax-exempt investors the possibility of higher return with less risk than our universe in August, 1976. The taxable investor also sees what he might consider attractive buys in the very issues which are inappropriate for non-taxpayers.

Neither of these investors should purchase a fund tied to the Standard & Poor's "500" since it contains issues which do not fit their individual requirements. It has been suggested that one could construct new indices to accommodate different needs: for example, a "high-yield index," a "growth index." *It is only a small step further to suggest that advisors return to*

TICKER SYMBOL	PRICE 2/27/76	ESTIMATED TANGIBLE BOOK VALUE 12/31/75	FORECAST RETURN ON EQUITY 1978-1980
IBM	255-5/8	75.90	17.5
T	55-3/4	52.02	11.0
XON	87-1/8	72.85	13.5
GM	65-7/8	43.65	16.0
EK	108	22.85	18.5
S	71-1/2	34.45	12.5
DOW	110-7/8	24.60	16.0
GE	53-3/8	21.45	15.5
DD	152-1/4	72.85	13.5
PG	84-7/8	25.27	17.0
TX	25	34.10	13.5
MMM	57-1/4	15.40	17.0
SN	42-7/8	38.20	14.0
AEP	33-1/8	4.90	26.0
RD	42-5/8	62.00	12.0
MOB	53-3/4	65.15	14.5
WY	42-1/2	12.20	17.5
KC	84-1/2	17.10	22.0
MRK	67-1/2	12.50	23.5
SD	30	39.15	14.5
XRX	66-1/2	23.70	16.0
JNJ	85-1/4	19.50	16.5
GO	23-1/8	34.40	12.0
F	51-1/8	63.65	13.0
CAT	86-1/4	30.70	16.5
UK	74-1/8	44.15	13.5
X	79-1/8	86.90	12.5
SLB	73-1/8	17.75	19.0
P	50-3/8	32.00	16.0
BGE	101-5/8	32.60	12.5
KG	35-3/4	9.50	14.0
ARC	81-3/4	56.30	17.0
LLY	51-3/4	13.50	18.5
GTE	27-1/4	21.15	11.5
CLL	63-5/8	44.80	14.5
SUO	49-1/4	57.10	11.5
IP	74	31.95	15.5
MTC	93-3/4	51.65	15.0
MO	53-1/4	17.25	16.0
GET	159-1/8	107.60	13.5
JCP	54-7/8	26.20	11.5
HAL	148-5/8	51.95	15.0
GF	50-1/4	16.52	16.5
SGP	50	10.80	20.5
RJR	65-3/4	32.05	16.5
WLA	31-3/4	13.30	15.5
TXN	119-1/2	25.55	15.0
ITT	28-7/8	24.00	11.0
MCD	62-3/4	10.25	17.5
N	31-7/8	19.20	18.0

the performance of one of their primary functions that has been long neglected: construction of portfolios to meet their clients' unique requirements.

FORECAST PAYOUT RATIO 1978-1980	PE RATIO ON FORECAST ROE 2/27/76	FORECAST IMPLIED GROWTH 1978-1980	FORECAST TOTAL RETURN 1978-1980
48	19.25	9.10	11.59
65	9.74	3.85	10.53
43	8.86	7.70	12.53
62	9.44	6.06	12.65
46	25.57	9.99	11.79
42	16.64	7.25	9.77
29	28.19	11.36	12.39
43	16.06	8.84	11.51
67	15.48	4.46	8.78
49	19.76	8.67	11.15
49	5.41	6.89	15.95
44	21.88	9.52	11.53
31	8.00	9.66	13.54
49	26.00	13.26	15.14
38	5.75	7.44	14.05
33	5.72	9.72	15.48
39	19.89	10.68	12.64
50	22.45	11.00	13.23
53	22.98	11.05	13.35
36	5.31	9.28	16.06
41	17.56	9.44	11.77
23	26.48	12.71	13.57
36	5.58	7.68	14.13
37	6.15	8.19	14.20
35	17.03	10.73	12.78
35	12.44	8.78	11.59
44	7.28	7.00	13.04
25	21.68	14.25	15.40
27	9.81	11.68	14.43
19	24.96	10.13	10.89
18	26.86	11.48	12.15
30	8.53	11.90	15.42
37	20.70	11.66	13.44
63	11.22	4.26	9.87
32	9.79	9.86	13.13
35	7.48	7.48	12.16
46	14.97	8.37	11.44
47	12.13	7.95	11.82
22	19.31	12.48	13.62
16	10.96	11.34	12.80
35	18.26	7.48	9.39
16	19.07	12.60	13.44
34	18.42	10.89	12.74
32	22.59	13.94	15.36
42	12.42	9.57	12.95
36	15.42	9.92	12.25
23	31.20	11.55	12.29
37	10.91	6.93	10.32
--	34.97	17.50	17.50
59	9.22	7.38	13.78

[1] VALUE LINE® forecasts of average return on tangible equity and dividend payout ratios for the period 1978 through 1980 were extracted from the thirteen weeks of VALUE LINE® publications ending February 22, 1976. Estimated year-end 1975 tangible book values and prices as of February 27, 1976 were used to construct normalized price/earnings ratios and expected returns. Copies of the estimates and our calculations of anticipated returns may be obtained by writing Mr. Gerald W. Bollman, Assistant Vice President, Crum & Forster Insurance Companies, P. O. Box 2387, Morristown, New Jersey 07960. His comments and technical assistance were essential to the preparation of this article.

[2] It is less surprising that there is a strong negative correlation between projected pre-tax yield and price/earnings ratios.

Slope:	−3.03
Intercept:	25.64
Coefficient Of Determination:	0.71

SECURITY
SELECTION
AND ACTIVE
PORTFOLIO
MANAGEMENT

How to beat those index funds

Use the Markowitz method to find efficient portfolios — and it's not that complicated.

Donald S. Shannon, Keith H. Johnson, and Gregory L. Neal

The threatening popularity of Index Funds is stirring up its share of commentary. Two notable illustrations are the lengthy feature article in the June, 1976 issue of *Fortune* describing the advent of this investment strategy,[1] and David Babson's article in the Spring, 1976 issue of this Journal comparing the superior performance of his firm's twelve growth stocks to the S & P 500.[2]

We agree with the thrust of Mr. Babson's comments. The towel should *not* be thrown in. It *is* possible to beat the S & P 500. Indeed, in this paper, we will describe the remarkable track record of a portfolio allocation strategy that nearly always beats the S & P Index.

1. Footnotes appear at the end of the article.

This strategy was first proposed by Harry Markowitz during the 1950s.[3] His work provided the impetus for the capital asset pricing model, which continues to preoccupy academic theorists. Surprisingly, however, relatively little attention has been given to the pragmatic evaluation of his portfolio selection strategy in a real-world setting. A question that has seldom been asked is, "How well would a portfolio have performed if it had been invested in accordance with the ideas proposed by Markowitz?"[4]

This lack of attention to the Markowitz strategy makes some sense when considered in the context of the random walk theory and the efficient market hypothesis. Both of these notions generally suggest that it is fruitless to attempt to beat the market. Comments such as *"any* diversified portfolio whose composite securities represent the spectrum of risk available in the market is likely to provide an adequate proxy for the market portfolio"[5] appear to be accepted by the majority. Thus, one method of allocating money across investments is viewed as being as good as another.

THE MARKOWITZ STRATEGY

The Markowitz strategy is based on a computer algorithm — or step-by-step set of rules for solving a problem — that has as its objective the identification of allocation schemes to produce the greatest expected portfolio rate of return for any particular level of risk. The desired level can be varied, resulting in new weighting schemes and new expected portfolio returns. The group of solutions associated with a variety of desired risk levels is referred to as the set of "efficient" portfolios. Again, each efficient portfolio has the characteristic of promising the maximum expected return for the level of risk or, conversely, promising the minimum risk for the particular return desired.

The most desirable of the efficient portfolios is the one offering the largest "premium" per unit of risk undertaken. The premium in this case is the portfolio

SECURITY
SELECTION
AND ACTIVE
PORTFOLIO
MANAGEMENT

rate of return expected in excess of the "riskless" rate obtainable by investment in U.S. Government securities. (In the event that the risk of this particular portfolio is judged to be excessive, it can be offset by investing a portion of the funds in the fixed securities.)

The noteworthy aspect of the Markowitz strategy is its strong reliance on correlation among securities — how their rates of return interact with one another over time. The variance of the rate of return of a portfolio of securities is a function of the rates of return of the individual securities, *and* of the correlations among these individual rates of return. When using the Markowitz algorithm, stocks with rates of return that are unrelated (zero correlation), or move in opposition to one another (negative correlation), are more likely to appear in a selected portfolio than stocks with positively correlated rates of return.

In the Markowitz algorithm, as stocks with low or negatively correlated rates of return are brought into the selected portfolio for purposes of reducing the overall portfolio variance, the final result is usually to *increase* the expected portfolio return by permitting a greater proportion of funds to be allocated to stocks with high expected returns.

DATA USED

The presumed inputs to the Markowitz model are intended to be expectations or forecasts. The inputs to the model that must be supplied by the portfolio manager include: the expected rates of return for each security, the variance of each security, and all pairwise covariances or correlations. All of these inputs are intended to pertain to events expected to occur during the *next* holding period. As with any investment scheme, the outcome is dependent to some extent on the accuracy of the forecasts employed. However, the results described in this paper do *not* stem from any superior ability to forecast rates of return. Each time the Markowitz algorithm was used, the expected rates of return for the next quarter were derived by taking simple arithmetic averages of historical quarterly rates of return in place of judgmental forecasts. Similarly, the variances and correlations of the rates of return were also derived from historical data.

More specifically, the data represent 345 companies included in the S & P 500 Index for which consecutive quarterly price and dividend data could be located on the Compustat Data Tapes through 1975. Using random selection without replacement, these 345 securities were broken down into six groups of fifty and one group of 45 companies. For each company in each group the first step consisted of calculating the quarterly rates of return (including capital gains and dividend yields).

The first allocation decision for each of the seven separate samples was presumed to have been made at the end of the second quarter of 1965. Inputs derived from data up to the end of the *second* quarter of 1965 were fed into the Markowitz algorithm and the solution weights were recorded. These weights represent the proportion of the portfolio funds that should be invested in each security throughout the *third* quarter of 1965.[6]

The selection procedure involves calculating the expected return for each security (in our case, the mean of the returns over past periods), the variance of each (again, based on past experience in this case), and, finally, the covariance of each security with each of the others in its group. With this as input, the computer algorithm selects those portfolios that are most efficient.

The Appendix to this article provides a simplified example, worked out arithmetically, showing how the investor would actually use this procedure. Consequently, we suggest that you turn to the Appendix for edification if the following algebra is unclear. It is less awesome than it appears, however, as it simply describes in general terms the procedure used to form a portfolio on July 1, 1965 that used seven years (28 quarters) of historical data to provide the necessary

SECURITY
SELECTION
AND ACTIVE
PORTFOLIO
MANAGEMENT

expectational inputs. These are the calculations that you would perform:

$$\bar{R}_i = \text{expected return for security i}$$

$$= \sum_{j=0}^{27} r_{i,t-j}/28. \text{ and } t = \text{second quarter, 1965}$$

$$V(R_i) = \text{variance of the return on security i}$$

$$= \sum_{j=0}^{27} (r_{i,t-j} - \bar{R}_i)^2/28.$$

$$C(R_i, R_k) = \text{covariance of returns between security i and k}$$

$$= \sum_{j=0}^{27} (r_{i,t-j} - \bar{R}_i)(r_{k,t-j} - \bar{R}_k)/28.$$

The general form of the model is then given by:

$$\text{Max } \lambda \sum_{i}^{50} w_i \bar{R}_i - \sum_{i}^{50} w_i^2 V(R) - \sum_{i=j}^{50} \sum_{j}^{50} w_i w_j C(R_i, R_j)$$

$$\text{subject to } \sum_{i}^{50} w_i = 1$$

$$\text{all} \quad w_i \geq 0$$

where w_i represents the proportion of assets to be invested in security i. By letting λ vary from 0 to infinity, the entire efficient frontier can be determined — i.e., those values for w_i that give the maximum expected portfolio return for a given level of risk (or minimum risk for a specified expected return). This efficient frontier is depicted as the curve AA' in Figure 1.

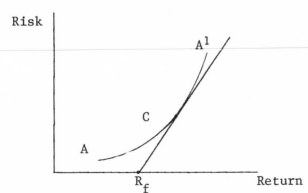

If one allows for a risk-free rate of return, R_f,

(say the return on 90-day T-bills), then the point of tangency depicted by the line from R_f tangent to the frontier at C yields the optimal tangency portfolio. These investment proportions or weights, w_i, at point C represent the proportion of the portfolio funds that should be invested in each security throughout the *third* quarter of 1965. Applying these weights to the actual rates of return for the third quarter of 1965 produces the portfolio rate of return that would have been *realized* if the Markowitz strategy had been utilized during that quarter. In this manner, realized portfolio returns were determined for each of the seven samples, for the 42 quarters beginning with the third quarter of 1965 (a total of 294 portfolios). The allocation decision made at the beginning of each quarter was based on data inputs that included the rates of return calculated from the immediately preceding quarter. Thus, no superior forecasting ability was presumed.

RESULTS

A summary of the results is given in Table 1. It is interesting to note that the rate of return (including

TABLE 1

RESULTS OF INVESTMENT IN S. & P. 500, T-BILLS, AND SEVEN SEPARATE PORTFOLIOS REALLOCATED

QUARTERLY, USING THE MARKOWITZ ALGORITHM – FROM THIRD QUARTER 1965 THROUGH 1975

	S & P 500	T-Bills	1	2	3	4	5	6	7
Average quarterly rate of return	1.44%	1.39%	3.62%	3.44%	1.94%	3.28%	1.46%	1.88%	1.22%
Standard Deviation	8.99%	–	11.57%	12.25%	11.76%	16.77%	9.94%	12.63%	13.06%
Premium per unit of risk	0.0056%	–	0.19%	0.17%	0.05%	0.11%	0.00%	0.04%	(neg)
Correlation with S & P 500	–	–	-0.25%	+0.80	+0.80	+0.81	+0.82	+0.72	+0.76	+0.87
Portfolio Beta	–	–	1.11	1.09	1.05	1.54	0.80	1.07	1.26

SECURITY
SELECTION
AND ACTIVE
PORTFOLIO
MANAGEMENT

dividend yield) for the S & P 500 was not a formidable hurdle. For the 42 quarters from mid-1965 through 1975, the quarterly rate of return averaged only 1.44%, only slightly more than the rate of 1.39% which could have been earned by investing in U.S. Treasury bills.

This is particularly interesting in light of the additional uncertainty associated with investment in the S & P 500 relative to the U.S. Treasury bills.

All but one of the seven groups selected by means of the Markowitz algorithm outperformed the S & P 500. Their average quarterly rates of return were as much as 250% as large as the quarterly rate of return on the S & P Index. This is quite an accomplishment in that the S & P Index return represents a "buy-and-hold" strategy and is not penalized for transactions costs whereas the Markowitz strategy necessitated trading every quarter, thus incurring considerable transactions costs.[7]

In addition to the rate of return measure, the premium per unit of risk was calculated for the rates of return on each of the seven groups and the S & P Index. The premium per unit of risk is calculated by

$$\text{Premium} = \frac{\text{Avg. Portfolio R.O.R.} - \text{Avg. T-Bill Rate}}{\text{Standard deviation of Portfolio R. O. R.}}$$

This measure was negligible for the S & P Index. Here again, all but one of the seven groups essentially equaled or outperformed the S & P 500.[8]

An additional analysis was made in an attempt to evaluate the desirability of the Markowitz strategy. First, the realized quarterly geometric mean returns were calculated for the eight stock groupings (six groups of fifty stocks, one group of 45, and the S & P 500 Index) over every possible consecutive combination of quarters from mid-1965 through 1975. The S & P 500 geometric mean was deducted from the comparable average of the seven geometric means of the samples. A part of the results is shown in Table 2. In the complete table there were 903 cells. Of these 903 possibilities, 747 were positive, indicating that in 83% of the cases the average of the seven rates of return from the Markowitz strategy outperformed the S & P Index.

Finally, the Treynor Performance Index was

TABLE 2

DIFFERENCES IN QUARTERLY GEOMETRIC MEAN PERCENTAGE RETURNS

FOR THE AVERAGE OF THE SEVEN SAMPLES MINUS THE S .& P. 500

(PARTIAL TABLE)

From Beginning of Quarter	To end of Quarter					
	1965 3	1965 4	1966 1	...	1975 3	1975 4
1965 3	+2.37	+0.85	+0.52	...	+0.73	+0.61
1965 4		−0.52	−0.28	...	+0.69	+0.57
1966 1			−0.02	...	+0.72	+0.60
.					.	.
.					.	.
.					.	.
1975 2					+3.09	+0.53
1975 3					+2.46	−0.85
1975 4						−4.29

calculated for each of the eight strategies over every possible combination of ten or more quarters from mid-1965 through 1975.[9] Using this criterion, the seven samples were compared to the S & P 500. Partial results are given in Table 3. In the complete table there were 561 cells, which when multiplied by seven would give a maximum total score of 3927. The actual total was 2664, which indicates that the Treynor Performance Index would have rated the Markowitz portfolios as being superior 68% of the time.

NOT A BAD SYSTEM FOR BEATING THE MARKET

Concisely put, we like the odds. We think the Markowitz allocation strategy warrants a close look. We should emphasize that it is not a selection strategy, but an allocation technique. You have control over selecting the securities that are the inputs to the model. (We used random selection.) The Markowitz strategy simply indicates what your investment proportions in each security should be to maximize return for a given level of risk. Also, you have the freedom to provide your own expectations as to returns and/or variability and/or covariability. We chose to be naive

212

SECURITY
SELECTION
AND ACTIVE
PORTFOLIO
MANAGEMENT

TABLE 3

NUMBER OF TIMES THE TREYNOR PERFORMANCE INDEX FOR THE SAMPLES

EXCEEDED THE SAME MEASURE APPLIED TO THE S. & P. 500 INDEX[a]
(PARTIAL TABLE)

From Beginning of Quarter	To end of Quarter					
	1967 4	1968 1	1968 2	...	1975 3	1975 4
1965 3	2	2	4	...	6	6
1965 4		2	4	...	5	5
1966 1			4	...	6	5
.					.	.
.					.	.
.					.	.
1973 2					6	5
1973 3						6

[a] maximum is 7.

by using random selection and past averages to represent our expectations.

One criticism of using the Markowitz strategy sometimes voiced is that too few securities are selected (in our case, from five to twenty). Managers of large funds thus may have difficulties with the "prudent man" rule. A simple alternative might be to develop several Markowitz portfolios, as we did here, and invest some of the funds in each portfolio. With our data, if we allocate 1/7 of our investment to each of the seven portfolios, our average return is 2.41% and the standard deviation is 10.80% which compares quite favorably to the index performance.

From a theoretical perspective, these results presented here pose an intriguing question. Can the S & P 500 really be used as a proxy for the "market portfolio"?

[1] A. F. Ehrbar, "Index Funds — an Idea Whose Time is Coming," *Fortune,* June, 1976, pp. 145-154.

[2] David L. Babson, "Index Funds: Why Throw in the Towel?," *Journal of Portfolio Management,* Spring, 1976, pp. 53-55.

[3] Harry Markowitz, "Portfolio Selection," *Journal of Finance,* March, 1952, pp. 77-91.

[4] For some information on this subject see: K. H. Johnson and D. S. Shannon, "A Note on Diversification and the Reduction of Dispersion," *The Journal of Financial Economics,* December, 1974; and D. S. Shannon and K. H. Johnson, "Portfolio Maintenance Strategies Revisited," *The Atlantic Economic Journal,* April, 1975.

[5] Eugene F. Fama, "Risk and the Evaluation of Pension Fund Portfolio Performance," in *Modern Developments in Investment Management: A Book of Readings,* edited by James Lorie and Richard Brealey (New York, N.Y.: Praeger Publishers, 1972), p. 494.

[6] The weights were selected from the "most desirable" of the efficient portfolios; that is, the efficient portfolio offering the largest "premium" per unit of risk. In this regard, the riskless rate used was 1.29%, the average quarterly rate of return on U.S. Treasury bills from 1963 through 1975.

[7] Our transactions costs were estimated by using the coefficient of agreement from one period to the next which is calculated as $J = 1 - \Sigma \mid w_{it} - w_{it-1} \mid /2$. This coefficient has a maximum value of 1 if all the investment proportions are exactly the same and a value of 0 if there was a complete turnover in the portfolio. Assuming transactions changes to be at the rate of .5% of the value of the portfolio churned, the approximation for these charges is then $(1-J) \times 2 \times .5$ which is deducted from the return on the portfolio for each period. Without transactions costs, the average returns for the seven portfolios are: 3.98%, 3.86%, 2.38%, 3.72%, 2.15%, 2.32%, and 1.65%.

[8] Some readers might be interested to note that these results (from the seven groups) were achieved with portfolios which were correlated +.81 with the S & P Index.

[9] J. L. Treynor, "How to Rate Management of Investment Funds," *Harvard Business Review,* January-February, 1965, pp. 63-75.

APPENDIX

The purpose of this appendix is to present a simple illustration of the Markowitz allocation technique. In this connection, Exhibit I presents some hypothetical rates of return for four stocks, A,B,C, and D over the last four years. Exhibit II includes four possible ways one might have allocated his money across these four stocks. Exhibit III in-

214
SECURITY
SELECTION
AND ACTIVE
PORTFOLIO
MANAGEMENT

cludes the portfolio yields that would have been earned if each of the allocation schemes suggested in Exhibit II had been implemented.

Exhibit I -- Rates of Return				
	Stocks			
Year	A	B	C	D
1976	9%	13%	21%	15%
1975	9%	17%	15%	10%
1974	11%	13%	21%	13%
1973	11%	17%	23%	12%

Exhibit II -- Allocation Schemes				
	Proportion invested in:			
Scheme	A	B	C	D
1	.2500	.2500	.2500	.2500
2	0	.4938	.0854	.4208
3	0	.5097	.2928	.1975
4	.1360	.4140	0	.4500

Before interpreting Exhibit III, it might be instructive to trace its construction from Exhibits I and II. The 15.342% portfolio rate of return earned when Scheme 3 is used in the year 1974 comes from applying the allocation proportions specified in Exhibit II to the individual returns earned during 1974, i.e.:

$$15.342\% = 0\,(11\%) + .5097\,(13\%) + .2928\,(21\%) + .1975\,(13\%).$$

Exhibit III -- Portfolio Rates of Return resulting from various allocation schemes				
	Allocation Scheme			
Year	1	2	3	4
1976	14.500%	14.525%	15.737%	13.356%
1975	12.750%	13.884%	15.032%	12.762%
1974	14.500%	13.683%	15.342%	12.728%
1973	15.750%	15.408%	17.769%	13.934%
Average	14.375%	14.375%	15.970%	13.195%
Variance	1.141	.452	1.141	.244
Standard Deviation	1.068	.672	1.068	.494
Premium per unit of risk	7.842	12.463	9.335	14.570

The averages in Exhibit III are the simple average portfolio rates of return for the four years. The variances are calculated by taking the average of the squares of the annual deviations from the four year means. For example, for Scheme 3,

$$1.141 = [(15.737 - 15.970)^2 + (15.032 - 15.970)^2 + (15.342 - 15.970)^2 + (17.769 - 15.970)^2]/4.$$

The standard deviation is the square root of the variance. Finally, the premium is a measure of the return, in excess of the riskless rate of 6.00%, per unit of standard deviation. Again, for Scheme 3:

$$9.335 = (15.970 - 6.000)/1.068.$$

For expository purposes in the text of the article, we derived expectations about next period's rates of return from past experience. This is *not* a requirement for the actual implementation of the model. A variety of ways are available for forming expectations, including seat-of-the-pants judgment, and other less sophisticated techniques. Nevertheless, the sense of the model is most efficiently conveyed if one temporarily accepts the notion that an unmodified condensation of past experience will provide the best guess of what will happen next period.

Given this interpretation, the averages in Exhibit III can be viewed as the expected portfolio returns over the next period, i.e., during 1977. Similarly, the standard deviations can be viewed as measures of uncertainty associated with each expected portfolio return.

Notice that the first scheme implies equal allocation across the four stocks and results in an expected return of 14.375% and a standard deviation of 1.068%. This naive allocation method is inferior to Schemes 2 and 3. The second scheme results in the same average portfolio return but reduces uncertainty to a standard deviation of .672%, even though only three stocks are considered. The third allocation scheme maintains the same level of uncertainty (as the first) but results in the higher expected return of 15.970%.

Portfolio 2 is "efficient," since no scheme can be found that will produce an average return greater than 14.375% while maintaining a standard deviation of .672%. Likewise, no scheme can be found that will produce a standard deviation of less than .672% while maintaining the average at 14.375%. Similar statements can be made about "efficient" portfolio 3.

This, in a nutshell, is what the Markowitz model is all about. The mathematical technique used to solve the problem is called quadratic programming. This technique finds all the efficient allocation schemes that exist for any specified data set.

Normally, we use statistics pertaining to individual stocks as the inputs to computer quadratic programming algorithms developed to select efficient portfolios. That is precisely what the algebra in the article proper is designed to do. It shows how we proceed from the calculation of the average rates of return for each available security for the period under consideration to the calculation of the variances of each and then to the covariance of each to the others. What results is that combination where we weight each security in such a way that we have maximized return for the portfolio as a whole at the same time that we have minimized its total variance.

We can work out this procedure arithmetically by using the individual stock statistics in Exhibit IV, where we see the expected return for each stock (simple arithmetic means of the four years' results shown in Exhibit I), the variance for each (the average of the squares of the annual deviations from the four-year means), the standard deviation for each (the square root of the variances), and then the covariance of each stock with the other three (or two, as the case may be).

Statistic	Stock			
	A	B	C	D
Expected return	10%	15%	20%	12.5%
Variance	1	4	9	3.25
Standard deviation	1	2	3	1.803
Covariance with A		0	2	0
Covariance with B			-2	-3
Covariance with C				3.5
Correlation with A		0	.67	0
Correlation with B			-.33	-.83
Correlation with C				.65

Exhibit IV -- Summary of statistics describing the future returns on stocks A,B,C & D

We calculate the covariance by multiplying the correlation coefficients by the related standard deviations. For example, to find the covariance of stocks B and C, we multiply their correlation coefficient of −.33 by their respective standard deviations (2)(3) to produce the result of −2. This statistic provides a measure of the extent to which the two rates of return move together over time; a major objective of the exercise is to produce portfolios that minimize this characteristic.

If, now, we wish to develop the expected return for a

portfolio constructed in accordance with Scheme 3 in Exhibit II, we would multiply the expected return for each security by the weighting scheme assumed in this example; thus:

$$.5097 \, (15\%) + .2928 \, (20\%) + .1975 \, (12.5\%) = 15.970\%$$

In order to determine the efficiency of this portfolio, however, we must also know its variance, which will obviously be a function of both the variances of its individual components and their respective covariances. In accordance with the general form of the model described algebraically in the main text of the article, we first take the sum of the products of the variance for each security times the square of its weight in the portfolio, and then add to that the sum of each of the weights multiplied by the weight of each of the others times twice their respective covariance.

That sounds complicated in words, but our arithmetic should make it clear enough. All the numbers in the calculation come from Exhibits II and IV:

$$.5097^2 \, (4) + .2928^2 \, (9) + .1975^2 \, (3.25)$$
$$+ \, 2 \, (.5097) \, (.2928) \, (-2) + 2 \, (.5097) \, (.1975) \, (-3)$$
$$+ \, 2 \, (.2928) \, (.1975) \, (3.5)$$
$$= 1.141$$

Thus, once we have the expected returns, variances, and covariances for each of the individual securities under consideration for the portfolio, we can readily calculate the rates of return and variances for any combination of them taken together. The purpose of the quadratic programming algorithm is to find those proportions, or schemes, that produce efficient portfolios.

Optimal portfolios from simple ranking devices

The math here is less formidable than it appears; the solutions can be extraordinarily helpful in finding efficient portfolios.

Edwin J. Elton, Martin J. Gruber, and Manfred W. Padberg

Modern portfolio analysis dates from Markowitz' [9 and 10] pioneering article published in 1952 and subsequent book. While the concept of modern portfolio analysis has been around for a quarter of a century, the implementation of modern portfolio analysis has been at best slow, and some would say nonexistent. There are two potential reasons for this lack of implementation: the size and nature of input requirements and the complexity and nonintuitive nature of the computational procedure.

The first problem that hindered implementation was the need to estimate a huge number of expected returns, standard deviations of returns, and either covariances or correlation coefficients. While it seemed possible for analysts to estimate expected returns and possibly standard deviation of returns, the number and difficulty of estimating covariances made analyst estimation impossible. Furthermore, historical covariances were poor estimates of future covariances. To overcome this problem, a number of models were developed which, when fitted on historical data, produced good estimates of future covariances. The best known of these is the single index or beta model, which assumes that the source of joint movement of securities comes about because of a common response to market movements. Other examples of models that can be used to estimate the covariance structure fall into two categories:

1. multi-index models, which assume firms move together because of a combination of economy-wide influences and industry-wide influences, and
2. models that employ an average of past correlation relationships, either on an economy-wide or an industry-wide basis.

Elton and Gruber [1] have examined these alternative models, compared their performances, and have shown them to be reasonable ways of estimating covariance structures. Thus, the first problem in implementing modern portfolio theory is no longer a bottleneck to its use. The second problem that hindered implementation was the necessity to solve a quadratic programming problem in order to determine an optimal portfolio.

Portfolio selection has always been a top management job. Few portfolio managers are willing to turn over their job to a black box. What increases the uneasiness of managers still more is that one could not predict which securities would be included in any optimum solution to the quadratic programming problem. Securities are included because they have desirable risk-return characteristics. Anyone who has tried to implement portfolio theory, however, knows that one just can't predict ahead of time which securities will be included and why. Furthermore, when the problem is solved, there are always securities that are included in the portfolio that are a source of surprise and puzzlement to both the security analyst and portfolio manager.

220
SECURITY
SELECTION
AND ACTIVE
PORTFOLIO
MANAGEMENT

HOW TO MAKE LIFE SIMPLER

In a series of papers [2], [3], [4], [5], and [6], we have shown that, if one is willing to make the assumptions underlying any of the existing models for forecasting covariances, then a *simple ranking device* exists that one can use to determine the optimal portfolio. In fact, the portfolio selected by any of these simple ranking devices is exactly the same portfolio that would be produced by solving the appropriate quadratic programming problem. In addition, by using the ranking devices, the computations necessary to find an optimal portfolio are simplified to the point where the use of a computer is no longer necessary and the criteria that make a stock desirable or undesirable are easy to understand and relate to.

Even if a portfolio manager is unwilling to utilize the simple ranking device for selecting his optimal portfolio, he can still use the ranking device to see which securities in his portfolio would *not* be included if he had used modern portfolio theory.

In this paper we will only present the simple ranking device that results from the assumptions underlying the single index or beta model. We have chosen this model because it is the one that is most familiar to practising portfolio managers.

The simple ranking devices that result from making the assumptions underlying other models for forecasting the covariance structure are found in Elton, Gruber and Padberg [2], [3], [4],]5], and [6]. While the proofs that these ranking devices do indeed produce optimal portfolios are mathematically challenging, the simple ranking devices are themselves easily understood. Thus, there is no remaining justification for the portfolio manager not to utilize modern portfolio analysis in his decision making process.

We are going to proceed with our analysis as follows. We will first assert the ranking criteria that can be used to order stocks for selection for the optimal portfolio. We will give an intuitive explanation for these ranking criteria. We will then present the technique for employing this ranking device to form an optimum portfolio, along with a logical explanation for why it works. After presenting the criteria for the composition of an optimal portfolio, we will demonstrate its use with a simple example. Finally, we will show how rules can be devised for the revision of an optimal portfolio as new securities enter the analyst's decision set.

THE FORMATION OF OPTIMAL PORTFOLIOS

The calculation of optimal portfolios would be greatly facilitated, and the ability of practicing security analysts and portfolio managers to relate to the construction of optimal portfolios greatly enhanced, if there were a single number that measured the desirability of including a stock in the optimal portfolio. If one is willing to accept the standard form of the single index or beta model as describing the comovement between securities, such a number exists. In this case, the desirability of any stock is directly related to its excess return to beta ratio. Excess return is the difference between the expected returns on the stock and the riskless rate of interest such as the rate on a Treasury bill. The excess return to beta ratio measures the additional return on a security, beyond that offered by a riskless asset, per unit of non-diversifiable risk.

The form of this ratio should lead to its easy interpretation and acceptance by security analysts and portfolio managers, for they are used to thinking in terms of the relationship between potential rewards and risk. In addition, Treynor [11] has argued for the use of this same ratio as a measure of portfolio performance. He suggests ranking portfolios by their excess return to beta ratio, with the best portfolio being the one with the highest ratio. It is intuitively appealing to rank stocks by the same criteria as one uses to rank portfolios, and in fact it has been shown (see [2]) that it is mathematically correct to do so.

More formally, the index we use to rank stocks is "Excess return to Beta" or $(\bar{R}_i - R_F)/\beta_i$ where,

$\bar{R}_i$ = the expected return on stock i

R_F = the return on a riskless asset

β_i = the expected change in the rate of return on stock i associated with a 1% change in the market return.

If stocks are ranked by excess return to beta (from highest to lowest) the ranking represents the desirability of any stock's inclusion in a portfolio. In other words, if a stock with a particular ratio of $(\bar{R}_i - R_F)/\beta_i$ is included in an optimal portfolio, all stocks with a higher ratio will also be included. On the other hand, if a stock with a particular $(\bar{R}_i - R_F)/\beta_i$ is excluded from an optimal portfolio, all stocks with lower ratios will be excluded (or if short selling is allowed, sold short). This means that there is a unique cut-off rate, such that all stocks with higher ratios of $(\bar{R}_i - R_F)/\beta_i$ will be included and all stock with lower ratios excluded. We will call this cut-off rate C*.

In this paper we will concern ourselves with the case where short sales are not allowed, for this is the relevant case for most financial institutions. For an extension to the case where short selling is permitted, the interested reader should refer to [2].

The rules for determining which stocks are included in the optimum portfolio are as follows:
1. Find the "excess return to beta" ratio for each stock under consideration; rank from highest to lowest.
2. The optimum portfolio consists of investing in all stocks for which $(\bar{R}_i - R_F)/\beta_i$ is greater than a particular cut-off point C*. Shortly, we will define C* and interpret its economic significance.

The previous procedure is extremely simple. Once C* has been determined, the securities to be included can be selected by inspection. Furthermore, the amount to invest in each security is equally simple to determine and will be discussed shortly.

RANKING SECURITIES

In Tables 1 and 2 we present an example that

illustrates this procedure.

Table 1 contains the data necessary to apply our simple ranking device to determine an optimal portfolio. It is the normal output generated from a single index or beta model, plus the ratio of excess return to beta. This same data could alternatively be

Table 1. Data Required to Determine Optimal Portfolio $R_F=5$

1	2	3	4	5	6
Security No. i	Mean Return $\overline{R}_i$	Excess Return $\overline{R}_i - R_F$	Beta β_i	Unsystematic Risk $\sigma^2_{\varepsilon_i}$	Excess Return Over Beta $\frac{\overline{R}_i - R_F}{\beta_i}$
1	15	10	1	50	10
2	17	12	1.5	40	8
3	12	7	1	20	7
4	17	12	2	10	6
5	11	6	1	40	6
6	11	6	1.5	30	4
7	11	6	2	40	3
8	7	2	.8	16	2.5
9	7	2	1	20	2
10	5.6	.6	.6	6	1.0

generated by analysts' subjective estimates. There are ten securities in the tables. For the readers' convenience, we have already ranked the securities according to $(\overline{R}_i - R_F)/\beta_i$ and have used numbers that make the calculations easy to follow. The application of rule 2 involves the comparison of $(\overline{R}_i - R_F)/\beta_i$ with C^*. Accept that $C^* = 5.45$ for the moment; we will shortly present a procedure for its calculation. Examining Table 1 shows that for securities 1 to 5 $(\overline{R}_i - R_F)/\beta_i$ is greater than C^* while for security 6 it is less than C^*. Hence, an optimal portfolio consists of securities 1 to 5.

SETTING THE CUTOFF RATE (C*)

As discussed earlier, C^* is the cut-off rate. All securities whose excess return to risk ratio are above the cut-off rate are selected and all whose ratios are below are rejected. The value of C^* depends on the characteristics of the securities that belong in the optimum portfolio. To determine C^* it is necessary to calculate its value as if there were different numbers of securities in the optimum portfolio.

Since securities are ranked from highest excess return to beta to lowest, we know that if a particular security belongs in the optimal portfolio, all higher ranked securities also belong in the optimal portfolio. We proceed to calculate values of a variable C_i (the procedure is outlined below) as if the first ranked securities were in the optimal portfolio ($i = 1$), and second ranked and the first ranked securities were in the optimal portfolio ($i = 2$), etc. These C_i are candidates for C^*. We know we have found the optimum C_i that is C^*, when all securities used in the calculation of C_i have excess returns to beta above C_i, and all securities not used to calculate C_i have excess return to betas below C_i. For example, column 7 of Table 2 shows the C_i for alternative values of i. Examining the table shows that C_5 is the only value of C_i for which all se-

1	2	3	4	5	6	7
Security No. i	$(\bar{R}_i - R_F)/\beta_i$	$\dfrac{(R_i - R_F)\beta_i}{\sigma_{\epsilon_i}^2}$	$\dfrac{\beta_i^2}{\sigma_{\epsilon_i}^2}$	$\displaystyle\sum_{i=1}^{i} \dfrac{(\bar{R}_i - R_F)\beta_i}{\sigma_{\epsilon_i}^2}$	$\displaystyle\sum_{j=1}^{i} \dfrac{\beta_i^2}{\sigma_{\epsilon_i}^2}$	C_i
1	10	2/10	2/100	2/10	2/100	1.67
2	8	4.5/10	5.625/100	6.5/10	7.625/100	3.69
3	7	3.5/10	5/100	10/10	12.625/100	4.42
4	6	24/10	40/100	34/10	52.625/100	5.43
5	6	1.5/10	2.5/100	35.5/10	55.125/100	5.45
6	4	3/10	7.5/100	38.5/10	62.625/100	5.30
7	3	3/10	10/100	41.5/10	72.625/100	5.02
8	2.5	1/10	4/100	42.5/10	76.625/100	4.91
9	2.0	1/10	5/100	43.5/10	81.625/100	4.75
10	1.0	.6/10	6/100	44.1/10	87.625/100	4.52

Table 2. Calculations for Determining an Optimum Portfolio with $\sigma_m^2 = 10$

curities used in the calculation of i have a ratio of excess return to beta above C_i, and all securities not used in the calculation of C_i have an excess return to beta ratio below C_i. Hence $C^* = C_5 = 5.45$.

CALCULATING THE CUT-OFF RATE C*

Recall that stocks are ranked by excess return

to risk from highest to lowest. For a portfolio of i stocks, C_i is

$$C_i = \frac{\sigma_m^2 \left(\sum_{j=1}^{i} \frac{(\bar{R}_j - R_F)\beta_j}{\sigma_{\epsilon j}^2} \right)}{1 + \sigma_m^2 \sum_{j=1}^{i} \frac{\beta_j^2}{\sigma_{\epsilon j}^2}} \qquad (1)$$

where:

σ_m^2 = the variance in the market index

$\sigma_{\epsilon j}^2$ = the variance of a stock's movement that is not associated with the movement of the market index. This is usually referred to as a stock's non-systematic risk.

This looks horrible. But a moment's reflection combined with a peek at the following example will show that it is not as hard to compute as it looks. While equation (1) is the form that should actually be used to compute C_i, this expression can be stated in a mathematically equivalent way that clarifies the meaning of C_i.

$$C_i = \frac{\beta_{ip}(\bar{R}_p - R_F)}{\beta_i} \qquad (2)$$

where

(1) β_{ip} = the expected change in the rate of return on stock i associated with a 1% change in the return on the optimal portfolio.

(2) all other terms as before.

β_{ip} and $\bar{R}_p$ are, of course, not known until the optimal portfolio is determined. Hence, equation (2) could not be used to actually determine the optimum portfolio; rather, equation (1) must be used. However, this expression for C_i is useful in interpreting the economic significance of our procedure. Recall that securities are added to the portfolio as long as

$$\frac{\bar{R}_i - R_F}{\beta_i} > C_i$$

Rearranging and substituting in equation (2) yields

$$(\bar{R}_i - R_F) > B_{ip}(\bar{R}_p - R_F)$$

The right hand side is nothing more than the

expected excess return on a particular stock based solely on the expected performance of the optimum portfolio. The term on the left hand side is the security analyst's estimate of the expected excess return on the individual stock. Thus if the analysis of a particular stock leads the portfolio manager to believe that it will perform better than would be expected based on its relationship to the optimal portfolio, it should be added to the portfolio.

Now let us look at how (1) can be used to determine the value of C_i for our example. While equation (1) might look complex, the ease with which it can be calculated is demonstrated by Table 2. Table 2 presents the intermediate calculations necessary to determine equation (1).

Let's work through the intermediate calculations shown in Table 2 and find the value for C_i for the first security in our list of securities. The numerator of equation (1) is

$$\sigma^2_m \sum_{j=1}^{i} \frac{(\bar{R}_j - R_F)\beta_j}{\sigma^2_{\epsilon_j}}.$$

Column 3 of Table 2 presents the value of

$$\frac{(\bar{R}_j - R_F)\beta_j}{\sigma^2_{\epsilon_j}}$$

for each security. This is necessary in order to determine the summation. For example, for the first security using the values shown in Table 1, it is

$$\frac{(15\text{-}5)}{50} = \frac{2}{10}.$$

Column 5 gives the value of the summation, or the running cumulative total of column 3. For the first security $i = 1$ and

$$\sum_{j=1}^{i} \frac{(\bar{R}_j - R_F)\beta_j}{\sigma^2_{\epsilon_j}} = \frac{(\bar{R}_1 - R_F)\beta_1}{\sigma^2_{\epsilon_1}}.$$

Thus column 5 of Table 2 is the same as column 3 for

security 1. The last term in the denominator of expression 1 is

$$\sum_{j=1}^{i} \frac{\beta^2_j}{\sigma^2_{\epsilon_j}}$$

which, since $i = 1$ for the first security, it is simply

$$\frac{\beta^2_1}{\sigma^2_{\epsilon_1}} = \frac{(1)^2}{50} = \frac{2}{100}.$$

This result is shown in column 4 and cumulated in column 6. We can now put these terms together to find C_1. Remembering that $\sigma_m^2 = 10$,

$$C_1 = \frac{\sigma_m^2 \left(\sum_{j=1}^{i} \frac{(\bar{R}_j - R_F)\beta_j}{\sigma^2_{\epsilon j}} \right)}{1 + \sigma_m^2 \sum_{j=1}^{i} \frac{\beta^2_j}{\sigma^2_{\epsilon_j}}} = \frac{\sigma^2_m (\text{column 5})}{1 + \sigma^2_m (\text{column 6})}$$

$$= \frac{10 \left(\frac{2}{10} \right)}{1 + 10 \left(\frac{2}{100} \right)} = 1.67$$

Let's now follow through the calculations for security 2 $(i = 2)$. Column 3 is found to be

$$\frac{(17 - 5)1.5}{40} = \frac{4.5}{10}.$$

Now column 5 is the sum of column 3 for security 1 and security 2 or

$$\frac{2}{10} + \frac{4.5}{10} = \frac{6.5}{10}.$$

Column 4 is

$$\frac{(1.5)^2}{40} = \frac{5.625}{100}.$$

228

SECURITY
SELECTION
AND ACTIVE
PORTFOLIO
MANAGEMENT

Column 6 is the sum of column 4 for security 1 and 2 or

$$\frac{2}{100} + \frac{5.625}{100} = \frac{7.625}{100}.$$

We can now find C_2 as

$$C_2 = \frac{\sigma_m^2 \text{ (column 5)}}{1 + \sigma_m^2 \text{ (column 6)}} = \frac{10\dfrac{6.5}{10}}{1 + 10\dfrac{7.625}{100}} = 3.68.$$

Proceeding in the same fashion we can find all the C_i's.

CONSTRUCTING THE OPTIMAL PORTFOLIO

Once the securities that are contained in the optimum portfolio are determined, we then have to calculate the percent invested in each security. The percentage invested in each security is

$$X_i^q = \frac{Z_i}{\sum_{j=1}^{N} Z_j}$$

Where

$$Z_i = \frac{\beta_i}{\sigma_{\epsilon_i}^2}\left(\frac{R_i - R_{F}}{\beta_i} - C^*\right).$$

This expression simply scales the weights on each security so they sum to one and thus insures that we are fully invested. Note that the residual variance on each security $\sigma_{\epsilon i}^2$ plays an important role in determining how much we invest in each security.
Applying this to our example, we have

$$Z_1 = \frac{2}{100}(10 - 5.45) = .091$$

$$Z_2 = \frac{3.75}{100}(8 - 5.45) = .095625$$

$$Z_3 = \frac{5}{100}(7 - 5.45) = .0775$$

$$Z_4 = \frac{20}{100}(6 - 5.45) = .110$$

$$Z_5 = \frac{2.5}{100}(6 - 5.45) = .01375$$

$$\sum_{i=1}^{5} Z_i = .387875$$

Dividing each Z_i by the sum of the Z_i, we find that we should invest 23.5% of our funds in security

1, 24.6% in security 2, 20% in security 3, 28.4% in security 4, and 3.5% in security 5.

Let us stress that this is identical to the result that would be achieved had the problem been solved using the established quadratic programming codes — except that the solution can be reached in a small fraction of the time with a set of relatively simple calculations.

Notice that the characteristics of a stock that make it desirable and the relative attractiveness of stocks can be determined before the calculations of an optimal portfolio are begun. The desirability of any stock is a function of its excess return to beta ratio.

Up to this point, we have assumed that all stocks have positive betas. We believe that there are sound economic reasons to expect all stocks to have positive betas and that the few negative beta stocks that are found in large samples are a result of measurement errors. As pointed out in [6], however, negative beta stocks (and zero beta stocks) are easily incorporated in the analysis.

Similarly, as shown elsewhere, the analysis can easily be extended to the case where unlimited short sales are allowed.

CONSIDERATION OF NEW SECURITIES

Not only do the techniques we have presented in this paper simplify the selection of optimal portfolios, they also vastly simplify the problem of revising portfolios as new securities enter the manager's decision set.

Remember that part of our procedure for designing the optimal portfolio was the selection of a cut-off rate C^*. The cut-off rate served to divide the included set from the excluded set. All securities whose excess return to beta ratio was above the cut-off rate were accepted. All whose ratio is below the cut-off rate were rejected. In our example, C^* was equal to 5.45; thus, if a new security is suggested that has an excess return to risk ratio of less than C^* (5.45), the manager would know that it could not enter into

230
SECURITY
SELECTION
AND ACTIVE
PORTFOLIO
MANAGEMENT

the optimum portfolio. The existence of a cut-off rate is extremely useful. It means that most new securities that are examined can be accepted or rejected without performing additional calculations.

Any security that has an excess return to beta ratio above 5.45 would have to be included in the optimal portfolio. Furthermore, the impact of this on which securities are included in the optimal portfolio is extremely easy to determine. For example, consider a security with an excess return of 9, a beta of 1, and residual risk of 10. Then, initially assuming that this security should be added to the previously optimum portfolio, we obtain a cut-off rate of 5.37. Since this is larger than the excess return to beta ratio for any security previously excluded from the portfolio, the optimum portfolio consists of the old portfolio with the addition of the new security. In some cases, the old portfolio will not remain optimal, but the change should at most involve a change in one or two of the securities whose excess return to beta ratio is close to the cut-off rate. Furthermore, the new optimal portfolio can be calculated in only a few simple steps.

BIBLIOGRAPHY

1. Elton, Edwin J. and Gruber, Martin J., "Determining the Dependence Structure of Share Prices: Implications for Portfolio Selection," *Journal of Finance* (December, 1973), pp. 1203-1233.

2. Elton, Edwin J., Gruber, Martin J., and Padberg, Manfred W., "Simple Criteria for Optimal Portfolio Selection," *Journal of Finance* (December, 1976), pp. 1241-1358.

3. ———,"Simple Criteria for Optimal Portfolio Selection: The Multi-Group Case," forthcoming *Journal of Financial and Quantitative Analysis*.

4. ———, "Simple Criteria for Optimal Portfolio Selection: Tracing Out the Full Efficient Frontier," Working Paper.

5. ———, "Simple Criteria for Optimal Portfolio Selection with Upper Bound Constraints," forthcoming *Operations Research*.

6. ———, "Simple Criteria for Optimal Portfolio Selection: The Multi-Index Case," Working Paper.

7. Elton, Edwin J., Gruber, Martin J., *Finance as a Dynamic Process* (Prentice-Hall, Englewood Cliffs, New Jersey, 1975).

8. Elton, Edwin J., Gruber, Martin J., and Padberg, Manfred W.,
   "Portfolio Selection — The Exploitation of Special Structures,"
   Bulletin of ORSA, Vol. 22, Supplement I (Spring, 1974), p. B-88
   (abstract).

9. Markowitz, Harry, *Portfolio Selection* (John T. Wiley & Sons,
   Inc., New York, 1959).

10. ——, "Portfolio Selection," *Journal of Finance* (March, 1952, pp.
    77-91.

11. Treynor, Jack, "How to Rate Management of Investment
    Funds," *Harvard Business Review,* January-February, 1965, pp.
    63-75.

SECURITY
SELECTION
AND ACTIVE
PORTFOLIO
MANAGEMENT

Core securities:
Widening the decision dimensions

By simplifying the Markowitz approach, we can build portfolios better suited to client needs.

Arun P. Sanghvi and Gordon H. Dash, Jr.

Modern portfolio theory is based largely on the seminal work of Markowitz[1] in the fifties.[2] To date, however, this theory has found limited acceptance by portfolio managers. Though often not understood, or misunderstood, modern portfolio theory is rightfully criticized for being two-dimensional in its scope: it deals only with risk relative to return. Traditional analysts correctly recognize the portfolio selection problem as having more dimensions than this. This gap between the modern approach and the traditional approach that is popular with many portfolio analysts today opens the discussion that follows. The notion of a core security is then introduced. Indeed, core securities, determined by the Markowitz model, are the missing links that help bridge the gap between the two approaches. Core securities were determined from the approved common stock list of the trust department of

[1] Footnotes appear at the end of the article.

a major New England bank, and are explored in an empirical analysis later on in the article.

THE GAP BETWEEN TRADITIONAL AND MODERN APPROACHES TO PORTFOLIO SELECTION

Portfolio selection is a decision making process under uncertainty, that begins with the determination of the investor's investment horizon and specific investment goals (dimensions). The return of an investment is generally regarded as an important determinant of the portfolio. In an uncertain environment, most investors also display the common trait of risk-aversion. The Markowitz model of portfolio selection views the risk and return dimensions as being the only determinants of a portfolio. Specifically, it has as its objective the minimization of portfolio risk for the desired return. This objective is also shared by the traditional approach. The traditional approach, however, generally has to incorporate other dimensions to accommodate the specific needs of the individual investor, such as a low downside risk, etc.

Herein lies a serious gap between the two approaches and a major reason for the unacceptance of the modern theory. In the next section, we show how the Markowitz model can help to determine certain core securities that are used as building blocks to provide a sound foundation for a portfolio. Additional securities are then added to the portfolio by the analyst to incorporate other dimensions important to the investor.

Since it is relevant to the discussion in subsequent sections, we note that even though the two approaches evaluate a portfolio in the risk dimension, the manner in which it is done is substantially different in each case. Specifically, under the traditional approach, a systematic and objective assessment of the risk of a security is not possible. Instead, qualitative comparative measures are developed. These range from statements about a firm's "quality," "maturity," etc., to developing comparative historical performance measures with various market indices. In contrast, the modern approach uses an objective numerical measure of risk to differentiate securities by their precise risk characteristics. This measure is called the standard deviation.

When building a portfolio, it is recognized by both approaches that the risk of the portfolio is generally dependent to a greater extent on the degree of intertemporal comovement (interdependence) in the returns of the member securities rather than their individual risks. Traditional analysts rely on their gut feeling, based upon years of experience, to subjectively assess the degree of comovement. In contrast, the modern approach relies on a numerical measure of the degree of intertemporal association, called the covariance. Covariances are easily computed and, together with the standard deviation of the securities, they provide an objective means of estimating the precise risk characteristics of a portfolio.

The point being made is immediately apparent when one realizes that, from an approved common stock list, an infinite number of portfolios can be built. The Markowitz model is easily programmed on a computer and affords the comparison of the risk-return characteristics of every possible mix of securities in a reasonable amount of time. On the other hand, traditional methods must rely on the subjective selection of a large assortment of "blue chip," "growth," and "balanced" securities across a wide spectrum of industries as a logical method of achieving diversification, since the determination and, hence, comparison of the precise risk characteristics of every portfolio, is difficult. This process inevitably leads to gross overdiversification and to a portfolio that is dominated by other portfolios in the risk and return dimensions.

CORE SECURITIES AND CORNER PORTFOLIOS

The expected return of a portfolio in a time period is measured as the price change plus dividend income as a percent of the price at the beginning of the period. For a desired expected return, the Markowitz model finds the minimum risk portfolio. The set of all such portfolios determines the risk-return trade-off curve. This curve is bounded by the maximum return portfolio on one end and the minimum risk portfolio on the other end. A typical curve is drawn in Exhibit 1.

Exhibit 1
A RISK - RETURN TRADE - OFF CURVE
(EFFICIENT FRONTIER)

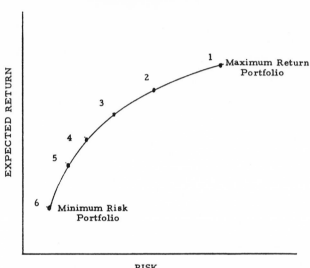

A portfolio is said to be efficient (undominated) if there is no other portfolio that has lower risk for any given expected return. The risk-return trade-off curve is, therefore, called the efficient frontier also.

Fortunately, it is not necessary to determine the risk-return characteristics of every point on the efficient frontier. This frontier is completely defined by a finite number of portfolios called *corner portfolios*. A corner portfolio is encountered when (i) at least one new security is added to the portfolio, or (ii) one or more member securities are dropped from the portfolio. Every other efficient portfolio is a weighted average of its adjacent corner portfolios.

The curve in Exhibit 1 has six corner portfolios, indicated by the dots. A typical numerical procedure determines the corner portfolios in order of decreasing

SECURITY
SELECTION
AND ACTIVE
PORTFOLIO
MANAGEMENT

return and risk, starting with the determination of corner portfolio 1 and stopping at portfolio 6. The composition of any efficient portfolio is a weighted combination of the securities that are contained in two adjacent corner portfolios.

Specifically, suppose that the expected return of corner portfolios 2 and 3, in Exhibit 1, are 6% and 4%, respectively, and the comparable risk characteristics are 2% and 1%, respectively. Furthermore, suppose that the compositions of the corner portfolios 2 and 3 are, respectively $(x_1=60\%, x_2=0\%, x_3=30\%, x_4=0\%, x_5=0\%, x_6=10\%)$, and $(x_1 = 50\%, x_2 = 0\%, x_3 = 20\%, x_4 = 30\%, x_5 = 0\%, x_6 = 0\%)$. The symbol x_i, $i = 1, 2, \ldots, 6$, denotes the percentage of the portfolio invested in security i. If an efficient portfolio with expected return of 5.2% is desired, its composition is obtained by taking $3/5$[a] of corner portfolio 2 and $2/5$[b] of corner portfolio 3. In other words, the composition of the undominated portfolio with an expected return of 5.2% is given by $(x_1=56\%, x_2=0\%, x_3=26\%, x_4=12\%, x_5=0\%, x_6=6\%)$.[c]

Once the composition and risk-return characteristics of every corner portfolio are computed, the composition of every other efficient portfolio can be determined by the simple procedure just outlined. Therefore, the problem of determining the efficient frontier is considerably simplified. No longer is it necessary to determine the characteristics of each one of the infinite number of portfolios on the frontier. Instead, one need only compute the finite, and typically very few, number of corner portfolios that essentially determine the entire frontier.

From the illustration in the preceding paragraph, it should be clear that any efficient portfolio

---

[a] This is obtained from the calculation $(5.2-4)/(6-4)=1.2/2=3/5$

[b] This is obtained from the calculation $(1-3/5)=2/5$

[c] e.g., $x_1=(3/5)(60) + (2/5)(50)$, and, $x_4=(3/5)(0) + (2/5)(30)$, and so on.

with an expected return between 4% and 6% must be made up of securities that make up the corner portfolios 2 and 3. This observation prompts the following concept. We define *core securities* to be securities that are present in a substantial amount (at least 5%) in one or more corner portfolios. In the previous example, the core securities in corner portfolios 2 and 3 are, respectively 1, 2, 6, and 1, 3, and 4. These core securities are important because, if risk and return are the only dimensions of concern to the investor, then significant portions of the portfolio are composed of core securities — the exact amounts are computed by the numerical procedure previously outlined. Every portfolio with expected return between 4 and 6% will be made up of securities 1, 3, 4, and 6.

In real life, however, portfolio management involves the selection of securities assembled to achieve the investment goals of the individual concerned, and these goals generally go beyond the risk and return dimensions incorporated in the Markowitz model. Safety of principal cannot be completely measured by the standard deviation of the portfolio. Many investors are more concerned about the downside risk of the portfolio. Others perceive a low price to expected earnings ratio as low risk. Still others have personal prejudices against selected companies or industries. Finally, in the Markowitz model, a high expected return can stem from high income and/or high capital growth; depending upon his/her income characteristics, financial status, and tax bracket, each of these sources of return can be viewed very differently by the investor. The core securities must, therefore, be augmented by securities that have the desirable characteristics in these other dimensions.

The experience and judgment of the analyst is vital in selecting these additional securities. The final result of this procedure will be a portfolio that is based upon the sound foundation of core securities, and that meets the investment objectives of the individual. The determination of core securities from the approved common stock list of the trust department of a major New England bank is illustrated in the next section.

EMPIRICAL RESULTS

In this section, the Markowitz model is used to generate the efficient frontier from the 116 securities on the approved common stock list of the trust department of a major New England bank. The estimates of risk (standard deviation) and degree of co-movement (covariances) for the approved securities were obtained from monthly time series data on prices and dividends for the eleven-year period 1965-1975.

As a point of interest, the trust department has subjectively identified a list of seven securities from the approved common stock list, with the recommendation to its analysts that every portfolio created from the approved common stock list contain these securities. Other securities can be added at the discretion of the analyst to meet the specific goals of the investor. These seven securities were called core securities by the trust department. We have borrowed the term core securities from them and also recommend that they be the foundation of every portfolio. The similarity, however, ends here. The methods that we use and recommend to determine the core securities are different.

The managed frontier obtained from the approved common stock list is displayed in Exhbit 2.[3] The maximum return is 3.6% (per month) with a risk of 21.09%, whereas the minimum risk portfolio has return and risk characteristics of .62% and 3.47%, respectively. There are 47 corner portfolios that determine the trade-off curve. These are not marked in Exhibit 2 for the sake of clarity. Instead, the risk-return characteristics and compositions of the 47 corner portfolios are displayed in Exhibit 5, at the end of this paper.

We reiterate that corner portfolios represent points on the risk-return trade-off curve where a new security is added to or one is dropped from the exist-

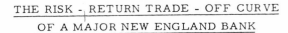
Exhibit 2

THE RISK - RETURN TRADE - OFF CURVE
OF A MAJOR NEW ENGLAND BANK

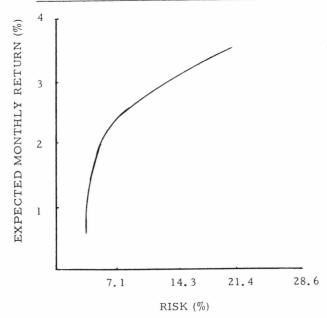

RISK (%)

ing portfolio. Exhibit 3 contains a list of securities that comprise substantial parts (at least 5%) of one or more corner portfolios. The maximum proportion ever acquired in any portfolio is indicated in column 5. Column 3 indicates the expected return of the first corner portfolio that contains at least 5% of the security. Column 4 indicates the expected return of the corner portfolio at which the security in question exists; e.g., the expected return of the first corner portfolio that contains at least 5% of BGH is 2.79%. This security forms at least 5% of every successive corner portfolio up to and including the corner portfolio with an expected return of 1.00%. This is abbreviated by saying that security BGH enters at 2.79% and exits at 1.00%. Furthermore, in this range the maximum proportion it ever achieves is 18.2%. Since every efficient portfolio is a weighted average of its adjacent corner portfolios, the implication is that

SECURITY
SELECTION
AND ACTIVE
PORTFOLIO
MANAGEMENT

Exhibit 3: CANDIDATE CORE SECURITIES

1	2	3	4	5
Security Ticker Symbol	Company	Expected return (%) at entry	Expected return (%) at exit	Maximum proportion (%)
DEC	Digital Equipment	3.60	2.11	100.0
KG	Kresge (S.S.)	3.44	1.47	36.8
BGH	Burroughs Corp.	2.79	1.00	18.2
SNAP	Snap-On Tools Corp.	2.79	2.24	6.9
ENG	Englehard Min.	2.79	1.97	9.9
HAL	Halliburton Co.	2.41	1.73	19.5
TYLR	Taylor Wine Co.	2.32	2.11	5.1
SGP	Schering-Plough	2.28	1.47	12.0
PEL	Panhandle E. Pipe	2.16	1.78	5.8
JNJ	Johnson & Johnson	2.16	.74	17.3
SN	Standard Oil (Ind)	1.97	.96	12.8
AMX	Amax Inc.	1.81	.63	8.2
FDU	Fidelity U. Bancorp.	1.81	1.20	5.4
PG	Proctor & Gamble	1.69	.63	11.8
T	Amer. Tele. & Teleg.	1.57	.63	28.6
XON	Exxon Corp.	1.22	.63	9.2
F	Ford Motor Co.	1.11	.74	6.3
DD	DuPont (E.I.)	.64	.63	7.8
IBM	Intl. Bus. Mach.	.64	.63	5.8

every efficient portfolio with an expected yield between 1.00% and 2.79% will contain substantial amounts (i.e., at least 5% but at most 18.2%) of security BGH.[4] As another example, IBM enters at .64% and leaves at .63%, achieving a maximum proportion of 5.8% only. Hence every "low" risk efficient portfolio with expected yield between .63% and .64% should contain IBM stock. Furthermore, IBM should not constitute more than 5.8% of the portfolio.

We can arrive at a list of core securities by reviewing the information in exhibit 3 in terms of the maximum and minimum possible expected yields of

Exhibit 4: CORE SECURITIES

Portfolio Type	Core Securities
Low Risk (.63% - 1.59%)[1]	KG, BGH, SGP, JNJ, SN, AMX, FDU, PG, T, XON, F, DD, IBM
Balanced (1.6% - 2.59%)[1]	DEC, KG, BGH, SNAP, ENG, HAL, TYLR, PEL, JNJ, SGP, SN, AMX, FDU, PG
Explorer (2.6% - 3.60%)[1]	DEC, KG, BGH, SNAP, ENG

[1] Expected monthly return.

3.60% and .63%, respectively. A method for doing so is the following: subdivide the range .63% - 3.60% into the three regions: (1) .63% -1.59%, (2) 1.6% - 2.59%, and (3) 2.6% - 3.60%. Portfolios with expected returns in regions 1, 2, and 3 for the data in this analysis can be characterized, respectively, as low risk, balanced, and growth (explorer) portfolios.

Exhibit 4 contains a list of core securities. It is derived from Exhibit 3 as follows. Suppose one seeks a low risk portfolio, i.e., one with an expected return between .63% and 1.59% from Exhibit 3. We know, for example, that security T will comprise at least 5% of such a portfolio. Similarly we know, from Exhibit 3, that security BGH will comprise at least 5% of every portfolio with expected return between 1% and 1.59%. For this reason, BGH is also listed as a core security for building low risk portfolios.

Several observations are in order. Some core securities appear in more than one portfolio type. This should not come as a surprise to the reader. This merely reflects the good risk and return characteristics that these securities enjoy to be included in two or more categories. More importantly, the covariance characteristics of the securities must make them favorable candidates for a large range of portfolios. For example, if a security tends to move against the market, or not to the extent the market moves, it might be an attractive candidate for a wide range of portfolios. Consequently, the presence of core securities KG and BGH in all three portfolio types only points to their robustness.

Of the seven core securities recommended by the trust department, only one (IBM) appears in Exhibit 4 in the low risk portfolio region. We can see from Exhibit 3 that the maximum proportion it ever assumes is 5.8%. The selection of core securities in the traditional approach involves a substantial degree of subjectivity, while in the modern approach these securities are determined after a thorough and objective analysis of the approved common stock list. Furthermore, the modern approach also sheds light on the

SECURITY
SELECTION
AND ACTIVE
PORTFOLIO
MANAGEMENT

amounts of the security present in the portfolio.

Exhibit 4 does not indicate the relative proportions of each core security to be included. There is a reason for this. The Markowitz model is two-dimensional in scope. The risk-return dimensions are important to most if not all investors. If these were the only dimensions of concern to the investor, then the core securities for the given range in Exhibit 3 should comprise at least 90% of the portfolio. The relative proportion of each security can be obtained by examining their proportions in the corresponding adjacent corner portfolios. Most investors' goals, however, necessitate the study of more than the two dimensions of return and risk. These dimensions were discussed in the preceding section. The analyst will need to add other securities to tailor the portfolio to the specific needs of the client.

Exhibit 5: COMPOSITIONS OF CORNER PORTFOLIOS

CORNER PORTFOLIO CHARACTERISTICS [1]

SECURITY	1	2	3	4	5	6	7	8	9	10	11	12	13	14	15	16
E	1.60	3.44	3.09	3.03	3.03	2.79	2.41	2.38	2.32	2.28	2.24	2.16	2.11	2.09	2.06	1.79
R	21.09	18.90	14.19	13.40	13.36	10.54	6.95	6.79	6.44	6.29	6.01	5.68	5.51	5.45	5.14	5.14
DEC	100	88.4	62.2	57.8	57.6	40.8	16.3	15.0	12.6	10.9	9.7	7.2	5.9	5.4	4.5	3.7
KG		11.6	33.4	36.7	36.8	35.7	25.4	25.1	23.3	21.5	20.2	17.4	16.0	15.4	14.4	13.5
SNAP			4.3	4.9	4.9	6.0	6.9	6.8	6.2	5.8	5.3	4.3	3.7	3.5	3.0	2.6
TYLR				.7	.7	2.2	4.6	4.7	5.0	5.1	5.1	5.0	5.0	4.9	4.9	4.8
ENG					.1	5.6	9.9	9.9	9.6	9.4	8.9	7.8	7.3	7.1	6.6	6.3
BGH						9.8	17.7	18.2	16.9	16.1	15.4	14.0	13.1	12.8	12.1	11.3
HAL							19.2	19.5	19.4	19.0	18.3	16.9	16.0	15.6	14.8	12.8
PEL								.9	2.2	3.3	4.1	5.6	5.8	5.8	5.8	5.6
SGP									4.8	8.2	8.9	10.4	11.3	11.6	12.0	11.7
ARC										.8	1.3	2.2	2.6	2.7	3.0	2.7
JNJ											2.9	9.0	11.7	12.5	14.1	15.3
EAF												.3	.1			
FDU													1.6	2.1	3.1	3.7
UCC														.6	1.6	1.6
SN																4.4
AMX																
WY																
PG																
NRD																
ABUD																
SQB																
T																
F																
XON																
LLY																
PSR																
MRK																
KN																
IBM																
DD																
SPP																
TXU																
AA																

1. E = Expected Return of the Portfolio (% per month)
   R = Risk of the Portfolio (% per month)

Exhibit 5 (continued): COMPOSITIONS OF CORNER PORTFOLIOS

CORNER PORTFOLIO CHARACTERISTICS

SECURITY / TICKER / SYMBOL																
KG	3.6	3.5	2.1	1.8	1.6	1.4	1.3	1.1	.9	.8	.7	.6	0.0			
SNAP	13.4	13.3	12.5	12.2	11.8	11.2	10.9	10.3	8.8	8.3	6.8	6.5	1.7	1.7	1.7	1.7
TTLR	2.5	2.4	1.6	1.4	1.2	1.1	1.0	.8	.5	.4	.1					
ENG	4.8	4.8	4.5	4.4	4.3	4.2	4.1	4.0	3.9	3.8	3.7	3.7	3.0	3.0	3.0	2.8
BGH	6.2	6.1	4.6	4.3	4.1	3.8	3.7	3.5	3.3	3.2	3.1	3.0	2.2	2.2	2.2	2.0
HAL	11.2	11.2	10.2	10.0	9.9	9.7	9.6	9.4	9.0	8.9	8.6	8.5	7.4	7.4	7.4	6.8
PEL	12.4	12.2	8.2	7.2	6.6	5.7	5.3	4.4	3.5	3.2	2.8	2.7	.9	.9	.9	.4
SGP	5.6	5.5	5.2	5.1	5.1	4.9	4.8	4.7	4.4	4.3	4.0	3.9	2.8	2.8	2.8	2.3
ARC	11.6	11.6	10.3	10.0	9.7	9.1	8.8	8.3	7.4	7.1	6.5	6.3	3.9	3.9	3.9	3.0
JNJ	2.7	2.7	2.4	2.3	2.3	2.3	2.3	2.3	2.3	2.3	2.4	2.4	2.2	2.2	2.2	2.2
EAF	15.4	15.5	17.0	17.3	17.3	17.1	17.0	16.7	16.4	16.2	15.8	15.8	14.0	14.0	14.0	13.0
FDU																
UGG	3.8	3.8	4.9	5.2	5.3	5.3	5.4	5.4	5.4	5.4	5.3	5.3	5.0	5.0	5.0	4.8
SN	1.5	1.5														
AMX	4.8	5.2	10.4	11.6	11.9	12.3	12.4	12.8	12.3	12.1	11.3	11.1	8.3	8.3	8.3	7.5
WY	.4	.6	4.6	5.5	6.0	6.6	6.9	7.4	7.8	7.9	8.1	8.1	8.2	8.2	8.2	8.0
PG			1.5	1.7	1.7	1.7	1.7	1.7	1.7	1.1	.9					
NRG				1.1	2.0	3.6	5.1	6.7	7.1	7.9	8.1	11.1	11.1	11.1	11.7	
ABUD						.6	.9	1.4	1.7	1.7	1.7	1.7	2.2	2.2	2.2	2.2
SQB								.1	.3	.4	.4	.5	.6	.6	.6	.6
T									.2	.2	.2	.2	.2	.2	.2	.2
F									4.2	5.4	8.0	8.6	17.0	17.0	17.0	19.6
XON										.3	1.3	1.5	4.1	4.1	4.1	5.0
LLY											1.3	1.3	5.0	5.1	5.1	6.3
PSR													0.0	0.0	1.2	
MRK																.5
KN																
IBM																
DD																
SPP																
TXU																
AA																

Consequently, the actual proportions of the core securities computed by the Markowitz model are no longer directly applicable. Still, the core securities should be included in the portfolio in "substantial" amounts. The selection of additional securities will largely be based upon the analyst's judgment and "feel" for the market. Once the analyst has decided upon a portfolio, however, its risk-return characteristics can be computed and plotted in Exhibit 3. The purpose of this is to compare the position of the created portfolio in relation to the trade-off curve. By picking a portfolio that differs from the exact proportions of core securities as indicated by the Markowitz model, the analyst will have forced the portfolio away from the trade-off curve, but this procedure helps to estimate the "loss" in performance in the risk-return dimensions that the investor must live with so that some other dimensions can be accommodated.

244
SECURITY
SELECTION
AND ACTIVE
PORTFOLIO
MANAGEMENT

Exhibit 5 (continued): COMPOSITIONS OF CORNER PORTFOLIOS

SECURITY TICKER SYMBOL	33	34	35	36	37	38	39	40	41	42	43	44	45	46	47
(characteristics)	1.10 / 3.48	1.10 / 3.48	1.10 / 3.62	· / 3.41	· / 3.40	· / 3.58	.95 / 3.58	· / 3.56	· / 3.53	· / 3.53	· / 3.53	· / 3.49	· / 3.48	· / 3.47	· / 3.47
DEC															
KG															
SNAP															
TYLR	2.8	2.7	2.6	2.5	2.5	2.5	2.4	2.3	2.2	2.2	2.2	2.0	2.0	1.7	1.7
ENG	1.8	1.8	1.2	1.1	1.0	.8	.7	.4	0.0	0.0					
BGH	6.6	6.5	5.5	5.4	5.2	4.7	4.5	3.7	2.5	2.5	2.4	.4			
HAL	.1														
PEL	2.1	2.1	1.6	1.6	1.5	1.4	1.3	1.1	.9	.9	.9	.4	.3		
SGP	2.7	2.6	.9	.8	.6										
ARC	2.2	2.2	1.9	1.9	1.9	1.8	1.8	1.7	1.6	1.6	1.6	1.4	1.3	1.2	1.1
JNJ	12.7	12.7	11.7	11.7	11.5	11.1	10.9	10.1	8.9	8.9	8.9	6.7	6.3	3.6	3.2
EAF															
FDU	4.8	4.8	4.5	4.5	4.4	4.3	4.3	4.2	4.1	4.1	4.1	3.9	3.8	3.3	3.3
UCC															
SN	7.3	7.2	6.0	5.9	5.8	5.3	5.2	4.8	4.2	4.2	4.2	3.6	3.5	2.4	2.2
AMX	8.0	8.0	8.0	7.9	7.9	7.7	7.7	7.4	6.8	6.8	6.8	5.9	5.7	5.0	4.9
WY															
PG	11.8	11.8	11.6	11.6	11.5	11.4	11.4	11.1	10.4	10.4	10.4	9.2	8.9	7.6	7.5
NRG	2.3	2.3	2.4	2.4	2.4	2.5	2.4	2.4	2.4	2.4	2.4	2.1	2.1	1.5	1.5
ABUD	.5	.5	0.0												
SQB	.2	.2	0.0	0.0											
T	20.4	20.5	23.1	23.3	23.7	24.6	24.9	25.8	26.8	26.8	26.8	27.6	27.7	28.5	28.6
F	5.1	5.1	5.6	5.6	5.7	5.9	6.0	6.3	5.9	5.9	5.9	5.3	5.1	4.3	4.2
XON	6.6	6.7	8.0	8.1	8.3	8.8	8.9	9.2	9.1	9.1	9.0	8.7	8.7	8.6	8.6
LLY	1.6	1.6	2.3	2.4	2.4	2.6	2.7	2.9	3.1	3.1	3.1	3.7	3.9	4.0	4.0
PSR	.6	.6	1.0	1.0	1.1	1.1	1.2	1.5	2.1	2.1	2.2	2.6	2.7	3.7	3.8
MRK		.1	2.0	2.1	2.4	3.0	3.1	3.3	3.7	3.7	3.7	4.0	4.1	4.3	4.3
KN				.1	.2		.4	.5	.8	1.3	1.3	1.3	1.3	1.1	1.1
IBM								.9	2.4	2.4	2.4	4.4	4.8	5.6	5.8
DD									1.7	1.7	1.7	4.2	4.7	7.4	7.8
SPP									0.0	0.0	1.5	1.8	3.2	3.3	
TXU											0.0	1.1	1.3	2.8	3.0
AA													0.0	.1	.1

[1] Markowitz, H. M. (1959), *Portfolio Selection: Efficient Diversification of Investments*, Wiley, New York.

[2] The terms "modern approach" and "Markowitz model" are used interchangeably in this paper.

[3] The analysis was performed using the portfolio analysis routine FRONTIER at the University of Rhode Island Computer Center. The algorithm and its theoretical development are contained in Sanghvi, "An Algorithm for Determining the Efficient Frontier," working paper, July, 1977. The routine was designed by the authors. FRONTIER extracts data from the COMPUSTAT tapes, computes the necessary statistical inputs for the portfolio model, and generates all the efficient corner portfolios.

[4] The exact proportion of BGH present in a portfolio with given expected yield is also computed by the numerical procedure outlined in the previous section.

CORE
SECURITIES:
WIDENING
THE DECISION
DIMENSIONS

A winning strategy for an efficient market *

How can the market be efficient and inefficient at the same time?

Burton G. Malkiel and Paul B. Firstenberg

T his article is addressed to the bright young money manager who has just been assigned his investment counseling firm's hottest potato: a very hefty institutional account whose investment committee has been captured from the old guard by a group of young Turks. The old guard believed fervently in their (and your firm's) ability to achieve superior performance through picking undervalued individual stocks and bonds. The young Turks have been indoctrinated in modern capital market theory. "Brainwashed" is the term your agitated seniors use.

Your designation as manager for this account makes you empathize with baseball managers, football coaches, and network programming vice presidents. You know that your appointment to the job

SECURITY SELECTION AND ACTIVE PORTFOLIO MANAGEMENT

* The authors are indebted to Frank Biondi for his invaluable help in preparing the exhibits.

1. Footnotes appear at the end of the article.

means it is now only a matter of time until you are fired; your professional demise is as assured as death and taxes.

Your senior in the firm was taken off the account because he could no longer control his rage in dealing with the young Turks. They sat at investment committee meetings with their calculators, asking him about the portfolio's alpha, beta, and R^2, and the risk premia for various investment media. They seemed to talk to each other in a jargon that sounded a good deal more like Greek than English. What really drove your senior up the wall was when an academic economist on the investment committee began arguing that efficient market research demonstrated that your firm's services weren't worth a fraction of what it is being paid. "That guy says his five year old could do better throwing darts . . ." your senior was heard to mutter as he was assigned to a corner office in the research department.

Now you have been tapped to save the account and your own precious neck is on the line. You need to come up with an investment strategy which calls for something other than buying the Standard & Poor's 500 stocks. If the account's portfolio is to be indexed, who needs your firm (and thus, who needs you)? Both will be replaced by a computer. But how do you come up with a program that employs the minds of people instead of a machine and still satisfy the efficient market theorists who now dominate the investment committee?

You quickly put aside notions of recommending a strategy of buying coins, paintings, or farm land; it may be that these investments will do better than stocks and bonds, but your firm has no expertise in these areas (it would be novel, however, if you lost this account to the Sotheby Parke-Bernet Galleries). The trick is to come up with a program that you can sell to the seniors in your firm, who believe the eleventh commandment provides that "managed money will consistently outperform the market on average over the long-term," and, at the same time, persuade the investment committee that you are not trying to pick undervalued securities.

If you are lucky enough to read this article in time, we have the solution for you. Let us begin by spelling out the implications for investment policy that your young Turks derive from modern capital market theory. You need to understand their game plan if you are to beat them.

THE STRATEGIC IMPLICATIONS OF EFFICIENT MARKET THEORY

Many studies indicate there is no evidence that professional firms can produce, on a sustained basis, above average returns from managing stock portfolios of equivalent risk, primarily because, in an organized central marketplace such as the stock market, prices at any time will usually reflect both the problems and opportunities inherent in any given stock. With countless security analysts thoroughly studying most securities — and certainly all major stocks held by institutional investors — the publicly available information that affects security prices is digested quickly and reflected in the prices at which securities are traded. This assumes, of course, that in fact a large number of investors understand the information that is available and make rational decisions.

A market where all developments are reflected quickly in security prices is characterized as an "efficient market"; one conclusion is that, in such an environment, few professional money managers can hope to be consistently wiser in analyzing stock values than their competitors, at least without the benefit of inside information. The market simply acts too quickly in digesting new data to enable even professional money managers to achieve consistently better returns than the market provides on average for assets of a given risk level. Accordingly, one can conclude that the primary difference in return to be expected in making stock investments is the differential compensation for assuming alternative levels of risk.

Experience shows that this is in fact the case. A

SECURITY
SELECTION
AND ACTIVE
PORTFOLIO
MANAGEMENT

study by Becker Securities Corp. last year showed that in the period 1967-1976, the S&P 500 Index outperformed 95% of the institutions surveyed. The study was recently updated to include performance in 1977. The study, which included the common stock investment performance of several hundred institutional investors, was almost as favorable to the S&P 500 as before, even though the average stock outperformed the S&P 500 during 1977. The results are shown in the following table.

	Percentage of Institutions Surveyed That Were Outperformed by S&P 500 Index
5 Years 1973 – 1977	79%
10 Years 1968 – 1977	83%
15 Years 1962 – 1977	85%

Clearly only a small minority of professional managers of pension fund equities was able to perform better than the Index during the periods measured. Experience over other fairly long periods — while perhaps not as devastating to professional money managers — does not show that the pros are able consistently to beat the market. Moreover, even investment professionals who insist that it is feasible to organize their analytical capability to make a superior selection of individual securities do not deny that it is exceedingly difficult to identify overvalued and undervalued stocks.

AN ALTERNATIVE TO INDEXING

Okay, you say, our explanation of an efficient market is reasonable enough and you don't have to know calculus to follow it. Moreover, there seems to be considerable evidence that supports the theory. But, you ask, isn't your point still that one ought to buy the market, or a proxy for the market, such as a fund that matches the holdings of stocks included in the S&P 500 Stock Index? How does that help me or my firm, you plead.

Patience, anguished account executive! There is an alternative strategy to the index fund — one that takes advantage of a current inefficiency in the market. Our suggested alternative should enable your client to achieve a somewhat better than average market return on equities but does not require you to persuade the random walkers on your investment committee to authorize you to select individual securities. Indeed, you can tell your random walkers that this is an investment strategy that enables you to buy a broadly diversified portfolio of common stocks — but at a discount from net asset value. That's right, you can offer your committee the chance, in effect, *to buy the market at a discount*. At the same time, you can tell your seniors in the firm that the firm's acumen will be needed to identify these investments and to insure that diversification is achieved. You will *not* be proposing to the client that it settle for average performance, as index funders are alleged to offer. (Incidentally, this critique of index funds misstates the claim of indexers. They do not offer "average performance" but maintain that, since few money managers can perform as well as the market as a whole, matching the market is performing way above the average of most professional money managers. But you do not need to make this point to your seniors unless, in fact, you want to get into another line of work.)

What is this investment that offers the prospect of outperforming the market? The vehicle is the closed-end investment company.

CLOSED-END INVESTMENT COMPANIES SELLING AT A DISCOUNT

Closed-end investment companies are similar to the more popular open-end mutual funds. They typically buy well-diversified portfolios. Unlike open-end companies, however, once the shares have been issued to the public, no new shares are issued, and current shares cannot be redeemed at net asset value. Instead, the shares trade in the open market (mostly on the New York Exchange) like any other securities. Therein lies their potential attraction, for the

SECURITY
SELECTION
AND ACTIVE
PORTFOLIO
MANAGEMENT

shares of closed-end investment companies typically trade at substantial discounts from their net asset values. This provides the investor a chance of obtaining a higher rate of return than could be obtained from a market portfolio. Assuming that the stocks and bonds owned by the closed-end fund do just as well as the market, and as long as the discount from asset value does not widen, it is possible to get a larger than average return: for every dollar you put into the fund you will have more than a dollar invested on which dividends can be earned. So, even if the fund just equals the market return, as academic research suggests it is likely to do, you will beat the averages. In addition, if the discount narrows by the time you have elected to sell, your shares will be further ahead than if you had simply purchased the underlying securities in the fund's portfolio.

One problem with the strategy of buying regular closed-end investment companies is that it is possible for discounts to widen in the future. While this risk is lower when discounts are larger than average historical discounts from net asset value, a particular type of closed-end fund, called a "dual purpose" fund, may mitigate this risk.

Dual purpose funds have two types of securities outstanding — each provides one half of the beginning assets of the fund. One is a Preferred or Income share, which is entitled to receive all of the dividend and interest income produced by the assets. The other is a Capital share, which is entitled to none of the income but all of the capital gains or losses produced by the fund. The Capital shares of the dual purpose funds alone are quite risky investment instruments. This is because the Capital shares are highly levered. Potentially, the Capital shares of some of the funds are over twice as volatile as would be a portfolio made up to parallel market indices.

There is, however, an investment strategy that enables the investor to undo the leverage and extra risk that go along with buying the Capital shares. The reason the Capital shares are riskier is that the Income shares have a prior claim on all the company's earnings. Also, the investment company has to pay off the Income shareholders at a predetermined price before the Capital shareholders get anything. But you can undo the leverage of the Capital shares. The general rule that works for most dual funds is to buy one Income share for every Capital share you own. This, in effect, gives you a direct share in the company's assets.

The advantage of this strategy of purchasing dual purpose funds over the simple strategy of buying regular closed-end funds is that all shares of the dual purpose funds are redeemable at a specific maturity date, which is generally between 1979 and 1985. Income shares are redeemed at a pre-determined price, typically around the original price the Income shareholders paid for their shares. The remaining assets belong to the Capital shareholders who may, if they wish, redeem their shares at full asset value on or about the maturity date. Thus, unlike the regular closed-end companies, the investor can be confident that the discount will be eliminated in the future.[1] It is this assured elimination of the discount that gives dual purpose funds their edge.

SPECULATION ABOUT "OPENING" FUNDS

Some analysts believe that pressure from shareholders will force the investment advisers who control regular closed-end funds to convert them to open status or that a powerful interest will "take over" such funds for the express purpose of liquidating them and realizing the gain on the excess of net asset values over share prices.[2] It is clear, however, that investment advisers of such funds will strongly resist the conversion to open status for fear that the funds will then suffer the same kind of redemptions by shareholders as open-ended equity funds have endured in recent years. If redemptions exceed new sales, as they have in recent years in the case of most open-ended equity funds, then there will be less assets to manage and the managements will have to accept either lower compensation and reduced staff or higher operating expense ratios for the funds. This spectre may compel advisers to resist the conversion of closed-end funds to open-end status.

Thus, the average discount for regular closed-end funds is likely to be larger than the "total discount from asset values" obtained by buying balanced positions of Capital and Income shares of dual purpose shares. Nevertheless, the possibility of a takeover bid will probably put pressure on many regular fund managements to pay regular capital distributions in addition to income dividends, and such payments are likely at least to help keep discounts from widening substantially.

SPECIAL RISK REDUCTION FEATURES

There is an important additional attraction to closed-end funds (both regular and dual purpose vehicles). Studies show that, more often than not, fund discounts tend to narrow when the market falls and increase when the market rises.[3] The explanation for this phenomenon is unclear, but the empirical regularity is observable. This negative covariance of the fund discounts with market movements (or, more simply, the narrowing or widening of the discount in a counter cyclical direction to the market) tends to lower the volatility of these funds and thus lessens their risk level. For instance, an investment in a group of closed-end funds, each of which holds a broadly diversified portfolio, could expect to produce about the same rate of return as the market on average, but such funds will tend to have an average beta of less than one (or be less volatile than the market on average) owing to the covariance feature of the fund.

This point may also be illustrated by the following comparison of the betas calculated on the market value of the shares of various types of closed-end funds for the period January, 1970–June, 1977 with the betas calculated on the basis of their underlying net assets for the same period.

January 1970 Through January 1978

	Historical Beta Calculated from Movements of Net Asset Value	Historical Beta Calculated from Movements of Share Prices
Selected Regular Closed-End Funds		
General Amer. Investors	1.062	1.047
Lehman	1.043	1.082
Madison	0.883	0.985
Niagara Share	0.951	0.842
Tri-Continental	1.057	0.871
Average of five funds	0.999	0.965
Selected Capital Shares of Dual Purpose Funds		
Am DualVest	2.073	1.588
Gemini	2.247	1.623
Income and Capital	2.100	1.774
Putnam	2.494	1.405
Scudder	1.594	1.343
Average of five funds	2.102	1.547

Notice that the volatility of the securities owned by the funds (that is, the betas based on net asset values) averages approximately one for the regular funds and above two for the levered Capital shares of dual purpose funds. The volatility assumed by the investor, however (based on market values), tends to be less than the volatility (beta) of the underlying portfolio, especially for the dual purpose Capital shares.

In sum closed-end funds represent an opportunity to lower investment risk without sacrificing return. Indeed, since you buy at a substantial discount, you will tend to earn larger returns than those that would be produced if you had bought the underlying portfolio. The random walkers on the investment committee should be no less than ecstatic.

WHY DO SUCH FUNDS SELL AT A DISCOUNT?

In some ways the behavior of closed-end funds discounts is like aspirin: We know it works but not exactly why. A number of reasons have been offered for the variations in the discounts:

- The built in capital gains tax liability investors face if they buy into a fund with substantial amounts of unrealized appreciation. The argument here is that share price should be discounted to some extent for a fund with significant amounts of unrealized appreciation because the realization of gains could produce unfavorable tax consequences for many investors.

- The holding by at least some of the funds of a significant portion of assets in securities whose sale is restricted. Since such shares are unregistered and are highly illiquid and hard to value, funds with large amounts of such holdings may sell at relatively large discounts.

- An exclusive commitment to invest in foreign securities. If at certain times investors cannot duplicate such holdings in their own right, either because exchange controls limit the opportunities to invest in foreign equities or U.S. tax provisions impose an added cost on buying off-shore securities, then such funds may be especially attractive. At other times when foreign investments seem relatively unattractive to investors, such funds may sell at a relatively large discount.

- The payment of regular capital gains distributions. Such distributions may lower average discounts significantly. This may be because these distributions appeal to investors who need dividends to cover their current spending requirements. Alternatively, investors may appreciate the partial liquidation of the fund since such distributions, in effect, enable investors to cash in a partial amount of their fund shares at net asset value.

- Other factors that might explain fund discounts include:

  a) The fund's past market performance, which some investors may regard as a good predictor of future performance; b) high portfolio turnover, which believers in an efficient market are persuaded does not produce sufficiently better investment returns to offset the heavy transactions costs incurred; and c) the level of management expenses, on the theory that investors will favor funds with the lowest amount of such costs

Many of the previously listed factors do in fact influence the discounts in the way we have suggested. In particular, the existence of unrealized appreciation, of letter stock, or of significant foreign holdings has in recent years tended to increase fund discounts, while large dividend payments (including capital gains distribution) tend to lower them. But statistical analysis indicates that these factors explain only a small portion of the average discounts available. Also, differences in the level of management fees do not appear to be related to the size of the discounts. Accordingly, some other explanation must also be important.[4]

In our judgment, the most reasonable possibility is that on average closed-end companies sell at discounts because they are not supported by an active marketing campaign. Once the fund has been established and closed, the investment advisor who typically organizes and brings out the fund does not stand to gain or lose, in terms of the fees he earns. Thus, the advisor has no financial interest in promoting such funds on a continuing basis, unless he fears that a large discount will engender a takeover bid that leaves the manager out of a job. Moreover, brokers, through whom shares must be purchased, may well prefer to sell load type open-end funds on which the broker will earn a larger commission. The truth of the matter is that, to the dismay of economists, investors don't *buy* investment funds, they are *sold* for such investments either by brokers or by other salesmen or, in the case of no-load funds, by a combination of advertising and direct solicitation. Since virtually no "sales" effort is made on behalf of closed-end funds — because there is no possible pay-off to such an effort in terms of increasing the fund's assets — the discounts may reflect scarcity of buyers relative to sellers.

A second and related possibility is that the discount on such funds is to some extent the functional equivalent of the redemption feature of open-end funds. Most open-end equity funds in recent years have suffered from redemptions in excess of new sales, reflecting the public's apparent aversion to the riskiness of common stocks and preference for the more stable money market or municipal bond vehicles. Since shares cannot be redeemed in a closed-end fund, the discounts may reflect the present state of the public's risk aversion to equities.

In any case, rational economic arguments can explain only a small part of the discounts that have typically existed. We suggest that at least to some extent the discounts represent a market inefficiency. As a result, closed-end funds offer an opportunity to, in effect, buy the "market at a discount," thus making them sufficiently attractive so that perhaps investors should regard them like a much needed aspirin in today's turbulent markets.

CRITERIA FOR SELECTING AMONG SUCH FUNDS

Both regular and dual purpose funds offer advantages. Purchase of the Income and Capital shares of dual purpose funds enables an investor to capitalize on the assured elimination of the discounts from net asset value upon termination of these funds. Purchase of regular closed funds may be attractive if their discounts are significantly higher than those discounts offered by dual purpose funds. While the discounts of these closed-end funds could widen, in many cases current discounts are now wider than general historical average discounts; this should, to some extent, mitigate this risk. Moreover, they may still be attractive enough relative to dual purpose funds to make them an appealing investment for a portion of an investor's funds.

Dual purpose funds may be selected for investment according to the following criteria:
1. *Attractiveness of discount.* Since the discounts are guaranteed to disappear on the maturity dates of

the funds, these discounts can be calculated as an annualized return to time of maturity to rank the attractiveness of the discount.

2. *Diversification and Performance.* The portfolio of the dual purpose funds should have a diversified position in equities. If funds appear equal on all other criteria, some investors may also wish to use past performance of the portfolio as a further criterion, though efficient market theorists would doubt that good past performance is a reliable predictor of future performance.

3. *Liquidity of Shares.* An investor must be able to purchase the Income and Capital shares of dual purpose funds in balanced proportions and at prices approximating the target discounts that appeal to the investor. The shares, conversely, must be readily marketable if the investor elects to use his capital for other projects or investments.

4. *Mix of Funds.* Purchase of more than one fund is recommended to hedge against the performance of any given fund's turning sour.

Regular closed-end funds may be selected for investment where the discounts from the net asset value of such funds are sufficiently larger than those available in dual purpose funds to offset the disadvantage that the discount is not guaranteed to disappear. In addition, if closed-end funds are selected, the discounts should be larger than the general historical average for the fund to mitigate the risk that the discount might widen. The other criteria listed for the dual funds are also applicable to the standard closed-end funds.

Detailed performance characteristics of a number of dual purpose and closed-end funds are available from the authors on request.

STRUCTURING A PORTFOLIO OF SUCH FUNDS

As you can see, there is a real role for an investment professional in selecting particular funds — and, indeed, you can assuage traditionalists by pointing out those funds and managers that have a track record of

SECURITY
SELECTION
AND ACTIVE
PORTFOLIO
MANAGEMENT

superior performance. More important, in structuring a portfolio of such funds, the risk preference of the investor should be taken into account. If the investor is willing to assume substantial risk, his portfolio can be weighted more heavily in favor of the capital shares of dual purpose funds; if he has conservative risk instincts, it can be weighted toward purchasing both sides of the dual purpose funds, particulary those with the closer maturity dates.

There are some minor limitations on the ability of a registered investment company to buy the securities of another registered investment company and, conversely, there is a limitation on so-called open-end investment companies to sell their securities to another registered investment company. The limitations are spelled out in Provision 12d of an Amendment to the Investment Act of 1940. They basically say that one registered investment company cannot own more than 3% of the stock of another, and that ownership cannot represent more than 5% of the owner's assets.

In addition, you will want to keep an eye on the degree of diversification of the underlying portfolio of the funds you recommend. A sample portfolio of funds can be constructed and the underlying stocks held by such funds classified according to industrial categories. The resulting underlying portfolio can then be examined to see whether in buying one grouping or another of funds, the investor's underlying portfolio is diversified to the extent desired, or is too light, in certain stocks or industries. If the latter is the case, then some weight can be given in structuring a portfolio of funds to selecting funds which will improve the diversification of the underlying securities.

Can such a strategy work? A recent empirical study by Rex Thompson suggests that it can.[5] Thompson showed it was possible to make up a simple strategy of buying closed-end investment company shares at a discount that outperformed a "market" portfolio of equivalent risk. The differences in return over the period of 1940 through 1975 were substantial and statistically significant.

My account executive friend, you still don't look happy — haven't we solved your problem? Ah . . . you are now concerned about what you do once you set up your client's portfolio. How do you occupy your time when you no longer have stocks and bonds to trade and your only duty is to monitor the performance of the funds you've selected? The answer is simple: write an article about your strategy.

---

[1] All dual purpose funds provide a method by which the Capital shareholders may realize the net asset value of the shares by a given date. In the case of funds such as the American DualVest Fund, it may be necessary for the stockholders to vote to make the fund open-end at the time the Income shares mature. We have no doubt but that the stockholders would not vote to have the fund remain closed since this would not be in their best interests.

[2] See Linda Snyder, "The Closed-End Funds May Be Opening Up," *Fortune*, February 13, 1978.

[3] See, for example, Burton G. Malkiel, "The Valuation of Closed-End Investment-Company Shares," *The Journal of Finance*, Vol. XXXII, No. 3, June, 1977.

[4] See Malkiel, *op. cit.*, and also Morris Mendelson, "Closed-End Fund Discounts Revisited," The Center for Study of Financial Institutions, University of Pennsylvania, 1977.

[5] See Rex Thompson, "Capital Market Efficiency and the Information Content of Discounts and Premiums on Closed-End Fund Shares: An Empirical Analysis," Working Paper #30, February, 1978, Graduate School of Industrial Administration, Carnegie-Mellon University.

260
SECURITY
SELECTION
AND ACTIVE
PORTFOLIO
MANAGEMENT

FURTHER
CONSIDERATIONS IN
SECURITY SELECTION

Multinationals are poor tools for diversification

Their stock prices behave too much like the prices of purely domestic firms.

Bertrand Jacquillat and Bruno Solnik

International portfolio investment and diversification are clearly desirable, as evidenced by numerous empirical studies: They offer higher average returns and simultaneously lower volatility of returns as compared with a well-diversified domestic portfolio. For example, Solnik has shown that international portfolios of fifty stocks equally invested on the major stock markets in the world are about three times less risky as measured by the amplitude of variation or standard deviation of returns than U.S. portfolios of similar size.[1] In a recent issue of this Journal,[2] Bergstrom presented the results of the experience of a U.S. managed international fund. The practical results were a higher average return because of investment in rapid growth economies and lower risk because of diversification.

To capitalize on the advantages of international

SECURITY
SELECTION
AND ACTIVE
PORTFOLIO
MANAGEMENT

1. Footnotes appear at the end of the article.

diversification, investors usually consider two main routes. One is to invest in U.S. multinational firms (MNF). Such companies are numerous, well-established, and draw an important part of their cash flows from sales generated in various countries. From the standpoint of portfolio managers, such a route is highly practical since U.S. multinationals tend to achieve the international diversification objectives for the investor without much pain.

The other route is to diversify among different stock markets. Although, actually, U.S. portfolio managers have not yet given much attention to it, our contention is that investing in U.S. multinational firms cannot be regarded as a valid substitute to international portfolio diversification. Such a conclusion is based on an extensive empirical study whose main results are summarized in this paper.[3]

INTERNATIONAL DIVERSIFICATION

The advantages of international diversification result from the relative independence between the various national economies and their stock price behavior. Although, as we have found in a recent study, the correlation between national stock indices movements has increased in recent times, it still offers opportunities for risk reduction. As can be inferred from Table 1, the average correlation coefficient of six of the largest European markets vis-à-vis the U.S. market is about .55. This means that, at most, 30% of stock market movements can be considered as common, the rest being diversifiable away. Another interesting conclusion that can be drawn from Table 1 is that, contrary to some a priori statements, the influence of exchange rate movements on stock prices is very weak and not systematic. Furthermore, the total variance of exchange risk is quite small compared to the variance of stock price movements (of the order of one-tenth).

Thus, these results imply that a well-diversified portfolio will have much lower risk than a purely domestic portfolio — even considering exchange risk, which tends to be diversified across several strong and

Table 1

Correlation Coefficients between Stock Index Returns and between Stock Index Returns and Exchange Rate Fluctuations

1974-1976

Stock Market Returns	Stock Market Returns*							Exchange Rate Fluctuations**						
	U.K.	Belgium	France	Germany	Netherlands	Switzerland	U.S.A.	British Pound	Belgian Franc	French Franc	German Mark	Dutch Guilder	Swiss Franc	U.S. Dollar
U.K.	1.000	.671	.635	.387	.708	.612	.578	-	.233	.128	.225	.091	.203	.103
Belgium		1.000	.717	.599	.816	.798	.621	-.218	-	.062	.095	-.083	-.108	-.358
France			1.000	.566	.740	.751	.542	-.252	-.057	-	.181	-.052	-.078	-.262
Germany				1.000	.632	.602	.335	-.026	.161	.354	-	.085	.151	.158
Netherlands					1.000	.807	.583	-.215	-.087	.090	.070	-	-.126	-.328
Switzerland						1.000	.685	-.101	.068	.172	.083	-.007	-	-.146
U.S.A.							1.000	.236	-.066	.046	.188	-.068	.097	-

* Rows and columns represent stock market returns measured on a monthly basis.

** A row represents a national stock index and a column represents a currency. A coefficient (e.g., .181) is the correlation between the row stock index return (e.g., the French Index) and the monthly exchange rate fluctuation of the column currency (e.g. the D.M.) expressed in terms of the stock index country currency (D.M. for French Francs).

Source: Capital International Perspective and IMF Statistics - various issues.

weak currencies. Given the relative independence of national economic growth and stock markets,[4] there also exist abroad investment opportunities that have no substitute domestically.

DO MULTINATIONAL FIRMS OFFER INTERNATIONAL PORTFOLIO DIVERSIFICATION?

The question is whether investment in MNF presents the same characteristics as international portfolio diversification. In other words, may MNF shares be regarded as an international portfolio with similar stock price behavior?

From the financial analyst's viewpoint, a positive factor might be the better stability of earnings of MNF as opposed to firms whose earnings depend on a single national market and labor force. Yet, such a conclusion seems to be altered by the recent implementation of the FASB statement No. 8, which creates an artificial volatility of the reported earnings of many companies because of exchange rate movements.

In any case, the investor must ultimately analyze the real "economic" earnings, their stability, and their translation in the stock market price behavior. So the question is whether the stock market recognizes the diversification aspects of multinational shares.

We have empirically investigated this question on a sample of approximately 300 European and 100 American firms whose monthly stock prices were available from April, 1966 to June, 1974. From these, 40 European firms and 23 American firms were selected as having the most multinational activities (according to *Business International* and *Fortune*). Extensive and usually confidential information on the geographical breakdown of their activities (sales, assets . . .) was collected.

A first conclusion is obtained by comparing the total variability of returns of a portfolio 1) invested in U.S. companies with little foreign activity, 2) invested in U.S. multinational firms, 3) equally invested on the

266

SECURITY
SELECTION
AND ACTIVE
PORTFOLIO
MANAGEMENT

Table 2
Average Betas of Portfolios of Country MNF with Selected National Indices

	US	Nether-lands	Belgium	Germany	Italy	Sweden	France	Switzer-land	U.K.	R^2 adj.	Single index beta	Single index R^2 adj
US MNF	.94	.12	-.05	-.01	-.04	.04	.02	-.01	-.07	.31	1.02	.29
Dutch MNF	.31	.76	.09	.16	-.02	-.28	.25	-.21	-.06	.63	.98	.50
Belgian MNF	-.27	.07	1.04	.06	.03	.19	.06	.08	.07	.58	1.03	.45
German MNF	.24	.03	-.21	1.18	-.02	-.01	.10	-.15	-.11	.74	1.18	.65
Italian MNF	-.10	.06	.10	.01	.83	.11	-.19	-.16	.20	.51	.91	.47
Swedish MNF	.06	-.15	-.02	.08	-.10	.96	.01	.15	.02	.50	.92	.42
French MNF	-.10	.14	.33	.18	.02	-.16	.95	-.22	.03	.62	1.08	.45
Swiss MNF	-.12	-.23	-.04	-.09	-.02	.16	-.11	1.74	.16	.75	1.39	.52
British MNF	-.10	-.11	.30	.09	-.04	-.13	-.09	.07	.84	.49	1.06	.44

Note: all R^2 are adjusted for the number of degrees of freedom.

major national stock markets. It turns out that the variability of returns measured by the standard deviation of the U.S. multinational portfolios is usually 90% of the risk of a purely domestic U.S. portfolio of the same size. The difference is much more striking for international portfolios of similar size, whose risk is only 30% to 50% of the risk of the U.S. domestic portfolio. Although multinational firms do perform some international diversification for the investor, this would suggest that MNF portfolios are poor substitutes for international portfolio diversification.

Further insights might be gained by looking directly at the factors that influence multinational stock prices.

MULTINATIONAL SHARE PRICE BEHAVIOR

The financial community is now familiar with the so-called β or market model. It describes the influence of the general (domestic) market movement on each common stock. Any well-diversified "domestic" portfolio will follow closely the domestic market movement. Such a behavior has been amply demonstrated on all major stock markets.[5] If a MNF share is indeed like an international portfolio, its stock price should be affected by foreign factors to the extent of its activities abroad. In periods of depressed American stock markets, MNF stock prices should be influenced by the bullish movements of other national stock markets[6] and therefore move against the general trend of American stock prices. Via U.S. multinational shares, portfolio managers would indirectly invest in rapid growth economies while getting the benefits of international diversification.

Unfortunately, the empirical examination leads to different conclusions. We regressed the stock returns of each MNF on all the various national stock indices to evaluate whether the foreign factors had a significant influence on MNF stock price behavior.[7] Some of the results are summarized in Table 2. The first part of the Table gives the average, by country of MNF headquarters, of all the "beta" coefficients of the international regression (and the R-square of the regression); the second part gives the results of the traditional (domestic) single index model.

The results are quite clear. With very few exceptions, only the domestic betas are significant and, on the average, they are close to one. The foreign betas are usually small and insignificant. Furthermore, the compounded influence of eight foreign indices explains only less than two additional percent of the stock price behavior of U.S. multinational firms. In other words, the international stock price behavior of U.S. MNF is negligible and there is not much difference between so-called multinational and the "average" domestic American shares.

The conclusions are somewhat different for MNF headquartered in smaller countries and having most of their activities abroad. For example, the foreign influence "explains" an additional 23% of Swiss MNF stock price behavior, which could be justified by the fact that their firms sell more than 95% of their product abroad (the adjusted R-square increases from 52% to 75%). Compared with the average national share, foreign factors influence 13% of Belgian and Dutch MNF price variations, which have 85% to 95% of their sales abroad. A fairly important foreign influence is also present for French MNF despite a lower level of foreign activities, but the difference between domestic and multinational firms from England, Italy, and even Germany is quite small.

In all cases, the extent of foreign influence on stock prices is unexpectedly limited compared to the extent of these firms' foreign involvement.

DIRECT VS. PORTFOLIO INTERNATIONAL DIVERSIFICATION

Finally, we ran a direct test of the relation between the geographical breakdown of each multinational activities and the national factor influencing its market value. According to those who believe that diversification via multinational firms is a good substitute for international portfolio management for the

SECURITY
SELECTION
AND ACTIVE
PORTFOLIO
MANAGEMENT

portfolio manager, the common stock of firms such as Colgate-Palmolive, which has about 50% of its sales, earnings, and assets abroad, should be considered as a sum of a purely domestic component (50%) and a foreign stock market component (50%). In other words, its stock price should follow the NYSE index for 50% of its price variation and a world index (excluding the U.S.) for the remaining 50%. Furthermore, this last component should be affected by exchange rate fluctuations to the extent that the multinational does not cover its foreign exchange risk exposure.

Without going into the mathematical, though simple, formulation of the model and its tests, summary results for American multinationals may be presented. The MNF price fluctuations were regressed against the domestic stock index, an aggregate foreign stock index and selected exchange rates (Deutsches Mark, French Franc, British Pound). The exchange rate influence seemed generally quite small and almost random in sign. However, on the average the coefficients were positive for the Mark and the Franc (.08 and .03). It implied that the strength of these two currencies during the period was recognized by Wall Street as having a positive effect. On the other side, MNF seemed to have *overhedged* their British assets and thereby benefited from the weakness of the Pound (an average negative coefficient of −.28). In all cases, these were very small factors.

For the stock markets' coefficients (betas), the influence of foreign factors on the value of the multinational firms was again much smaller than could be expected from the percentage of foreign activities[8] as seen in Table 3. Clearly the domestic beta coefficients seem too large compared to the domestic sales ratio (.97 and .97 compared to .62 and .41), while foreign coefficients are too small (.15 and .11 compared to .38 and .59). A similar conclusion is found for European MNF. To support these results in an international pricing context would require the domestic part of MNF to be much less risky than the average domestic firm and the international part of their activities to be much risk-

Table 3

Proportion of Geographical Influence on MNF Stock Prices

	US MNF		European MNF	
	Sales %	Betas	Sales %	Betas
Domestic	62	.97	.41	.97
Foreign	38	.15	.59	.11

ier than the average foreign firm. There is no evidence that such is the case.

Cross-sectional results reported below give more insight into this problem.

First, a regression among all firms (cross-section) between the domestic betas and the foreign betas of the following form was run

$$\beta_{\text{domestic}} = C_0 + C_1 \beta_{\text{foreign}}$$

In this portfolio context, we would expect C_0 to be equal to 1 and C_1 to -1.

This regression yields the following results for the U.S. MNF

$$\beta_{\text{domestic}} = 1.12 - 1.13 \beta_{\text{foreign}} \qquad R^2 = .56$$
$$(.22)$$

and for the European MNF

$$\beta_{\text{domestic}} = 1.09 - .66 \beta_{\text{foreign}} \qquad R^2 = .62$$
$$(.12)$$

The coefficients are not significantly different from their predicted values, while C_1 is significantly lower for European firms. However, the negative correlation between domestic and foreign β's is in both cases quite strong (R-square of .6) and all coefficients statistically different from zero (.01 level).

A regression among all U.S. MNF (cross-section) between the domestic betas and the percentage

270
SECURITY
SELECTION
AND ACTIVE
PORTFOLIO
MANAGEMENT

of domestic activities (domestic sales) yields the following result

$$\beta_{domestic} = .26 + 1.09 \text{ D.S.} \qquad R^2 = .07$$
$$(.88)$$

where D.S. is the ratio of domestic to total sales and the standard error is in parentheses.

The same regression for foreign betas is

$$\beta_{foreign} = -.23 + .98 \text{ F.S.} \qquad R^2 = .12$$
$$(.57)$$

where F.S. is the ratio of foreign to total sales. We would expect the intercept of the regression to be close to zero and the dependent variable coefficient to be close to one. While the relations are consistent with our expectations, they are very weak with low R-square.

CONCLUSIONS

In this paper we studied the multinational stock price behavior of American firms with extensive foreign activities. We did not address the question of the advantages of international investment, considering that there existed now numerous studies supporting, at least, a limited degree of international stock diversification with a selective policy among companies and national stock markets. The issue was rather whether investing in U.S. multinational firms could be regarded as a direct substitute to international portfolio diversification. The answer seems to be mostly negative.

The multinational stock prices do not seem to be extensively affected by foreign factors and behave much like the stock price of a purely domestic firm. Several explanations could be proposed, ranging from the importance of national control, government constraints, the influence of the major stock market where the stock is traded, or investors' poor judgement. In any case, this is another story that awaits another study.

[1] See B. Solnik, "Why not diversify internationally," *Financial Analysts Journal*, July, 1974.

[2] G. Bergstrom, "A new route to higher return and lower risk," *Journal of Portfolio Management*, Autumn, 1975.

[3] A portion of these results were presented in a talk at the Center for Research in Security Prices at the University of Chicago in May, 1977 and at a conference of the European Association of International Business, Jouy-en-Josas, 1977. The paper will be reprinted in the proceedings of this conference and copies are available from the authors at CESA, 78350 Jouy-en-Josas, France.

[4] For empirical evidence on the degree of dependence of economic variables such as GNP, see Alan Rugman, "Risk reduction by international diversification," *Journal of International Business Studies*, Fall, 1976. He finds correlation coefficients much lower than one would intuitively expect.

[5] See Pogue and Solnik, "The Market Model Applied to European Common Stocks," *Journal of Financial and Quantitative Analysis*, December, 1974.

[6] Given the fairly large degree of independence among national stock prices' behavior indicated earlier.

[7] The domestic beta-model can be written as: $\tilde{R} = \alpha + \beta \tilde{I}o$ where $\tilde{R}$ is the return on the common stock and $\tilde{I}o$ the return on the domestic market.
The international multi-index model used here has the following form:

$$\tilde{R} = \alpha + \beta_0 \tilde{I}o + \beta_1 \tilde{I}_1 + \ldots + \beta_n \tilde{I}_n$$

where $\tilde{I}_1, \ldots, \tilde{I}_n$ are the returns on the foreign stock markets.

[8] Rugman reports that measures of foreign activities such as assets, sales, net income, number of employees are highly correlated (correlation of .8 or more). Therefore, our conclusions would not be changed by the proxy used for foreign industrial activities. Alan Rugman, Letter to the Editor of the *Financial Analysts Journal*, March/April, 1976.

SECURITY
SELECTION
AND ACTIVE
PORTFOLIO
MANAGEMENT

Liquidity filters: Tools for better performance

How liquid is your portfolio? How liquid is the total market? How can the answers to these questions reduce risk and enhance returns?

Michael D. Hirsch

Common stock liquidity as a consideration in securities purchases and sales and in overall portfolio construction is a recent concept. In the past, primary emphasis was placed on fundamental factors and secondary emphasis on technical aspects, with liquidity (marketability) relegated to at best a third-class role. This was typified in some institutions by requiring no more than a "Good-Fair-Poor" rating of liquidity on investment committee reports, or by leaving it to the trading desk's "feel" for the stock at others.

With the ever-deepening liquidity crisis the stock market has been experiencing since the late '60s, the neglect in which this criterion was previously held is fast disappearing. In its stead there has evolved a need to develop a benchmark that accurately measures liquidity.

The historic benchmarks of liquidity have proven lacking. Shares Outstanding ignores the level of market price. Dollar Value Outstanding does not reflect holdings not available for trading (e.g., Shell Transport owns 40% of Shell Oil). Floating Supply statistics are not available, and even where reliable estimates can be derived, they do not reflect the rapidity of share turnover. Trading volume also ignores price level. Turnover is misleading in that low turnover is presumed to equal high liquidity, but may simply reflect low volume. Finally, Dollar Volume ignores the impact of market price.

THE LIQUIDITY RATIO

What is required, therefore, is a tool that will measure: (A) Dollar Volume Traded, and (B) that volume's impact on price. With this in mind, we developed in 1971 the Liquidity Ratio, which measures the Dollar Value Traded per each percent of price variation. For example, XYZ Corporation over five trading days has $500,000 in Dollar Value Traded. Over that period, the day-to-day percentage changes in price were: +1.2%, +1.0%, −1.0%, +0.8%, −1.0%. To arrive at the Liquidity Ratio for XYZ, we divide the Dollar Volume (500.000 — expressed in thousands) by the cumulative percentage change (5.0 — disregarding sign, since we are concerned with impact, not direction), giving us a Ratio of 100.0, or $100,000 of Dollar Value Traded per each percent of price variation.

With this as a base, we can proceed to construct comprehensive liquidity parameters for overall portfolios by developing Liquidity Ratios for all listed common stocks from which we can then ascertain a relative liquidity ranking for this universe; in addition, we can establish liquidity statistics by industry to facilitate portfolio construction.

But to be useful in any form, the Ratio must prove stable, particularly for institutional investors who in the main are concerned with a long-term time frame. Otherwise, even though the Ratio might be able to provide a "liquidity framework" for current purchases, it would be useless in determining what liquidity will be available when the time comes to liquidate positions.

SECURITY
SELECTION
AND ACTIVE
PORTFOLIO
MANAGEMENT

An extended test bore out the stability of the Liquidity Ratios. Tracking the Ratios of a random sample of 500 stocks over five years (1966-1970) on a quarter-to-quarter basis resulted in a correlation coefficient (by quarter) of .84. Fifty-stock portfolios randomly selected from this universe during the same period (which is more reflective of institutions, with their diversified portfolios) achieved a quarter-to-quarter correlation coefficient of .99! Further, this stability was maintained for more extended periods, with a .7 coefficient two years out and a .5 coefficient three years out for individual stocks in the sample. Again, in both time frames, the coefficient for portfolios was significantly higher.

Simply stated, this showed that individual stocks have "liquidity monikers" — liquid stocks remain liquid and illiquid stocks remain illiquid in most cases. As such, we can then rely upon the Liquidity Ratio as a filter upon which to base liquidity considerations for stock selection and portfolio construction.

THE LIQUIDITY BETA

Where we are considering the purchase of more than one issue and the maintenance of diversified portfolios, the liquidity concept can be carried a step further with the development of a Liquidity Beta for each stock. The Liquidity Beta measures *the sensitivity of a stock's liquidity relative to the entire market*. Or, what is the percentage change in a stock's liquidity which normally accompanies a 1% change in the market's liquidity?

In construction, the Liquidity Beta is similar to price beta, in that it is based on a regression analysis of the past 36 months' Liquidity Ratios (on a moving basis) for each stock and for the total market. The resulting Beta describes how much of the change in a stock's liquidity level can be ascribed to the change in liquidity of all stocks.

In purchasing an individual stock, this is obviously not of concern. But in purchases for portfolios, if diversification possibilities do exist whereby we can diversify the liquidity risk over a group of stocks and achieve (or come near) a *net* Liquidity Beta of 0 (minimal movement in the liquidity level of the total portfolio regardless of the direction and dynamics of liquidity movements for the overall market), then we can further insure the availability of a probable level of liquidity at any given point in the future (Liquidity Beta signs do offset). Thus, a portfolio consisting of Stock A with a Liquidity Beta of 1.0 and Stock B with a Liquidity Beta of −1.0 will have a net Liquidity Beta of 0.

USING THE TOOLS

Together, the Liquidity Ratio and the Liquidity Beta can act as meaningful filters and constraints for the portfolio manager, although, since a low Liquidity Beta by itself does not imply good liquidity, there should never be a situation where the Beta is used alone. Typical applications would be:

1. No stock will be considered for the portfolio unless it ranks among the 500 most liquid stocks; or,
2. No stock with a Liquidity Beta in excess of 1.0 will be eligible for the approved list; or,
3. The specific dollar amounts applied to each of a group of stocks I intend to purchase at present will be weighted by each stock's Liquidity Ratio, so that each purchase will have a similar impact on price.

On individual stock purchases, or where buying a limited number of issues is involved, the portfolio manager and trader can analyze the liquidity data to: (A) provide a benchmark for the timing of the order to minimize the effect that order might have on the issue's price; (B) serve as a relative gauge for offers received from the specialist, third market, or fourth market; and (C) act as final determinant in purchases between two or more equally favored stocks.

For instance, if a portfolio manager decided to establish a position in the paper industry, he would find that the three most liquid stocks in the group as of June, 1975 were: International Paper (latest three-

276
SECURITY
SELECTION
AND ACTIVE
PORTFOLIO
MANAGEMENT

month Ratio: 1255.8, Beta: .24), Crown Zellerbach (Ratio: 927.0, Beta: .42), and Union Camp (Ratio: 401.4, Beta: −.08). This presents him with the following alternatives:

1. If he has flexibility as to dollar amounts that he can apply to each purchase, then International Paper can absorb ⅓ more purchasing power than Crown Zellerbach and three times more than Union Camp without any greater impact on price;

2. If diversifying portfolio liquidity risk is a primary consideration, then Union Camp should be stressed as a purchase.

Particularly in the present market environment, with its substantial volatility and wide price swings — many of these caused by the impact of concentrated purchases and/or sales by institutions — such determinations can prove extremely helpful towards improving the profitability potential of the portfolio. Yet, in order to make any emphasis on liquidity meaningful and not simply an academic process, there should be a sufficient number of "institutional-quality" stocks available in the universe of stocks that meet basic liquidity minimums. As Table I indicates, there is a significant group.

The criteria used for inclusion on this list were: (A) a stock must rank among the top 500 by Liquidity Ratio (implying that they are liquid enough for institutional-size orders) and (B) a stock must have a Liquidity Beta below .50 (denoting that they gain or lose liquidity half as fast as the overall market). There were 153 issues that qualified, representing a cross section of industries and technical characteristics. Both in terms of their marketability levels and in their historical record of maintaining those levels in a relatively stable fashion relative to the overall market, they can be categorized as suitable for substantial investments.

WHICH IS THE BEST EXECUTION?

One last application for such liquidity data has taken on particular significance since the advent of fully negotiated rates and the concurrent emphasis on "best execution." Indeed, the emphasis put on execution capabilities by the Pension Reform Act of 1974 has placed additional import on a fiduciary's ability to judge trading impact through an objective, statistical system.

Utilizing the Liquidity Ratio as a base, one can create an "execution rating system" founded on price data to judge the absolute effectiveness of the execution relative to the trading range and the Ratio for the stock involved (in effect, to determine the "degree of difficulty" of the trade). A "good" execution in a stock with a low Ratio, or one with limited marketability, should be rated higher than a "good" execution in a stock with a high Ratio, or one easily marketable.

A less refined approach would be to utilize the Ratios on a trade-by-trade basis to determine effectiveness. For example, Broker A is given a buy order for 10,000 shares of ABC Corporation. ABC, currently selling at $50 per share, has a Ratio of 500.0. This implies that $500,000 of Dollar Volume (the value of the order with Broker A) should affect the price of ABC by no more than 50¢ per share (1% of $50). The institution, therefore, now has a benchmark by which to judge this broker (and other brokers on other trades) by recording how near he comes to the implied $50.50 upper limit on completing the order.

Thus, with a method available to statistically measure liquidity on an historical basis, the portfolio manager should no longer focus his attention strictly on fundamental and technical factors in developing a portfolio strategy and a buying and selling program: he can now give due regard to marketability. At a time when the marketplace is becoming ever more dominated by institutional orders, liquidity has "come of age" as a primary portfolio consideration.

SECURITY
SELECTION
AND ACTIVE
PORTFOLIO
MANAGEMENT

STOCKS WITH HIGH LIQUIDITY AND LOW LIQUIDITY RISK

COMPANY	JUNE, 1975 3-MONTH LIQUIDITY RATIO	RANK	JUNE, 1975 LIQUIDITY BETA	RANK
ASA Ltd.	619.9	152	-.80	7
Air Products & Chemical	717.0	129	.21	153
Alcan Aluminum	659.9	137	.03	79
Allied Chemical	689.6	134	.27	192
Aluminum Co. of America	1345.0	65	.06	84
Amax, Inc.	1135.6	83	.18	130
American Home Products	2868.0	17	.23	164
American Tel. & Tel.	13733.1	1	.46	368
AMP Inc.	657.2	139	.04	81
Amsted Industries	308.8	278	.42	332
Archer-Daniels-Midland	255.2	323	.34	246
Asarco	240.5	344	.33	239
Atlantic Richfield	3547.7	9	.12	110
Avery Products	175.5	434	.41	324
Baker Oil Tools	568.2	163	.43	337
Bates Manufacturing	152.9	477	.20	142

COMPANY	JUNE, 1975 3-MONTH LIQUIDITY RATIO	RANK	JUNE, 1975 LIQUIDITY BETA	RANK
Bausch & Lomb	538.6	167	.34	242
Baxter Laboratories	896.1	103	.37	267
Bethlehem Steel	1428.0	58	.35	248
Black & Decker Mfg.	730.2	125	.20	145
Boeing Co.	756.2	121	.38	282
British Petroleum	189.5	402	.27	189
Bucyrus Erie	921.3	99	-.02	63
Burlington Northern	407.8	221	.36	255
Burroughs Corp.	2228.2	31	.44	354
Campbell Red Lake	240.7	341	-.59	14
Caterpillar Tractor	2278.5	27	.40	309
Charter Co.	197.5	386	.32	219
Chemetron Corp.	421.3	214	.50	434
Chessie System	858.5	110	.27	194
Citicorp	1969.8	40	.48	389
Cleveland Cliffs Iron	267.4	309	.18	134
Coca-Cola Co.	1515.8	53	.32	228
Colt Industries	374.4	237	-.19	32
Crane Co.	269.0	305	-.11	44

Company				
Detroit Edison				
Diamond Shamrock	1095.6	86	.35	253
Digital Equipment	1985.3	39	.34	245
Dome Mines, Ltd.	276.9	300	-.37	25
Dow Chemical	4336.9	6	.16	125
Dresser Industries	1263.0	73	.45	361
DuPont	3580.1	8	.41	321
Duquesne Light	183.2	415	.38	275
Eastman Kodak	5431.3	3	.41	317
Emery Air Freight	233.5	356	.08	96
Falcon Seaboard	168.9	452	.12	111
Fluor Corp.	689.1	135	.36	266
Freeport Minerals	261.8	317	.43	336
Gearhart-Owen Ind.	162.9	464	.20	143
Getty Oil	1446.2	57	.11	108
Great Lakes Chemical	141.7	500	.23	159
Gulf Resources Chem.	481.6	187	.25	180
Halliburton	2805.2	18	.03	78
Harnischfeger	176.9	432	.01	67
H. J. Heinz	654.8	142	.49	404
Hercules	986.6	96	.25	179
Hewlett-Packard	1991.1	38	-.05	58
Homestake Mining	874.5	106	-.97	3

282

SECURITY
SELECTION
AND ACTIVE
PORTFOLIO
MANAGEMENT

COMPANY	JUNE, 1975 3-MONTH LIQUIDITY RATIO	RANK	JUNE, 1975 LIQUIDITY BETA	RANK
Ingersoll-Rand	1132.2	84	.09	99
Inland Steel	512.8	178	.35	249
Intl. Flav. & Frag.	476.8	190	.06	86
Intl. Min. & Chem.	1300.6	71	-.19	31
International Paper	1255.8	75	.24	169
Johnson & Johnson	2711.6	20	.36	264
Joy Manufacturing	729.1	126	.49	414
Kennecott Copper	1635.0	45	.07	90
Kerr McGee	2134.5	32	.39	284
Koppers Co.	188.5	404	.16	124
LTV Corp.	420.9	215	.10	105
Eli Lilly	2715.1	19	.37	273
Long Island Lighting	245.7	333	.48	399
Lykes Youngstown	177.8	429	-.06	53
Mapco	476.2	191	.21	146
Masonite Corp.	396.5	228	.24	167
J. Ray McDermott	1080.6	88	.21	147
McDonald's	2359.8	26	.33	236
Merck	2998.6	15	.16	122
Mesabi Trust	150.3			

Company				
Monsanto	209	.29	13	3143.6
Moore McCormack	64	-.02	181	498.6
Mountain Fuel Supply	294	.39	273	315.7
NL Industries	415	.49	274	315.6
Nat. Semiconductor	136	.19	87	1093.4
Nat. Starch	278	.38	438	173.9
Natomas	225	.32	173	523.3
Newmont Mining	265	.36	387	197.3
Niagra Mohawk Power	290	.39	312	266.0
No. Natural Gas	177	.25	192	473.7
Northrop	104	.10	446	169.8
Northwest Bancorp	391	.48	426	178.6
Ogden	235	.33	475	153.4
Owens-Corn. Fiberg.	429	.50	282	308.2
J. C. Penney	323	.41	48	1577.9
Penn. Power & Lt.	247	.34	293	289.0
Pennwalt	335	.43	454	168.3
Pennzoil	382	.47	199	455.2
Peoples Gas	272	.37	347	237.8
Perkin Elmer	322	.41	314	262.5
Phelps Dodge	285	.39	249	357.8
Phillips Petroleum	410	.49	54	1485.8
Pittston	310	.40	41	1763.9

284

SECURITY
SELECTION
AND ACTIVE
PORTFOLIO
MANAGEMENT

COMPANY	JUNE, 1975 3-MONTH LIQUIDITY RATIO	RANK	JUNE, 1975 LIQUIDITY BETA	RANK
Potlatch	274.5	303	.46	372
Procter & Gamble	2656.8	22	.01	69
Pub. Serv.-Colorado	241.0	340	.45	355
Pub. Serv.-Indiana	532.3	168	.29	210
Pullman	413.1	218	.09	97
Republic Steel	507.8	179	.49	412
R. J. Reynolds Inds.	2100.7	33	.44	349
Reynolds Metal	289.3	291	.39	295
Robintech	155.4	473	-.49	17
Rosario Resources	346.2	255	-.60	12
Rucker Co.	183.4	414	-.45	19
Safeway Stores	1270.1	72	.48	394
St. Joe Minerals	515.3	177	.13	113
St. Regis Paper	244.4	334	.43	342
Santa Fe Industries	519.4	175	.40	306
Schering-Plough	2267.7	29	.36	256
Schlumberger	2500.2	25	-.09	48
S. Car. Elec. & Gas.	178.7	424	.26	184
Southern Co.	973.1	97	.27	187
Southland Royalty	178.8	423	.27	195
A. E. Staley	268.1	308	.25	178

Sun Oil	279.4	297	.25	175
Syntex	1578.2	47	.42	333
Texaco	3094.8	14	.42	334
Texas Instruments	2507.0	24	.18	131
Texasgulf	651.3	143	.42	325
Tidewater Marine	142.1	499	.23	165
Tucson G. & E.	148.5	486	.50	424
UAL Inc.	397.1	227	.48	400
UV Industries	143.4	495	.29	208
Unilever	172.0	442	.45	358
Union Camp	401.4	224	-.08	51
Union Oil	769.1	120	.47	388
Union Pacific	1340.9	66	.04	80
U. S. Steel	3455.6	11	-.20	30
Upjohn	1481.9	55	.28	202
Utah Intl.	1261.1	74	.07	89
Utah Power	220.4	366	.47	387
Va. Elec. & Pow.	483.5	186	.48	392
Westvaco	177.7	430	.01	68
Weyerhaeuser	1335.6	67	.13	114
Williams Cos.	1309.2	69	-.05	57
Wisconsin Elec. Pwr.	429.0	210	.23	163
Xerox	4946.8	4	.39	293

Risk/return contrasts: NYSE, Amex, and OTC*

These markets do differ, but by how much?

Arthur A. Eubank, Jr.

The two primary objectives of this study are to compare the risk-return characteristics of different stock market segments and to test for the potential for improving risk-adjusted portfolio returns by diversifying across these market segments. The three stock market segments examined are: (1) the New York Stock Exchange (NYSE), (2) the American Stock Exchange (ASE), and (3) the Over-the-Counter Market (OTC). If portfolios composed of randomly selected securities from these three market segments exhibit risk-return characteristics which are significantly different for each market segment, this finding would indicate that there are, in fact, several distinct markets

* The author would like to acknowledge the data collection and computer programming efforts of Gerald H. Mock.

for common stocks.[1] Further, their existence and identification might provide the potential for improving portfolio performance by diversifying across these unique market segments.

Specific stock market segments have been examined in previous studies by Reilly [16,17], Jessup and Upson [11,12,23], Eubank [4,5], Hagerman and Richmond [9], and Blume and Husic [3]. The studies by Reilly were concerned with comparisons of the correlations of daily and weekly changes in the levels of the Dow Jones Industrial Average, the Standard and Poor's 425 Industrial Index, the NYSE Composite Index, the ASE Price Level Index, and the National Quotation Bureau Industrial Average for the OTC market. His findings provided some support for the existence of a segmented stock market. The Upson and Jessup studies compared the Minnesota OTC market, other regional OTC markets, and the NYSE, and concluded that these physically separate markets exhibit significantly different risk-return characteristics.[2] The studies by Eubank found significant differences among distributions of risk-return measures for individual stocks selected from the NYSE, ASE, and OTC segments. Hagerman and Richmond tested the market efficiency of OTC stocks; their results indicated that the monthly stock price changes of the sample of OTC stocks used were serially independent and were not unlike the results of earlier studies by Fama [7], and Fama and Blume [8], which used samples of NYSE stocks. Blume and Husic found significant differences between the monthly returns for NYSE and ASE portfolios having the same price and beta levels, although the signs of the differences alternated for different time periods.

The results of the present study indicate the three segments examined do exhibit significantly different risk-return characteristics. The results also suggest, however, that there is insufficient diversification potential to successfully improve risk-

1. Footnotes appear at the end of the article.

adjusted portfolio performance by diversifying across the three segments examined. The lack of sufficient diversification potential is attributable to the reasonably high correlation coefficients between the index returns for the three segments.

DATA AND METHODOLOGY

The data for this study were obtained from the Annual Industrial and Annual Over-the-Counter Compustat Tapes, *Standard and Poor's Corporation Records*, *Standard and Poor's Trade and Securities Statistics*, and monthly issues of the *Federal Reserve Bulletin*. All companies on the Annual Industrial and Over-the-Counter Compustat Tapes that had at least two consecutive annual closing stock price, dividend, and adjustment factor data were included in the sample.[3] The time period used was 1960 through 1973, which provided thirteen annual returns for each company having a complete set of closing stock price, dividend, and adjustment factor data over the sample period.

After all companies with sufficient data on the Compustat tapes were identified, each company was checked in the *Standard and Poor's Corporation Records* to determine its market trading location for each year, in order to categorize it by market segment for each year of its data availability. This procedure was necessary since some companies shown on the Compustat tapes as currently NYSE-listed companies were, in fact, listed on the ASE or traded in the OTC market for parts of the sample period. Several companies were found to have followed the OTC-ASE-NYSE progression of trading location. An annual breakdown according to trading location of the number of companies with sufficient data for each year is shown in Table I.

After identifying the proper market segment for each company for each year of its data availability on the Compustat tapes, an index for each of the three segments was constructed by computing an arithmetic average of the annual returns of all companies in each segment for each respective year. Following the calculation of each segment index, an equally weighted

SECURITY SELECTION AND ACTIVE PORTFOLIO MANAGEMENT

TABLE I

Number of Companies Used From Each Segment (1961-1973)

Year	NYSE	ASE	OTC
1961	541	255	357
1962	566	275	397
1963	596	308	467
1964	625	332	482
1965	657	364	468
1966	702	389	465
1967	746	413	458
1968	781	451	442
1969	842	467	465
1970	896	488	517
1971	933	479	526
1972	989	483	548
1973	944	430	448

index was also constructed from the three segment indexes. To determine the relationships among the individual indexes, the equally weighted index, and the Standard and Poor's 425 Industrial Index, correlation analyses were performed for each pair of indexes.

After performing the index correlations, a systematic random sampling technique was employed to select twenty portfolios from each of the three market segments for each year of the study to be used to make comparisons among these segments (e.g., NYSE:ASE, NYSE:OTC, and ASE:OTC).[4] This sampling technique selected every twentieth security beginning with the first security for the first portfolio and continuing until the list of available securities for a particular segment was exhausted in a given year.[5] A systematic random sampling technique was employed to ensure that each portfolio was composed of a representative cross section of industries, since the ordering of the companies on the Compustat tape is by industry. This portfolio selection process was used to eliminate the potential bias associated with using companies that were either traded in the OTC market or listed on the ASE for the entire sample period.[6]

Following the initial comparisons of portfolios from the three market segments, portfolio comparisons were also made between pairs of segments and combinations of the segments as well as between pairs of different segment combinations. A systematic random sampling technique was also used to select securities for inclusion into the portfolio sets of the segments and combinations. In order to ensure independence within and between the two portfolio sets in each pair, no security in a given year was included in more than one portfolio for a specific pair. Based upon the earlier empirical findings of serial independence by Fama [7] and Fama and Blume [8], it was assumed that the portfolio returns for different time periods are independent. The segment compositions of each of the four combinations which were used in the comparisons are as follows:

Combinations

1. NYSE-ASE (N-A)
2. NYSE-OTC (N-O)
3. ASE-OTC (A-O)
4. NYSE-ASE-OTC (N-A-O)

If a particular segment were included in both members of a pair when making a comparison between a segment and a combination (e.g., NYSE:N-A) or between two combinations (e.g., N-A:N-O), then every odd-numbered fortieth security from the segment was selected for inclusion into each of the respective twenty portfolios of the first pair, and every even-numbered fortieth security was placed into each of the respective twenty portfolios of the second pair for each year. In order to ensure proper weighting of the segments within combinations having unequal numbers of securities from each segment, the average return for each segment included in the combination was calculated, and the segment returns were then equally weighted to obtain a particular combination's annual return.

The risk-return measures used to compare the portfolio sets are as follows:

1. annual arithmetic mean return (AMR), [7]
2. annual geometric mean return (GMR),
3. Standard deviation about the annual arithmetic mean return (SD),
4. beta (systematic risk) coefficient (β),[8]
5. coefficient of determination (R^2),
6. the Jensen [10] alpha coefficient (α),
7. the Sharpe [19] reward-to-variability measure (SRV), and
8. the Treynor [22] reward-to-volatility measure (TRV).[9]

The capital market measures (α, β, R^2) were obtained by regressing each portfolio's continuously compounded[10] excess returns ($R_{it} - R_{ft}$) on the continuously compounded excess returns ($R_{mt} - R_{ft}$) of the equally weighted index (constructed from the three market segments) according to Equation (1) which follows:

$$(R_{it} - R_{ft}) = \alpha_i + \beta_i (R_{mt} - R_{ft}) + e_{it}, \quad (1)$$

where

R_{ft} = Ln (one plus the annualized 90-day Treasury bill rate)

R_{it} = Ln (one plus the portfolio annual return)

R_{mt} = Ln (one plus the equally weighted index annual return)

The final step in the study was to test for significant differences among the distributions of the various risk-return measures. Because earlier test results indicated non-normality, the non-parametric, independent sample Mann-Whitney U-test was used to detect differences of central tendency, while the Kolmogorov-Smirnov two-sample test was used to test for significant differences of central tendency

and/or dispersion among the distributions of the re-
pective portfolio risk-return measures for the three
market segments and for the four combinations of the
segments.[11]

EMPIRICAL RESULTS

The results of the correlation analysis of the returns for the three market segment indexes, the
equally weighted index, and the Standard and Poor's
425 Industrial Index are given in Table II. Although the
NYSE, ASE, and OTC indexes are highly correlated
with each other, the results also demonstrate that the
indexes of the three market segments are all more
highly correlated with the equally weighted index
than with the S&P 425 Industrial Index.[12]

TABLE II

Correlations of the Returns for the Segment Indexes,
the Equally Weighted Index, and the S&P 425 Index

	NYSE	ASE	OTC	Equally Weighted	S&P 425
NYSE	1.000	.951	.982	.983	.877
ASE		1.000	.975	.990	.740
OTC			1.000	.995	.792
Equally Weighted				1.000	.797
S&P 425					1.000

The mean ($\overline{X}$) and standard deviation (σ) of the
respective distributions of the eight risk-return measures for each market segment and for each combination of the segments are presented in Table III. An examination of the results for the three market segments
reported in Table III reveals that during the 1961-1973
period, the OTC and ASE segments demonstrated
higher average portfolio arithmetic mean returns
than the NYSE portfolios. The average geometric
mean returns for the NYSE and ASE, however, were
almost identical to each other, but both were below the

SECURITY
SELECTION
AND ACTIVE
PORTFOLIO
MANAGEMENT

TABLE III

Means ($\overline{X}$) and Standard Deviations (σ) of the Distributions
of Risk-Return Measures for 20 Randomly Selected Portfolios from
Each Market Segment and Each Combination of Segments

		NYSE	ASE	OTC	N-A	N-O	A-O	N-A-O
Arithmetic	$\overline{X}$	.116	.162	.205	.139	.161	.177	.161
Mean Return	σ	.011	.034	.037	.021	.019	.037	.020
Geometric	$\overline{X}$	.091	.090	.147	.094	.122	.114	.114
Mean Return	σ	.011	.029	.028	.020	.016	.029	.018
Standard	$\overline{X}$	.237	.371	.437	.328	.301	.395	.336
Deviation	σ	.015	.054	.044	.022	.029	.041	.022
Beta	$\overline{X}$	.751	1.181	1.047	.968	.909	1.123	.996
	σ	.042	.085	.113	.054	.065	.064	.047
R^2	$\overline{X}$	.944	.925	.910	.959	.949	.949	.972
	σ	.020	.030	.036	.023	.017	.018	.011
Jensen	$\overline{X}$	-.006	-.035	.025	-.017	.012	-.009	-.001
"Alpha"	σ	.011	.027	.022	.020	.014	.024	.016
Sharpe Reward-to-	$\overline{X}$	.292	.262	.418	.280	.375	.324	.336
Variability	σ	.044	.071	.057	.060	.043	.064	.047
Treynor Reward-to-	$\overline{X}$	.095	.099	.151	.097	.127	.116	.116
Volatility	σ	.016	.028	.026	.022	.018	.028	.019

average OTC geometric mean returns.[13] Furthermore, although the average OTC portfolio arithmetic mean returns were higher than the ASE returns, the means of the distributions of portfolio standard deviations and beta values indicate that there were smaller differences during the period between these risk measures for the OTC and ASE portfolios compared to the differences between each of them and the much lower risk measure values for the NYSE portfolios. In terms of the risk-adjusted performance measures (α, SRV, TRV), the OTC segment outperformed the ASE and NYSE segments for all three measures.[14] Also, although the average arithmetic mean return was higher for the ASE than for the NYSE, the three risk-adjusted performance measures indicate conflicting results for the ASE when compared to the NYSE.

An examination of the risk-return measures for

RISK/RETURN
CONTRASTS:
NYSE, AMEX,
AND OTC

the four sets of combinations (listed in the last four columns of Table III) reveals that the A-O combination had arithmetic mean and geometric mean return performances superior to the other combinations as well as to the ASE and NYSE segments. The standard deviations and betas associated with the combinations indicate that the N-A, N-O, and N-A-O combinations had lower risks than the OTC and ASE segments and the A-O combination. The three risk-adjusted performance measures for the combinations indicate that the N-O combination portfolios outperformed all other combinations and segments, with the single exception of the OTC segment. The OTC segment portfolio performance, however, proved to be superior to those of all other segments and combinations. This result indicates a lack of diversification potential among the segments, since the OTC segment was superior on a risk-adjusted basis to all other combinations for the time period examined.[15]

In order to depict graphically the arithmetic mean returns and standard deviations as well as the arithmetic mean returns and betas, Figure I-a presents the locations of the means of the distributions of arithmetic mean returns and standard deviations for each of the seven portfolio sets, i.e., the three individual stock market segments and their four combinations; similarly, Figure I-b presents the locations of the

FIGURE I-a[16]

Comparisons of the Location of the Mean AMR's ($\overline{AMR}$) and SD's ($\overline{\sigma}$)
for Portfolios from Each Segment and Each Combination

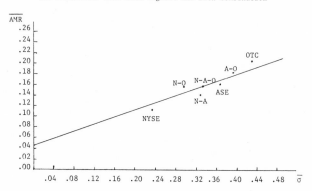

SECURITY
SELECTION
AND ACTIVE
PORTFOLIO
MANAGEMENT

FIGURE I-b

Location of the Mean AMR's ($\overline{AMR}$) and Betas ($\overline{\beta}$) for
Portfolios from Each Segment and Each Combination

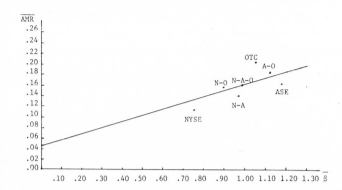

means of the distributions of arithmetic mean returns
and systematic risk (beta) levels.

Table IV shows the results of the tests for significant differences between the distributions of each

TABLE IV

Summary of Mann-Whitney U Test z-values and Two-Sample Kolmogorov-Smirnov
K_D Values ( ) for Tests of Differences Between all Possible Pairs of
Distributions of Portfolio Risk-Return Measures for the
Market Segments and Combinations

Pairs of Segments
& Combinations   Risk-Return Measures for Sets of 20 Randomly Selected Portfolios

	AMR	GMR	SD	β	R^2	α	SRV	TRV
NYSE:ASE	4.517** (16.0)	0.379 (6.0)	5.410** (20.0)**	5.410** (20.0)**	1.948 (6.0)	3.652** (12.0)**	1.190 (5.0)	1.028 (4.0)
NYSE:OTC	5.410** (20.0)**	5.410** (18.0)**	5.410** (20.0)**	5.410** (20.0)**	2.921** (9.0)*	4.436** (13.0)**	5.085** (16.0)**	5.275** (16.0)**
ASE:OTC	3.219** (10.0)*	4.680** (14.0)**	3.544** (12.0)**	3.381** (12.0)**	1.325 (6.0)	5.167** (17.0)**	5.194** (16.0)**	4.544** (13.0)**
NYSE:N-A	2.894** (12.0)**	1.082 (7.0)	5.410** (19.0)**	5.356** (19.0)**	4.599** (14.0)**	1.163 (5.0)	0.135 (2.0)	0.839 (4.0)
NYSE:N-O	4.301** (15.0)**	3.922** (15.0)**	4.409** (14.0)**	4.842** (15.0)**	4.842** (14.0)**	3.246** (12.0)**	3.868** (14.0)**	3.517** (13.0)**
NYSE:A-O	5.031** (19.0)**	4.544** (16.0)**	5.410** (20.0)**	5.410** (20.0)**	2.326* (7.0)	0.839 (4.0)	3.327** (10.0)*	4.166** (12.0)**
NYSE:N-A-O	4.463** (15.0)**	3.381** (13.0)**	5.410** (20.0)**	5.410** (19.0)**	5.356** (19.0)**	1.434 (7.0)	2.813** (10.0)*	2.786** (11.0)*
ASE:N-A	0.514 (5.0)	2.380* (8.0)	4.680** (15.0)**	4.490** (14.0)**	3.976** (13.0)**	3.273** (11.0)**	2.137* (7.0)	1.866 (6.0)
ASE:N-O	0.568 (3.0)	3.517** (12.0)**	5.302** (19.0)**	5.302** (19.0)**	3.652** (10.0)*	5.248** (17.0)**	4.977** (15.0)**	3.273** (13.0)**
ASE:A-O	2.732** (9.0)*	3.814** (14.0)**	1.785 (7.0)	2.029* (7.0)	4.274** (13.0)**	4.328** (15.0)**	4.084** (13.0)**	3.652** (13.0)**
ASE:N-A-O	1.028 (8.0)	3.571** (14.0)**	4.680** (14.0)**	4.139** (14.0)**	5.221** (18.0)**	4.355** (16.0)**	3.814** (13.0)**	3.300** (12.0)*
OTC:N-A	5.031** (16.0)**	5.031** (15.0)**	2.543* (10.0)*	2.218* (9.0)*	4.734** (15.0)**	5.031** (16.0)**	5.194** (16.0)**	5.140** (17.0)**
OTC:N-O	4.003** (13.0)**	3.435** (11.0)**	4.382** (13.0)**	3.598** (10.0)*	4.193** (15.0)**	2.732** (9.0)*	2.570* (9.0)*	3.598** (12.0)**
OTC:A-O	2.840** (9.0)*	3.408** (10.0)*	0.595 (4.0)	2.867** (11.0)**	4.490** (15.0)**	4.003** (12.0)**	3.814** (13.0)**	3.652** (12.0)**
OTC:N-A-O	3.976** (13.0)**	3.949** (13.0)**	3.003** (11.0)**	0.325 (5.0)	5.031** (18.0)**	3.949** (13.0)**	3.976** (13.0)**	4.301** (14.0)**
N-A:N-O	2.516* (8.0)	3.598** (10.0)*	3.544** (11.0)**	3.598** (10.0)*	1.894 (7.0)	4.274** (12.0)**	4.382** (13.0)**	3.625** (11.0)**
N-A:A-O	4.490** (14.0)**	4.301** (13.0)**	4.166** (13.0)**	3.868** (11.0)**	1.785 (8.0)	3.787** (11.0)**	4.193** (11.0)**	4.274** (13.0)**
N-A:N-A-O	3.381** (12.0)**	3.733** (12.0)**	0.730 (3.0)	0.081 (2.0)	3.084** (12.0)**	3.868** (13.0)**	3.922** (11.0)**	3.571** (13.0)**
N-O:A-O	1.948 (5.0)	1.082 (3.0)	4.788** (17.0)**	5.140** (18.0)**	0.135 (3.0)	3.381** (10.0)*	2.705** (9.0)*	1.623 (5.0)
N-O:N-A-O	0.920 (6.0)	2.435* (9.0)*	3.111** (11.0)**	3.679** (12.0)**	2.516* (10.0)*	3.111** (10.0)*	2.732** (11.0)**	2.597** (10.0)*
A-O:N-A-O	1.894 (8.0)	0.757 (5.0)	4.085** (14.0)**	3.841** (12.0)**	3.192** (9.0)*	0.649 (4.0)	0.243 (5.0)	0.947 (4.0)

*Significant at the α = .05 level.
**Significant at the α = .01 level.

risk-return measure for all pairs of stock market segments and segment combinations as determined by the Mann-Whitney U-test and the Kolmogorov-Smirnov two-sample test. These results indicate that the average geometric mean returns, as well as the average Sharpe reward-to-variability and Treynor reward-to-volatility values, of the NYSE and ASE segments are not significantly different and that, with the exception of the average coefficients of determination, the remaining distributions of risk-return measures for the three common stock market segments are significantly different from each other. The statistical results for the eighteen additional pairs of segments and combinations reveal that the OTC segment is significantly superior to the four combinations for the two return measures and for all three risk-adjusted performance measures.

CONCLUSIONS AND IMPLICATIONS

The results of this study indicate that there are, in fact, significant differences among the risk-return performances of the NYSE, ASE, and OTC stock market segments. These findings suggest that conclusions reached by previous studies concerning common stocks using only NYSE stocks may not be applicable to the ASE and OTC stock market segments. This study further indicates, however, that although there are significant differences among the NYSE, ASE, and OTC segments, these differences are not sufficient to provide an adequate opportunity for diversification and a resulting improvement in the risk-adjusted performance of sets of randomly selected portfolios.

The superior performance of the OTC segment may not provide conclusive support for the superiority of its investment potential over the NYSE and ASE, since factors not directly measured by a portfolio's standard deviation or systematic risk level may explain the differences among the segments. For example, the three segments may attract distinctly different types of investor clientele who behave differently during various market conditions. Another factor that might ex-

SECURITY
SELECTION
AND ACTIVE
PORTFOLIO
MANAGEMENT

plain the difference is the possibility of different levels of marketability risk associated with individual securities from different segments. The results of this study do, however, clearly indicate the potential as well as the need for more research in this area.

[1] Previous empirical studies by, for example, Blume [2], Black, Jensen, and Scholes [1], and Sharpe and Cooper [20] concerning common stocks have been limited to an examination of NYSE stocks. These studies have made generalizations about NYSE stocks; however, their conclusions are not applicable to ASE and OTC stocks unless common stocks from all three segments are from the same population.

[2] The results of the Jessup and Upson studies showed that the NYSE provided, in general, superior returns compared to those of the Minnesota OTC market as well as to the other regional OTC markets.

[3] An additional screen was used to exclude companies with annual returns above 10.0 or below −.95 in order to eliminate outliers and potential data errors.

[4] On the basis of data availability (See Table I) and considering both the number of portfolios needed for the statistical tests and the number of securities needed for each portfolio to provide an adequate amount of portfolio diversification according to the earlier findings of Evans and Archer [6], it was felt that twenty portfolios per segment would be satisfactory. The mean R^2 values for the portfolios from each of the segments and each of the combinations indicate that the use of twenty portfolios permitted an adequate number of securities to be included into the portfolios for the elimination of most of the unsystematic risk of the portfolios.

[5] This sampling procedure was repeated for each of the thirteen years of annual returns used in the study. Since the company sets for each segment changed from year to year, the company composition of each of the twenty portfolios also changed each year. The securities were equally weighted within each of the portfolios for each year.

[6] Companies that remain in the OTC or ASE segments for the entire time period of the study may form samples of companies that have different risk-return characteristics compared to those companies that prosper and move from the OTC to the ASE or NYSE segment or from the ASE to the NYSE segment.

[7] The annual arithmetic mean return is the annual price change plus cash dividends received during the year divided by the beginning of year price (with appropriate adjustments for stock splits and stock dividends).

[8] The systematic risk or beta coefficient is associated with the "capital asset pricing model" developed earlier by Sharpe [18], Lintner [14], and Mossin [15].

[9] The α, SRV, and TRV one-parameter measures of portfolio performance are used in the study to provide additional information concerning the performance of the various portfolio sets; a discussion of the criticisms of the underlying capital asset pricing model is beyond the scope of this study.

[10] For a justification of the use of continuously compounded rates of return in a "capital asset pricing model" setting, see Jensen [10: 392].

[11] See Siegel [21] for a discussion of these tests. Independent sample tests are used because the risk-return comparisons are made with respect to summary risk-return measures calculated over the complete thirteen-year time frame of the study. Market factors associated with changing economic conditions are assumed to affect all common stocks in a similar manner over the sample period. Therefore, the portfolio samples of size twenty associated with the member of each pair are assumed to be independent samples whose differences are attributable to their different respective trading locations.

[12] These correlations are higher than those reported earlier by Reilly [16]. This difference in results may be due to the present study's use of annual differencing intervals compared to daily and weekly differencing intervals used by Reilly.

[13] The greater difference between the mean arithmetic and geometric mean returns for the ASE compared to the respective difference for the NYSE is attributed to the significantly larger mean standard deviation of the mean arithmetic mean return of the ASE segment compared to that of the NYSE segment.

[14] The superiority of the OTC over the NYSE is consistent with the earlier findings of Eubank [4,5] for individual stocks; however, the results differ from those of Jessup and Upson [11, 12, 23]. Possible explanations of this difference are that, first, the present study uses only OTC companies which are sufficiently large to be included on the Compustat tapes, while there was no size requirement for the Jessup and Upson OTC samples. Second, the OTC sample obtained from the Compustat tapes contains only companies which have not failed, while the Jessup and Upson annual OTC

samples include returns from some OTC companies which did, in fact, fail during a later time period.

[15] This method of examining naively diversified portfolios is similar to a technique used earlier by Lessard [13] to examine the potential for international portfolio diversification. His results differ from those of the present study; they indicated a risk-adjusted return improvement from the internationally diversified portfolio compared to the best portfolio from a single country, while this study shows no improvement in risk-adjusted portfolio returns for the combinations compared to the superior OTC risk-adjusted portfolio performance.

[16] The intercept for each graph is the average, annualized Treasury bill rate over the sample period (.045).

REFERENCES

1. Black, Fisher, Michael C. Jensen, and Myron Scholes, "The Capital Asset Pricing Model: Some Emprical Tests," in *Studies in the Theory of Capital Markets*, M. C. Jensen, ed., New York: Praeger Publishing Co., 1972.

2. Blume, Marshall E., "On the Assessment of Risk," *Journal of Finance*, XXVI (March, 1971), 1-10.

3. —— and Frank Husic, "Price, Beta, and Exchange Listing," *Journal of Finance*, XXVIII (May, 1973), 283-99.

4. Eubank, Arthur A., Jr., "Risk-Return Comparisons Among Different Market Segments," *Eastern Finance Association Proceedings* (April, 1973), 94-99.

5. ——, "Comparison of Systematic Risks Among Stocks from Different Market Segments," *Southwestern Finance Association Proceedings* (March, 1973), 108-17.

6. Evans, J. L. and S. H. Archer, "Diversification and the Reduction of Dispersion: An Empirical Analysis," *Journal of Finance*, XXIII (December, 1968), 761-67.

7. Fama, Eugene F., "The Behavior of Stock Market Prices," *Journal of Business*, XXXVIII (January, 1965), 34-105.

8. —— and Marshall E. Blume, "Filter Rules and Stock Market Trading." *Journal of Business*, XXVIII (January, 1966), 226-41.

9. Hagerman, Robert L. and Richard D. Richmond, "Random Walks, Martingales and the OTC," *Journal of Finance*, XXVIII (September, 1973), 897-909.

10. Jensen, Michael C., "The Performance of Mutual Funds in the Period 1945-64," *Journal of Finance*, XXIII (May, 1968), 389-416.

11. Jessup, Paul F. and Roger B. Upson, "Opportunities in Regional Markets," *Financial Analysts Journal*, XXVI (March/April, 1970), 75-79.

12. ——, *Returns in Over-the-Counter Stock Markets*, Minneapolis: University of Minnesota Press, 1973.

13. Lessard, Donald R., "International Portfolio Diversification: A Multivariate Analysis for a Group of Latin American Countries," *Journal of Finance*, XXVII (June, 1973), 619-33.

14. Lintner, John, "Security Prices, Risk, and Maximal Gains from Diversification," *Journal of Finance*, XX (December, 1965), 587-615.

15. Mossin, Jan, "Equilibrium in a Capital Asset Market," *Econometrica*, XXXIV (October, 1966), 768-83.

16. Reilly, Frank K., "Evidence Regarding a Segmented Stock Market," *Journal of Finance*, XXVII (June, 1972), 607-27.

17. —— "Stock Price Changes by Market Segment," *Financial Analysts Journal*, XXVII (March/April, 1971), 54-59.

18. Sharpe, William F., "Capital Asset Prices: A Theory of Market Equilibrium Under Conditions of Risk," *Journal of Finance*, XIX (September, 1964), 425-42.

19. ——, "Mutual Fund Performance," *Journal of Business*, XXXIX (January, 1966), 119-38.

20. —— and Guy M. Cooper, "Risk-Return Classes of New York Stock Exchange Common Stocks, 1931-67," *Financial Analysts Journal*, XXVIII (March/April, 1972), 46-54, 81, 95-100.

21. Siegel, Sidney, *Nonparametric Statistics for the Social Sciences*, New York: McGraw-Hill Book Company, 1956.

22. Treynor, Jack L., "How to Rate Management of Investment Funds," *Harvard Business Review*, XLIII (January-February, 1965), 63-75.

23. Upson, Roger B. and Paul F. Jessup, "Risk-Return Relationships in Regional Securities Markets," *Journal of Financial and Quantitative Analysis*, IV (January, 1970), 677-95.

SECURITY
SELECTION
AND ACTIVE
PORTFOLIO
MANAGEMENT

The non-efficient market is not for institutions

It is not only too costly and risky: we have plenty to accomplish in the efficient area.

Stephen B. Timbers

One of the continuously intriguing choices of portfolio strategy and research direction is whether to spend money and time analyzing stocks in the so-called efficient sector of the market or to concentrate on the non-efficient, seldom researched sector of the market. Although most institutions do the former, thereby helping to create the efficiency of the market, a small group have applied their efforts to investigating industries and companies where there is little institutional ownership or research in an effort to discover undervalued or misvalued stocks in the vast — in numbers of issues but small in capitalization — non-efficient sector. Their premise is that eventually other investors will follow them to the discovery of the inherent value of these stocks. These contrarians have always existed, but their approach to stock selection seems to be talked about more now than usual.

    My opinion, however, is that most large institutions should continue for the most part what they are doing now and leave the non-efficient market alone because of the costs, organizational problems, and even returns involved in doing otherwise. In fact, I believe that the only change required by institutions to accommodate the implications of the efficient market dialogue is one of emphasis: to concentrate more on the non-efficient aspects of the stocks they are currently organized to analyze.

No one seriously engaged in portfolio management today disagrees that certain companies grouped together do comprise a relatively efficient and large market. One may argue how many and which individual stocks comprise this market, but essentially these stocks have similar characteristics in that they enjoy large capitalizations, exhibit regularly substantial trading volume with small daily price fluctuations, elicit a significant number of articles in the financial press and research reports from brokerage houses and institutions, and are already owned by most large institutional portfolios.

One may also argue how efficient this market is. The proponents of the Efficient Market Hypothesis tell us that, to be perfectly efficient, a market would have to preclude opportunities for above average returns on a risk-adjusted basis, because all available information has been already discounted in share prices. Their task has been to prove that this condition exists in the stock market. They keep trying, and some of their work is compelling. But although I do concede that in aggregate a large sector of the market is relatively efficient, I, like most investors, am still unconvinced that the efficient marketeers have proved a conclusive case for absolute efficiency.

WHY GO "NON-EFFICIENT"?

While a necessary byproduct of my discussion is to question the extent of efficiency in the market, my principal intention here is to ask whether it is reasonable for institutions to continue to research and invest primarily in stocks with the characteristics I previously enumerated. Initially, we must examine how far this

SECURITY
SELECTION
AND ACTIVE
PORTFOLIO
MANAGEMENT

discussion has come. The current interest that money managers have in exploiting the non-efficient part of the market may be attributed to a number of reasons.

First, institutional common stock results in 1973 and 1974 were generally abysmal, and compounded annual returns over the past decade have not been good. Certainly if an investor does poorly over an extended period owning a certain group of stocks, he is at least likely to be receptive to a different approach. Second, our diligent critics, the academics, have been bombarding professional investors with books, articles, and models over the last decade proving beyond a shadow of a standard deviation — to deny them their due — that we should either throw darts at a page of stock listings or fit tangent lines to optimal universes. These publications have left most money managers uneasy, exhausted, and even thinking the unthinkable: that the academics might just be on to something.

Then not long ago, an extraordinarily thoughtful article[1] by Charles Ellis received wide circulation and caused a stir among institutional money managers. It pointed out that, since institutions currently dominate the trading in the stock market to the point of, in effect, being the market, and since the stock market is essentially a zero-sum game,[2] results from institutional portfolios should tend to group very closely around the results of the broad market indices — and may even fall consistently below because of transactions costs. The implication is that, if one invests as the institutions have, one's results will tend to approximate the market averages or worse.

Finally, such revelations in the environment I have described have helped to revive the old concept of the index fund, the ultimate abdication and threat to the careers of active money managers. Not surprisingly, a few rather creditable organizations are offering index funds that seem to be accomplishing their admittedly unambitious objectives. After all this, one is forced to ask: are traditional portfolio management

1. Footnotes appear at the end of the article.

and research practices wrong-headed and doomed to be unefficacious over the long run — or is what we have been doing still valid?

THE MANAGERS' DREAM

Logic dictates that there should be superior returns to superior intelligence or extraordinary industry, and therefore the more intelligent or industrious organization *should* be able to devise a method to beat the average performance consistently. Although a lot of evidence points to the failure of this premise, that may be discouraging but not conclusive. Certainly even today there are a number of money managers whose records are superior over the long term. The trouble is that the apologists for the efficient market theory point out that the number of these superior managers is not statistically very meaningful nor are their strategies sufficiently similar to be helpful to the rest of us.[3]

Still, the idea persists that an intelligent and resourceful portfolio manager can outperform the market. Interestingly, it even seems to exist in the enemy's camp. For example, Batterymarch Financial Management offers both an index fund and a fundamentally grounded portfolio management service. Its strategy is that the index fund will take care of the efficient sector of the market nicely and the other service will identify the opportunities in the non-efficient sector. This concept is logical and a necessary consequence of our current environment.

I do not mean to focus on Batterymarch, but its President, Dean LeBaron, is one of the most eloquent proponents of the philosophy of exploiting the imperfections in a generally efficient market, and their efforts are conscientious and creditable. Nevertheless, they part company with the efficient market absolutist by insisting that there are certain stocks, mostly of small companies or at least of companies with little representation in the dollar-weighted indices, that may be mispriced because they have been overlooked.[4] This failure of investors to analyze stocks on the same basis creates an imperfection or opportunity. Imperfections occur usually because of information lags and the several structural and organizational problems of institutions. These problems include the tendency of institutions to act as a group, the acceptance of a premium price for liquidity or glamor, ERISA concerns, and the conventionality and inbred resistance to change in large organizations.

There is of course another, almost definitional, reason for directing their attention to the imperfect or non-efficient sector of the market: the competition is less. It follows that an application of intelligence or industry should result in a high return in an arena with few intelligent or industrious competitors. Thus, with this strategy one can satisfy the natural tendency to think one can outperform the competition, while accepting the inevitability of failure that will come to one who is not savvy enough to limit his sphere of interest and activity in the market.

THE COST BURDENS

Unfortunately, this philosophy of investing is not a nostrum, nor, I hope to point out, is it even appropriate for most institutional investors. First of all, I cannot imagine a more costly form of analysis. Companies that are most likely to be found in the non-efficient sector of the market have small market capitalizations and are probably smallish companies also in terms of assets and sales. These companies typically do not provide a vast amount of financial or business information to investors, and there are very few professional researchers who are willing to analyze that information, even if it is provided. Therefore, to research these companies adequately requires great individual effort to dig out information and permits few opportunities for crosschecking findings. Obviously, this process is extremely time-consuming and fraught with the potential for error. Moreover, analysts trained in researching these kinds of companies are impossible to find in numbers large enough to satisfy the research department requirements of institutions, were this philosophy of investing suddenly to become popular. Of course, analysts could be trained differently, but the attendant high initial costs and the long training period, during which time portfolio managers would be even more distrustful of the quality of investment analysts' work than now, could be prohibitive.

Assuming, however, an institution could obtain suitably trained analysts and had ample resources, how costly would this effort be? An organization managing $1 billion of common stocks might typically employ twelve analysts and have a research department budget of $800,000. This group would follow the approximately 100 companies owned in the portfolios and 200 more that would be possible candidates, meaning about 25 companies per analyst. Currently almost all of these 300 companies would enjoy relatively efficient characteristics as stocks.

A serious program of investing in non-efficient sector stocks probably would entail a switch of 20% of the portfolio into these kinds of stocks. Because of the smaller market capitalization and the dearth of available information about these stocks, prudence would dictate holding a greater number of stocks in the new 20% of the portfolio than the old. I contend that this ratio would be at least three to one. The result would be a new portfolio of 140 stocks or 40% more and probably a comparable increase in the stocks followed but not held. The cost implications are obvious. An analyst would now have to follow 35 instead of 25 stocks or the institution would have to hire another five analysts to maintain the same intensity of coverage as before. Since these newer companies would be more difficult to follow than the efficient sector stocks, more travel, industry conferences, subscriptions, field work, and perhaps specialized analytical techniques would be required. To be specific, I estimate the cost of five analysts and necessary support today might run conservatively $250,000.

What does this incremental cost figure mean?

At a one half of 1% of assets management fee, an institution would have to earn $50 million more for its clients — a 5% additional return — yearly on a $1 billion asset base to recover the costs alone. Considering historical returns on common stocks, I do not think an incremental 5% return realistic.

This cost example, of course, is not a comprehensive analysis, only instructive. Yet it is clear that either costs would have to increase substantially or the quality of existing analysis would deteriorate significantly, unless an institution altered its method of operation in another way. Further, it is clear that an institution would have to have ample resources indeed to implement this strategy.

HOW TO BE RIGHT AND WRONG SIMULTANEOUSLY

Beyond the research cost factors, one could also be faced with the dilemma of being right and wrong at the same time. A proponent of this philosophy will always be right by his standards, assuming he assiduously discovers mispriced stocks in this sector of the marketplace. If, however, others fail to discover these stocks in turn, one could be very wrong by others' standards and the performance standards of one's clients. The proof of a particular strategy will always be in the higher bid by the next buyer. If that bid never materializes, one may have incurred substantial opportunity costs. Only philosophers can afford to be philosophically correct but financially wrong.

Timing is important. In today's ERISA-dominated environment, one might also risk more than opportunity cost if these stocks are never discovered. In spite of whatever value an investor may find in a stock or portfolio, the thrust of ERISA seems to define prudence as whatever is acceptable by the majority of other professional investors. By this standard, contrarians had better be right sooner than later.

The crux of the successful employment of the non-efficient market approach to investing is to attract others to the value one has found without spoiling the game. Since word of a successful strategy travels fast, one has to fear a wave of mightily staffed, heavily financed institutions gearing up to exploit the non-efficient sector and thereby increasing its degree of efficiency. It would be sweet if institutions bought one or two of these undervalued stocks at a time and never caught on to the game being played — merely assumed that the value they found was an extension of the fruits of their continuing research into their normal stalwarts like IBM, Caterpillar, and Kresge. So success depends on others bidding up non-efficient stocks but continuing to reject the methodology, or at least on only a few competitors embracing this strategy. I find the life-line of this strategy very fragile.

Because of the extraordinary costs involved, the higher risk of being wrong fundamentally, the legal and investment returns implications of poor timing, and the rather tenuous validity of the philosophy as a long-term strategy because of the tendency of success to attract a crowd, I am obliged to conclude that it is inappropriate today for most institutional investors to devote much research time to the non-efficient sector of the market. The onus then is on the organization to show that research on and investment in those stocks generally perceived to be included in the efficient sector of the market can produce consistent returns superior to those of the market averages or their investment vehicle proxy, the index funds, or can result in a successful investment relationship.

CAN YOU WIN IN THE EFFICIENT SECTOR?

The most comforting fact is that some managers have outperformed the averages — maybe not always a large number, but some is better than none.[5] Incidentally, these managers hardly think that they were merely lucky. Thus, the question we are addressing is one of distribution — how great is the dispersion of investment results around the median? The fact that the aggregate of institutional investors' performances approximate the return of the market averages does not gainsay the possibility that a significant number of institutions could do significantly better or worse than the median result. I have seen many periods when this situation has occurred. Still everyone does admire consistency and the studies invariably state performance in terms of systematic returns.

However, the current performance records may be more evidence that institutions do not manage money very well during down markets than an invalidation of their attempts to combine prudence and performance with the purchase and sale of efficient market stocks such as ATT, U.S. Steel, and Coca-Cola. In other words, the recent performance may be more of a function of timing and asset allocation than research and stock selection. This point is important, because the types of questions I have been discussing always seem to be popular after bear markets and fade during other periods. How many institutions were slightly embarrassed to compare their five- and ten-year records against the Dow Jones Industrial Average in 1971, 1972, and 1973, when even their unsophisticated clients understood that that Average was only full of dull, outmoded, underperforming companies? Times change, and likewise it may well be impossible to sell the index fund concept to a client in a few years, if a large group of money managers have new impressive performance records to show as they have had in the past.

THE ROLE OF RESEARCH

The next point is more subtle but very real to any daily participant of the market. In discussing the degree of efficiency in the market, one encounters a real problem in dealing with aggregates rather than the particular. In the aggregate, stocks with certain characteristics may function nearly efficiently but individually they may not from time to time. For example, holders of much followed Ingersoll-Rand in September of 1976 saw the stock drop 10% on the news that quarterly earnings would be quite disappointing. The reasons for this short-fall from expectations were several, but most were what I would call reasonable

—at least the information could have been discovered by a skeptical and hard-working analyst a few weeks in advance if he visited production lines and warehouses and kept a detailed record of revenue exposure to certain foreign countries. Yet the brokerage and institutional research communities largely missed these developments. No one would argue that Ingersoll-Rand does not have the characteristics of a stock belonging to the efficient sector of the market.

Maybe this event was an exception and maybe institutions tend to own too many stocks so that the impact of discovering or not discovering this kind of occurrence early enough to act would have been slight, but I cannot believe that this kind of situation is insignificant or rare. I could name at least fifty other situations similar to this one in big, liquid, and "owned" stocks during the past two years and any other research director could do the same. Moreover, the case of Ingersoll-Rand was largely only a failure to garner information. The instances of differences in interpretation of information are by far more numerous.[6] Perhaps these occurrences are meaningless in the aggregate, but I remain unconvinced portfolio results would not have been enhanced by a better research job on them.[7]

WHAT IS THE PROPER STRATEGY?

My final point is one of tone. I have always admired mathematics with its simple, elegant explanation of seemingly complex phenomena. On the other hand, I have always distrusted mathematicians, because they tend so easily to take on a moral superiority, as their solutions follow so logically and absolutely. Once we have accepted their assumptions, the exercise is practically over. Our problem is in accepting the assumptions. The assumption in the investment business is that performance is the only consideration. I reject that assumption. Performance is important but is not the only investment consideration. Prudence, a sense of well-being, an active communication of objectives and interests, a sense of the rightness of a philosophy are qualitative factors, all important in the relationship between the money manager and his client and the money manager and himself. I believe the argument that deals exclusively with quantitative performance fails to capture the tone of a complete investment relationship.

If a strategy of directing a substantial research effort at the non-efficient sector of the market is too costly and probably inappropriate for most institutions and if there is reason to believe that what institutions have been doing all along may not be so misguided after all, can we improve our performances while continuing to operate in the more efficient, more familiar sector of the market? We should start by admitting that, while the conclusions and implications of the Efficient Market Hypothesis may run against much of our observed market experience and logic, it describes enough of the market action to be valuable. I do not pretend that most of the research done by institutions is not redundant and needlessly costly. We read too many essentially repetitive reports, attend too many fruitless meetings, analyze individually too many of the same financial statistics to deny that the current system could not be improved greatly. Moreover, we continually observe with disappointment that most of our analysts' findings are generally known in a relatively short time and presumably are in the price of a stock. In short, we are guilty of producing a vast amount of research behind the thick walls of our institutions that is neither unique nor useful.[8]

My suggestion is to let outside sources such as brokerage houses, correspondent services, or research consultants do much of this maintenance research — to let them process the standard information that the market will discount immediately. Rather, the value-added in today's research efforts by institutions should be in the collection of significant information from novel sources, the creative employment of analytical techniques, the original juxtaposition of data, the development of specialized expertise, and the informed interpretation of these and conventional information inputs. Naturally, research directors will answer that they already encourage their analysts to do these things, but my impressions are that 80% of the analyst's job is still maintenance in character. If research directors really believed in my approach, the ratio of time spent would be altered significantly.

The implications of such an approach are several. First, costs should be less. If one purchases most of one's maintenance research services outside, the costs of that outside operation would be determined on an incremental cost basis. It seems reasonable that this price could be less than internal duplication costs. The institution then would have the choice of cutting its internal research staff or redirecting all of them to the more creative type of research I have described. Second, morale and productivity could increase significantly as essentially bright individuals are loosened from their housekeeping chores and turned towards more stimulating tasks. Next, client relations could improve as institutions would have a more cogent and lucid explanation of their research activities. Most clients today do not simply equate size of research staff with quality of output. Finally, portfolio returns should theoretically improve. With the research organization actively engaged in more creative avenues of analysis, their chances of coming upon anomalies, new information, or correct interpretations must be greater. The periodic and often lucky stumbling on significant information could become much more systematic. Presumably, this improved input would be translated into better portfolio results. I don't mean that everyone embracing this approach will succeed, but the exercise of research will be infinitely more interesting, and those who continue with present methods will enhance their chances of being left behind.

A critical aspect of this approach, of course, is the enthusiastic support and portfolio implementation by the management of the investment department and the portfolio managers. Institutions naturally must overcome any structural features in their organizations that inhibit implementation of useful ideas.[9] It may be, however, that present organizational rigidity is merely a function of too many unoriginal, fully discounted ideas that have been passed on by research departments. New useful ideas might by their very nature ensure timely adoption.

My conclusion is that our current problems are not a function of defining the right market sector on which to concentrate but a function of the way we do our work. It has always been attractive to investors to conceive of a lotus-eaters' land where they would find undiscovered riches and opportunities and little competition to inhibit them. That dream underlies the thinking of the proponents of non-efficient market investing. My advice is to stop dreaming and clean our own houses. Once we are organized properly, we shall have a chance to prove our worth again.

---

[1] Charles D. Ellis, "The Loser's Game," *Financial Analysts Journal* Vol. 31, No. 4 (July-August, 1975), pp. 19-26.

[2] Mr. Ellis, *ibid.*, does not make this point explicitly, but I feel it is a necessary given in his argument. Strangely this concept is the subject of some controversy, but why I don't know. The net new money flowing into the stock market is very small relative to the capitalization of the total market and the cost leakages are likewise not major.

[3] Michael C. Jensen, "Risk, The Pricing of Capital Assets, and the Evaluation of Investment Portfolios," *The Journal of Business* Vol. 42, No. 2 (April, 1969), pp. 167-247.

[4] There is some disagreement regarding how much of the market does not exhibit efficient characteristics. Figures I have heard run from 5 to 20% — noteworthy exceptions but not enough to invalidate the thrust of the Efficient Market Hypothesis, *per se*.

[5] A simple, heuristic approach to this question is to compare the compounded annual rates of return of the mutual fund industry, as a proxy for institutional investors, to the Standard and Poor's Composite Index with dividends reinvested. Even with a particularly negative end year as 1974,

for example, we were able to identify 67 mutual funds out of a sample of 410 which outperformed the market index over a five-year period and 158 out of 223 over a ten-year period. Not surprisingly, most of the superior-performing funds in the shorter period outperformed in the latter period as well.

[6] Arthur Zeikel in his article, "The Random Walk and Murphy's Law," *The Journal of Portfolio Management* Vol. 1, No. 1 (Fall, 1974), pp. 20-30, described several instances when interested investors responded to new developments and assessed information differently.

[7] Interestingly, efficient market theorists like Jensen, *ibid.*, do not think that it is inconsistent with their hypothesis that analysts may be able to predict stock prices. They merely contend that institutional misorganization prevents the timely implementation of these predictions. Keith Ambachtsheer in his "Profit Potential in an 'Almost Efficient' Market," *The Journal of Portfolio Management* Vol. 1, No. 1 (Fall, 1974), pp. 84-87, provided some empirical evidence to support this notion that analysts can predict security price changes to a useful, if limited, extent.

[8] Ironically, the validity of the Efficient Market Hypothesis requires analysts. As Leopold H. Bernstein in his "In Defense of Fundamental Investment Analysis," *Financial Analysts Journal* Vol. 31, No. 1 (January-February, 1975), p. 59, remarked in attacking the cynical position of the efficient market advocates, "it (security analysis) is something one encourages others to practice."

[9] The literature on this subject usually refers to this problem as "friction," that is, the organizational constraints that vitiate the benefits of useful information. See Jensen, p. 244.

SECURITY
SELECTION
AND ACTIVE
PORTFOLIO
MANAGEMENT

Authors

KEITH P. AMBACHTSHEER is a Director of Canavest House in Toronto, where he has management responsibility for their entire research effort. He developed forecasting and investment management methods for Sun Life prior to joining Canavest in 1972.

CLINTON M. BIDWELL III is Visiting Associate Professor at the University of North Carolina, Chapel Hill. He was formerly Director of Research for a New York Stock Exchange member firm and Assistant Professor of Business Administration at Fort Lewis College, Durango, Colorado.

MARSHALL E. BLUME is currently Visiting Professor at the European Institute of Advanced Studies in Management in Belgium and also at the Stockholm School of Economics. He has been Professor of Finance at The Wharton School since 1974, where he is also Associate Director of the Rodney L. White Center For Financial Research. A distinguished scholar in the field of institutional investing, he is currently at work on a Twentieth Century Fund study of the individual investor, co-authored with Irwin Friend.

CHARLES T. CASAZZA is a technical analyst at William D. Witter, Inc. He has also done technical work for Eaton & Howard, Inc. in Boston and for the Provident National Bank of Philadelphia.

JOHN D. CONNOLLY is a Vice President of Faulkner, Dawkins & Sullivan, Inc., where he has specialized in automobiles and retail trade since 1971. A Chartered Financial Analyst with an M.B.A. in Finance from Stanford, he formerly followed autos at First National City Bank and National Securities and Research.

GORDON H. DASH, JR. is Assistant Professor of Finance at the University of Rhode Island. A consultant to several investment funds in the use of computerized analysis, he is developing extended mathematical programming techniques for bank optimization models.

EDWIN J. ELTON is Professor of Finance at New York University. The author of more than forty articles and three books in the area of finance, he is associate editor of *The Journal of Finance* and *Management Science*. He is also co-editor of the Monograph Series in Finance and Economics at the Salomon Center at NYU.

ARTHUR A. EUBANK, JR. is Associate Professor of Finance at DePaul University of Chicago. He was previously on the faculties of the University of Missouri-Columbia and the University of Illinois at Urbana-Champaign. He is also President of Eubank Securities, a market making firm on the Midwest Options Exchange.

PAUL B. FIRSTENBERG is Executive Vice President and Chairman of the Finance Committee of Children's Television Workshop and a director of the Vanguard group of investment companies. He was formerly Financial Vice President of Princeton and is co-author of a book on endowment portfolio management with Burton G. Malkiel.

RUSSELL J. FULLER is Assistant Professor of Finance at Washington State University and a General Partner and portfolio manager for Capital Investment Group of Lincoln, Nebraska. He holds a Ph.D. in finance from the University of Nebraska and is a Chartered Financial Analyst.

JOHN C. GROTH is Assistant Professor of Finance at Texas A & M University, where he teaches corporation finance and investments. He holds a Ph.D. from Purdue.

MARTIN J. GRUBER is Professor of Finance at New York University. With five books and many articles to his credit, he has also served as associate editor of *The Journal of Finance.* He is a member of the Advisory Board of the Computer Applications Committee of the New York Society of Security Analysts and co-editor of the Monograph Series in Finance and Economics at the Salomon Center at NYU.

GEORGE A. HARBEN is an associate in the Dean Witter Economics Department. He has also been with Hemphill Noyes, Merrill Lynch, and Bache. Now doing graduate work at Pace, he is a graduate of Princeton.

MICHAEL D. HIRSCH is Vice President of Amivest Corporation, a New York-based NYSE member firm providing specialized research services for institutional clients. Mr. Hirsch began his Wall Street career as a security analyst with the Value Line Investment Survey.

BERTRAND JACQUILLAT is Professor of Finance at CESA, a French business school, and is currently Visiting Professor at Stanford University. He is the Director of the CESA Investment Management Program in Paris, a consultant for several prominent French and American institutions, and an authoritative writer on Modern Portfolio Theory.

KEITH H. JOHNSON is Associate Professor in the Department of Business Administration at the University of Kentucky, where he is M.B.A. coordinator and advisor and teaches data processing, statistics, and quantitative business analysis.

JOSEPH A. LAVELY is Associate Professor and Chairman of the Department of Finance at Indiana University-Purdue University at Fort Wayne. A frequent writer in the field of finance, he has also served as a consultant to business and professional firms.

RONALD C. LEASE is Associate Professor of Finance at the University of Utah and holds a Ph.D. from Purdue.

WILBUR G. LEWELLEN is Professor of Industrial Management at the Krannert Graduate School of Management, Purdue University. A Ph.D. from MIT, he has written profusely in the fields of corporate financial policy and investments.

ROBERT M. LOVELL, JR. is Senior Vice President-Financial of Crum & Forster, which he joined in 1970. He has also been with Halsey Stuart & Co., Lehman Brothers, and New Court Securities. He is a graduate of Princeton.

BURTON G. MALKIEL is Chairman of the Economics Department at Princeton, where he has been on the faculty since 1964, with the exception of a stint (1975-77) as a Member of the Council of Economic Advisors. An MBA from Harvard and a Ph.D. from Princeton, he is the author of five books and countless articles in the field of finance and securities. He is currently President of the American Finance Association.

ARNOLD X. MOSKOWITZ is Vice President and Chief Economist of Dean Witter Reynolds in New York. Prior to joining Dean Witter in 1970, he was an econometrician for Grumman Aircraft.

GREGORY LYNN NEAL is Assistant Professor of Finance at Northern Arizona University. He was formerly an instructor in finance at the University of Kentucky, where he received a degree of Doctor of Business Administration in August, 1977.

CHARLES F. O'HAY is Director of Investment Strategy at William D. Witter, Inc. He was formerly Senior Vice President and Director of Research at the Provident National Bank of Philadelphia and has also done financial work at Manufacturers Hanover, Salomon Brothers, and Shearson Hammill.

MANFRED W. PADBERG is Associate Professor of Operations Research and Finance at New York University. His main interest lies in the field of mathematical programming. He has published extensively in that area as well as in the field of portfolio management and is an editor of *Math Programming*.

DONALD M. PETERSON is a consultant to Marine Midland Bank-New York, and Computer Directions Advisors in Silver Spring, Maryland. He holds advanced degrees from Rensselaer

Polytechnic Institute, Wharton, and American University. He is the author of the recently published book, *Financial Ratios and Investment Results*.

JAMES B. REA is President of James B. Rea & Associates, a broker dealer, investment advisor, and consultant to top managements on diversification, ventures, and policy. He has had a long career in consulting and played a major role in the development of the Whittaker Corp. He also had a distinguished career as an aeronautical engineer and inventor as well as a test pilot and a flight captain on overseas routes for Pan American from 1941 to 1944. Born in Hawaii, he is an avid surfer and plays piano in a jazz orchestra.

ARUN P. SANGHVI is with the consulting firm, MATHEMATICA, Inc. in Princeton, N.J. Dr. Sanghvi holds a Ph.D. in Operations Research from Yale and specializes in the application of those techniques to empirical problems, particularly in the field of investments.

GARY G. SCHLARBAUM is Associate Professor of Management at the Krannert Graduate School of Management, Purdue University. He holds a Ph.D. from the University of Pennsylvania and has published frequently in the field of investments and finance.

DONALD S. SHANNON is Associate Professor at the College of Business and Economics, University of Kentucky. A.C.P.A. and a Ph.D. from the University of North Carolina, he specializes in the fields of financial theory and corporate financial policy.

BRUNO SOLNIK is Professor of Finance at CESA. Formerly on the faculty at Stanford, he holds an engineering degree from Ecole Polytechnique and a Ph.D. from MIT.

STEPHEN B. TIMBERS is Assistant Vice President and Director of Research for Equity Investments at The Mutual Life Insurance Company of New York. He is also Vice President of MONY Advisers, Inc. He has a degree in English Literature from Yale and an M.B.A. from the Harvard Business School.